CONSTRUCTIVE YEARS

The U.S. Economy Under Eisenhower

Raymond J. Saulnier

UNIVERSITY
PRESS OF
AMERICA

Lanham • New York • London

Copyright © 1991 by
University Press of America®, Inc.
4720 Boston Way
Lanham, Maryland 20706

3 Henrietta Street
London WC2E 8LU England

Library of Congress Cataloging-in-Publication Data

Saulnier, Raymond Joseph, 1908-
Constructive years : the U.S. economy under Eisenhower /
Raymond J. Saulnier.
p.   cm.
Includes index.
1. United States—Economic policy—1945-1960.
2. Eisenhower, Dwight D. (Dwight David), 1890-1969.
I. Title..
HC106.5.S336   1991
338.9'009'045—dc20   91-22856 CIP

ISBN 0–8191–8367–9 (hard : alk. paper)
ISBN 0–8191–8368–7 (pbk. : alk. paper)

 ™ The paper used in this publication meets the minimum requirements of
American National Standard for Information Sciences—Permanence
of Paper for Printed Library Materials, ANSI Z39.48–1984.

To Estelle

Acknowledgements

No one has done more to help me bring this book to completion than my wife, Estelle, to whom I have dedicated it as an expression of my gratitude. The reward for her, as it is for me, is at long last to have on the record an account of what we both perceive to be the approach to national economic policy best suited to serve our country's interests. It is hard for me to see how the work could have been done without her moral support and editorial help.

Among others, first from the corporate world, I want especially to mention Harold Geneen, Gerald Saltarelli and Arthur Viner, each with a deep interest in and understanding of scholarship and government and helpful to me in many ways. Among former students, from whose friendship and advice I continue to benefit, I mention Theodore P. Kovaleff, Richard J. Epstein and Anthony Low-Beer. Among those who were in the White House complex when I was there, and have encouraged and aided me in this enterprise, there is Roemer McPhee, Andrew Goodpaster and John S. D. Eisenhower. And in a large circle of academic friends I am particularly indebted to Robert Connery, a colleague and confidant for many years. I am indebted also to Marie Milton for a meticulous and thoughtful preparation of the manuscript for printing.

Finally, at Barnard College, in Columbia University, I have had the unfailing support of a succession of presidents and deans, among whom I want especially to mention Presidents Martha Peterson, Millicent McIntosh and Ellen Futter, and Professor Henry Boorse, Dean of the Faculty during many of my teaching years.

For the encouragement and support of all these friends, and many others, I am deeply grateful; for the book's shortcomings, which I trust are not large, I am of course alone responsible.

RAYMOND J. SAULNIER

Contents

Prologue

Some time ago, puzzling over what might be a proper title for this book, a colleague from the 1950s who was a prominent member of Eisenhower's White House staff suggested—not altogether seriously, I expect—that I call it "Holy Mike, Ike Was Right."

There could very well be a book for which my friend's title would do wonderfully well, but it was not, sad to say, a usable idea for the one I had in mind. All the same, it captures two major elements of the Eisenhower story. The first is its implication, which I trust this book will support, that the US economy functions best under policies such as Eisenhower advocated and practiced. The second is its recognition of the "revisionist" trend in which, thirty years after the close of his presidency, an increasing number of people, including some who earlier were among his severest critics, are coming to see the merit in Eisenhower's economic views, often with some astonishment at the discovery.

But my friend's proposal could be easily read as claiming too much. No president can be right in everything he undertakes; and no matter how well advised his policies may be, not everything turns out as planned. The business of the presidency is too big, too complicated, and affected by too much over which the president has little or no control to make such a record even a remote possibility. What can be fairly expected is that the president will be right in his philosophy of government, right in what he strives to do, and right in the fundamentals of how he seeks to do it. And we can, of course, hold a president responsible for guiding the nation toward fuller and more satisfying political and economic life. It is in these crucial respects that, in my view, "Ike was right."

*   *   *

Granted this has not been everyone's opinion. As we will see, much of what Eisenhower attempted was at the time opposed in Congress by members, often in controlling numbers, who took a totally different view of what should be done and how to do it. There were many in the media for whom large parts of what he stood for went down badly. And, on the whole, the academic community dealt with him severely. When a poll of seventy-five leading students of American history was taken shortly after Eisenhower left the White House he was placed twenty-second in their rating of presidents to that date, next to the bottom of the group whose performance was judged to have been only average.[1]

But presidential ratings were not a matter over which Eisenhower was inclined to agonize. When he was asked in one of his last presidential news conferences how he thought his place in history would be affected by certain policy reverses he had recently suffered, he remarked only that the question would be "decided by historians," implying that it would take time and scholarship to put the record in perspective.[2]

So it has, and it is fair to say that time and scholarship have worked in Eisenhower's favor. There are still critics of what he stood for in economic policy, as there are critics of what he did in other areas of presidential responsibility, but they are fewer than in the past and they make their case with diminishing effect. And along the way there have been some remarkable conversions.

Nostalgia may have something to do with this. There is a tendency nowadays (not entirely warranted) to look on the 1950s as somehow a quiet time, and the wish to recapture something of such a quality, even by scholars, is understandable. Also, one must assign some credit for the rise in Eisenhower's posthumous fortunes to the vastly increased amount of material now available for study of his presidency, and to its increasing use. The papers gathered at the perior capability in production, which Eisenhower recognized full well, his case for it went deeper. It was his conviction that a market-directed economy, primarily because of the diffusion of power that it entailed, was the only type of economy consistent with democratic political institutions. Accordingly, it was the system best able to offer the individual meaningful opportunities for personal fulfillment. Deeply opposed as he was to any form of statism (he exclaimed at one of his first presidential press conferences: "I think I am as implacable a foe of the communistic theory as there is in this world"), he was thus on political and social grounds, as well as on economic grounds, a vigorous and consistent champion of the enterprise system.[2]

What brought him to this position was a belief—it set him apart not just from all socialists but from the great majority of liberals in his time—in what he called "the connectedness of freedoms." It was spelled out in October 1949 in a studiously prepared address to the American Bar Association entitled "The Middle of the Road: A Statement of Faith in America:"

> [A]ll our freedoms—personal, economic, social, political—freedom to buy, to work, to hire, to bargain, to save, to vote, to worship, to gather in a convention or join in mutual association; all these freedoms are a single bundle. Each is an indispensable part of a single whole. Destruction of any inevitably leads to the destruction of all.[3]

Putting it differently: a society that denies economic freedom, and denies the institutions of private property and individual responsibility that are basic to it, will sooner or later deny political freedom as well.

It was his belief in this proposition that set his basic goal in economic policy, which was to make the market-directed enterprise system work as efficiently as possible. To succeed in this would assure the strength and continuance of democratic institutions; to fail would put democratic institutions in danger. Understanding this interconnectedness is the key to understanding Eisenhower's economic program.

*   *   *

Eisenhower Presidential Library at Abilene, Kansas, to cite the principal collection, make it easier for the record to speak for itself, as do the personal letters and papers being prepared at The Johns Hopkins University by Professor Louis Galambos and being published by the Johns Hopkins University Press.

What these materials say is overwhelmingly favorable to Eisenhower, but doubtless more important than anything else in prompting a more positive view of his presidency is the perspective afforded by the passage of time, and by the opportunity this has provided to compare his record with results in other administrations under economic policies that in some cases departed sharply from those he favored.

Admittedly, these are controversial matters; moreover, they are so heavy with essentially ideological content that it is not easy for anyone to be entirely objective about them, least of all not for one who, like the writer, not only shares the philosophy underlying Eisenhower's strategies but had a hand in shaping economic policy under his presidency. But I have made an earnest effort to give a balanced and objective account of the period, and I am content to let the reader judge whether that has been fairly and adequately done.

Now, to get on with the story.

Notes

1. *New York Times,* July 29, 1962, Section VI, pp. 12–13.
2. *The Public Papers of the President, Dwight D. Eisenhower, 1960–61* (Office of the Federal Register, National Archives and Records Service, General Services Administration, Washington, D.C.), p. 553. (Hereafter cited as *Public Papers, DDE.*)

I. Eisenhower's Philosoph
and Goals

A president's personal style has much to do with tl
made about his performance, and Eisenhower
mistakable style in presidential matters. Dignity, e
ness, a deliberative turn of mind and attentiveness
and a strong sense of duty and love of country were c
qualities in it. So was the habit of putting long-te
above immediate gain. And, as it was put by Gabriel F
of his most relied-on aides in government, "the tow
was integrity."[1]

All of this was important in the public's percepti
man, but what gave the truly distinctive character to hi
istration of economic policy was the philosophy he br
the White House. In a word, it was individualism. At it
was a perception of the individual as a self-disci
basically self-reliant person, enjoying a whole battery o
and freedoms—religious, political, civil, and economic
just as it was the duty of government to protect those righ
individual had a parallel responsibility, which Eisenhowe
fidently expected would be honored, to have regard fo
rights and freedoms of others.

*   *   *

From this philosophical stance certain convictions follov
that were crucial in shaping the approaches he took to politi
and economic questions. First, it made him an ardent champi
of the competitive, market-directed, enterprise economy. Whi
the case for this system is typically made on the ground of i

Second, his individualism made him equally an advocate of limited government. There was ample room in his philosophy for government that would do for people what they needed to have done but for one reason or another could not do adequately for themselves; but there was no room in it for the big, federalized, interventionist, and increasingly paternalistic government that in his time had won many supporters and was winning more. The principle involved here is plain enough (the first formulation of it is commonly attributed to Lincoln), but nothing tested the talents of Eisenhower's speechwriters more than the task of devising a felicitous phrasing of it. According to Governor Sherman Adams, Eisenhower's first White House Chief of Staff, the president's preferred wording was this:

> The legitimate object of government is to do for a community of people whatever they need to have done, but cannot do at all, or cannot so well do, for themselves—in their separate and individual capacities. In all that people can individually do as well for themselves, government ought not to interfere.[4]

Eisenhower had been espousing the principle for years. In the October 1949 address to the American Bar Association, already alluded to, he acknowledged the need for government to "prevent or correct abuses springing from the unregulated practice of a private economy," but went on:

> We, in turn, carefully watch the Government—especially the ever-expanding Federal Government—to see that in performing the functions obviously falling within governmental responsibility it does not interfere more than is necessary in our daily lives. We instinctively have greater faith in the counterbalancing effect of many social, philosophic and economic forces than we do in arbitrary law.

Three months before that, in a long letter to a Texas friend, in which he wrote with some heat on ". . . ideas which, if adopted in our country, would merely advance us one more step toward total socialism, just beyond which lies total dictatorship," there was another spelling-out of his views on the proper scope of government:

The problem of our day and time is how to distinguish between all those things that government must do in order to perpetuate and maintain freedom for all . . . while, on the other hand, we combat remorselessly all those paternalistic and collectivistic ideas which, if adopted, will accomplish the gradual lessening of our individual rights and opportunities and finally the collapse of self-government.[5]

In 1949, newly established as president of Columbia University, he began the year by writing a long, reflective entry in his personal diary in which he put his position bluntly:

As between the so-called concept of the welfare state and the operation of a system of competitive enterprise there is no doubt where I stand. I am not on any fence.[6]

And a few years later, addressing himself from the White House to a Congress in which there were many of a different mind than his on the issue of big versus limited government, he put the point again:

This administration . . . follows two simple rules: first, the Federal Government should perform an essential task only when it cannot otherwise be adequately performed; and second, in performing that task our government must not impair the self-respect, freedom and incentive of the individual. As long as these two rules are observed, the government can fully meet its obligation without creating a dependent population or a domineering bureaucracy.[7]

Finally, as he left the presidency in January 1961 the concluding words of his last State of the Union Message were a plea to Congress to maintain "a reasonable balance between private and governmental responsibility."[8] After eight years contesting with Congress what would constitute "a reasonable balance," his own standard was clear. Naturally enough, the limits it put on the scope of government were all along a major point of contention between him and his political opposition.

*   *   *

Third, individualism made Eisenhower a decentralist on how

the responsibilities of government should be divided among federal, state and local authorities. Thus, a February 1954 news conference was warned: "when we relieve local communities, local populations, of all responsibility, all of the participation in the costs of (local projects), we are running a very dangerous course."[9] And in an interview five years after he had left the White House he reaffirmed what he had said when he first arrived there, saying: "I am perfectly certain that the best answer to overcentralized government is better local and state government."[10]

Underlying this preference for decentralized government was Eisenhower's confidence that citizens could be relied on to deal with local problems more economically and, in general, more constructively than could the federal government, acting alone and from a distance. And equity was involved. To the extent possible, states and localities should bear the cost of governmental services where they were the sole or principal beneficiaries of them, certainly they should bear a major share of the cost.

There is a good statement of this sharing or partnership principle in a note Eisenhower drafted early in his presidency for the guidance of his staff prior to meeting with a group interested in a joint federal/state power project:

> "[I]t seems logical to me that we should seek to have embedded in our pursuits the partnership principle—by which I mean that the Federal Government do its full share in any project, but that those localities or areas or groups especially benefitted by any project should bear a share of the burden. For this reason I have not been particularly concerned with precedent or the lack of precedent. I think it is far more important in the long term stability and success of our form of economy to make all these things conform to principles of logic and fairness than to be guided solely by what has been done in the past.[11]

Naturally enough, sharing did not go down well with those in Congress who favored more federalizing of government programs. And it went down no better with the majority of officials of state and local government, who were increasingly looking to Washington for funds to meet the cost even of projects and programs entirely local in nature. The issue was confronted repeatedly in legislative battles.

*   *   *

Taken together, these elements of Eisenhower's political and economic philosophy—his determination to strengthen the market-directed economy; his preference for limited government; and his decentralism—amounted to a wish to see economic and political power diffused to the fullest extent possible in domestic affairs. Side by side with them was a fourth element—his resolute internationalism.

Standing for internationalism was not always a comfortable position to take, no more so in Eisenhower's than in any president's time, and inevitably there were disappointments for him and for his supporters in his efforts to practice its precepts. As with every other head of government in modern times, it was Eisenhower's experience that the domestic interest, narrowly construed, collided frequently with what a fully internationalist viewpoint would dictate, and compromises had to be accepted to preserve what gains in the liberalizing of trade relations had already been made. It was often difficult for full-fledged free traders to concede a need for these concessions; but, as we will see, the concessions involved no abandonment of the basically internationalist position.

*   *   *

How did he come by these convictions? Their roots were first of all in the circumstances of his early life. Growing up in Kansas at the turn of the century in a family that lived quite literally by the Bible and made its way in the world by hard work and strict economy was not an absolute guarantee that his views would be such as those he espoused in later life. Others having substantially similar backgrounds had reached very different political positions. But it was a background obviously calculated to foster respect for the qualities of self-reliance and self-discipline that were basic to his individualism. And it was at the bottom of another major element in his political makeup: his confidence in the readiness of people, given the facts, to act responsibly and constructively in personal and civic affairs.

His loyalty to this background and the depth of the convictions it instilled in him are reflected in his reply to a letter he received while at Columbia that challenged the legitimacy of his views and asserted that while "Generals, Colonels, University Presidents and Corporation Heads (generally speaking) favor individualism and private initiatives . . . they are less keen about it in practice for the rank and file." With some irritation, Eisenhower responded:

> I cannot prove validity for my own particular chain of reasoning or for the conclusion resulting therefrom, but I do know that those ideas were *not* [his italics] absorbed because I was or am a Colonel, a General, a University President or a Corporation Head. I absorbed them from my father and mother as one of a large family of boys without any money or one atom of political influence. The teaching in that family was one of reward for hard work and the existence of opportunity, for the worker, on every hand. That entire group of boys is today as devoted to individualism as I am, and even if I seem to violate the limits of modesty I must say, in my opinion, that the group has proved the existence of opportunity as well as that society will still reasonably reward individuals who will put enough sweat and thought into their work. Everyone in the family was raised on such slogans as "Sink or swim, survive or perish," a favorite saying of a very wise, even if very poor, set of parents.[12]

*　　*　　*

But there was more to the shaping of his convictions than this family background. They took shape also as reactions to the drift of things in the United States. As he wrote to me in 1964 (as an aside to another matter), one of the reasons he undertook to run for the presidency in 1952 was that he "wanted to do something important in changing trends that were then prevailing."

To begin with, there was his concern about inflation. It made a mockery of personal traits which, as he saw it, were essential for the survival of a free economy and thus (on his "bundle of freedoms" theory) essential for the survival of political liberties. And America had had a good deal of inflation. In the twelve years ending in 1952 the value of the dollar had been cut

nearly in half. Immense military needs were in good part responsible for this, but the feeling grew on all sides, with
Eisenhower sharing it, that the methods followed in financing
World War II, in particular the ill-starred attempt to hold interest rates unchanged when market forces dictated that they rise,
and the reliance during those years on a price control system
that treated the symptoms of inflation rather than its causes,
also had a large part in what had happened. The price increases
between 1946 and 1948 that followed the release of wartime
controls confirmed these views. In short, history set the stage
for the return to monetary and fiscal orthodoxy that
Eisenhower advocated.

Other concerns also ran deeply. Chief among them was
Eisenhower's uneasiness about the increasing size and intru-
siveness of government. He wrote in *The White House Years*
how he and his associates viewed the drift of things in 1952–53:

> As we began our studies, many people believed that federal
> expenditures and the national debt had become so great and
> accompanying tax rates so high that we faced the distinct
> possibility of living in a permanently controlled economy. If this
> situation were allowed to continue indefinitely, the country
> could not long pretend to be one of private, competitive enter-
> prise; we would be accepting a controlled economy as a perma-
> nent feature of our society. The cloud of an unwanted socialism
> seemed to be, at least faintly, appearing on the economic hori-
> zon.[13]

There was reason to be concerned. Spending by government,
counting outlays at all levels, had risen from 12 percent of
national income in 1929 to 23 percent in 1940. Then, after rising
to nearly 57 percent during World War II, dropping back in the
postwar years, and rising again during the Korean Conflict, the
ratio settled at around 33 percent in 1952. And within the total
of government spending there was more and more a concentration at the federal level. Washington's share had risen
from about a quarter in 1929 to about a half just before World
War II began and to three-quarters by the first Eisenhower
year.[14]

Higher taxation had accompanied higher spending. The "tax take" had risen from 12 percent of national output in 1930 to 18.5 in 1940 and to 27.5 in 1952, with the percentage claimed by the federal government nearly six times as large at the end of the period as at the beginning. Even so, government was not raising enough money to cover its expenses.[15] Except in war-time, budget deficits were small compared to those incurred in the 1970s and 1980s (in relative as well as absolute terms), but the tripling of public debt between 1942 and 1952 was viewed with much concern, certainly by Eisenhower. It was, of course, essentially a wartime phenomenon, but it was also a reminder of a rule on which he put heavy emphasis: a government, like a family, should aim over some reasonable period to bring its expenditures into balance with its income. As he remarked to a 1959 news conference: "I think it is rather a good thing to be a bit frugal and say that we can live within our income."[16]

In addition, there were connections between federal budget deficits and the expansion of money supply that made a budget balance important to inflation control. As he stated in a 1959 speech, "when part of the [Treasury's] borrowing . . . comes from commercial banks, the money supply is increased and the conditions are created for an inflationary price rise."[17]

It is not surprising that the increases he and his associates had been witnessing in spending, in taxes, and in the inflation rate fired them with zeal for a conservative conduct of the federal government's fiscal affairs. Expressing this, Eisenhower's first State of the Union Message declared that "the first order of business is the elimination of the annual deficit."[18] And the task was approached vigorously in 1953: first, through restraints on spending; second, by urging Congress to defer certain tax reductions already legislated (mainly, rollbacks to pre-Korean levels) and that in other circumstances the new administration would have been anxious to support.

As we will see, the request to Congress to hold the line on taxes was withdrawn when it became apparent later in 1953 that the economy was turning into recession; but expenditures (as shown in the national income and product accounts) were all the same cut nearly 10 percent between the calendar years

1953 and 1954, and the deficit was reduced by 15 percent. In short, the fiscal principles were quickly put to work.

*   *   *

It goes without saying that in his individualism and noninterventionism Eisenhower was not running with the intellectual tide. Everywhere, ideas were gaining ground that were in fundamental conflict with what he set himself and his administration to do. In the United States, the issue came to a head as World War II ended in discussions of how much government intervention would be needed to assure a satisfactory transition from war to peace. Interventionists argued that only a massive federal effort would prevent unemployment from soaring to unprecedented heights. Taking an opposite stand, noninterventionists maintained that there were no serious imbalances in the economy and that, given a favorable monetary environment, demand would by itself expand sufficiently to provide the needed solution.

History bore out the noninterventionists, perhaps more fully than even they had expected. Thanks to savings that consumers had accumulated during the war (when incomes were high and buying opportunities were limited) and to a large additional use of installment credit (which their improved financial status permitted), the shortage of demand did not materialize. Goods and services bought by the federal government dropped between 1944 and 1946 from something over 40 percent of total national output to only 9 percent, but a combination of greatly increased consumer buying, a more than doubling of business spending on capital goods, a restocking of inventories by businesses, and the beginning of an export boom held the overall decline in physical output to 20 percent. Civilian employment rose by 2.4 percent a year and, despite a reduction of 8 million in the armed forces, the unemployment rate had risen by 1946 to only 3.9 percent from an abnormally low level (1.2 percent) in 1944.[19]

Despite this success, support for some form of national economic planning continued, coming to the forefront in the debate over what was in the end enacted as the Employment

Act of 1946.[20] Also, a disposition to favor central planning seemed implicit in the "national economic budgets" that were a prominent part of the Economic Reports prepared under the Employment Act for President Truman.[21] While the planning implied in these budgets was only "indicative," the possibility of it developing along "directed" lines was sufficiently high to warrant viewing it as likely to lead to basically undemocratic changes in the nation's economic and political institutions.

Eisenhower feared it might do so. As he wrote in his White House memoirs, reflecting on what led him to stand for the presidency:

> By 1952 I fervently believed that . . . the Republicans had to win or abjectly accept the conclusion that a "centralized" power philosophy was permanently supplanting our once-proud tradition of depending for national progress upon individual initiative, self-reliance, and private, competitive enterprise.[22]

That was what the Republican Party meant when it said in the 1952 presidential campaign that it was "Time for a Change." And that was what Eisenhower meant when, in accepting the Party's nomination to run in that year as its presidential candidate, he said that "You have summoned me . . . to a Great Crusade."[23] It would be a return to a more traditional scheme of things.

Notes

1. In an interview for the Columbia University Oral History Project.

2. *Public Papers, DDE*, 1953, p. 432.

3. *American Bar Association Journal*, October 1949, Vol. 35, p. 812.

4. From *Firsthand Report: The Story of the Eisenhower Administration* (p. 299), which is Sherman Adams's account of his service as Eisenhower's first White House Chief of Staff. The book was published in 1961 by Harper Brothers, New York, and reprinted in 1974 by Greenwood Press. It is an indispensable source of information and comment on the Eisenhower presidency.

5. *The Papers Of Dwight David Eisenhower*, Vol. X, no. 482 (The Johns Hopkins University Press, Baltimore, 1984), pp. 665–669.

(Hereafter cited as *Eisenhower Papers*). This volume and a number of others in the series were edited by Professor Louis Galambos of Johns Hopkins University.

6. *The Eisenhower Diaries*, edited by Robert H. Ferrell (W. W. Norton and Company, New York, 1981), p. 170. (Hereafter cited as *Eisenhower Diaries*.)

7. *Public Papers, DDE*, 1955, p. 22. There are statements by Eisenhower of his philosophy in numerous other places. A long one was quoted by Kevin McCann in his book, *America's Man of Destiny, An Intimate Biography of General Eisenhower* (William Heinemann Ltd., London, 1952), pp. 189–97. Other relevant papers are Eisenhower's London Guildhall Address, delivered in June 1944; the May 26, 1946 entry in *Eisenhower Diaries;* the May 1946 memorandum written by Eisenhower while Chief of Staff of the United States Army (McCann, *America's Man of Destiny,* pp. 120–21); his 1947 letter to Everett "Swede" Hazlett, a longtime Abilene friend and frequent correspondent, which gives his reasons for accepting the presidency of Columbia University (McCann, *America's Man of Destiny,* pp. 128–129); and his 1957 address to Republican women (*Public Papers, DDE*, 1957, pp. 250–59).

8. *Public Papers, DDE*, 1960–61, p. 930.

9. *Public Papers, DDE*, 1954, p. 273.

10. *Nation's Business*, October 1965, Vol. 53, no. 10, pp. 34–7.

11. From a draft of a teletype message to Governor Sherman Adams, December 20, 1954, in papers at the Dwight D. Eisenhower Presidential Library, Abilene, Kansas (DDE Diary Series, Box 8, December 1954 [10]). Hereafter cited as *Abilene Papers*.)

12. *Eisenhower Papers*, Vol. X, no. 447, pp. 612–14.

13. *The White House Years, Vol. I, Mandate for Change, 1953–1956* (Doubleday and Company, New York, 1965), p. 128. (Hereafter cited as *The White House Years*.)

14. G. Warren Nutter, *Growth Of Government in the West* (American Enterprise Institute, Washington, D.C., 1978), pp. 1–18 and Appendix Tables B-4 and B-6.

15. The concept of "tax take" is that used by the Tax Foundation in *Facts and Figures on Government Finance, 22nd Biennial Edition, 1983*, p. 45.

16. *Public Papers, DDE*, 1959, p. 197. The question of having the federal government use a capital budget did not arise as a practical issue in Eisenhower's time, and one can only speculate on how he would have reacted to it: I expect not favorably.

17. A speech to the U.S. Savings Bond Conference, *Public Papers, DDE*, 1959, p. 221.

18. *Public Papers, DDE*, 1953, p. 20.

19. *Economic Report of the President*, February 1984, Tables B-02

and B-29. (Hereafter cited as *Economic Report*) Also, *Historical Statistics of the United States, Colonial Times to 1970*, Part 1, p. 126. (Hereafter cited as *Historical Statistics*)

20. Stephen Kemp Bailey notes in his book *Congress Makes a Law, The Story Behind The Employment Act of 1946* (Columbia University Press, 1950) that "Congressional debate over the Full Employment Bill was presaged by the struggle between conservative and liberal legislators over reconversion policy" (p. 35).

21. For example, in the *January 1949 Economic Report* (Harcourt Brace and Company, New York, 1949), pp. 30–35.

22. *The White House Years,* Vol. II, p. 651.

23. *New York Times,* July 12, 1952, p. 4.

II. Implications of the Philosophy for Policies and Programs

It is not always easy to identify the philosophy that underlies a president's policies other than to say it is pragmatism, and it is true that government decisions are typically made with an eye to their practicality. Eisenhower's administration of government was no exception. But pragmatism, as has been said, is less a philosophy than a way of doing without one, and to say of Eisenhower that he was a pragmatist, as every now and then it is, not only says little that would distinguish him from almost anyone else in the presidency of the United States but misses any notion of how his philosophical leanings—his ideology—shaped his thinking on economic policy.

*   *   *

To begin with, it was inherent in Eisenhower's individualism that economic progress depended less on what government did than on the intiative and enterprise of individuals seeking to better themselves through their own efforts. Accordingly, the proper role of government, for him, was to create an environment that would give maximum encouragement to the initiatives undertaken by individuals, acting separately or in groups. This acknowledged that government would provide basic safeguards of personal economic security and the essential services that individuals or groups could not provide adequately for themselves, that it would seek to keep prices stable and markets competitive, and that it would do all it could do constructively to promote saving and investment. Beyond that, government would abstain from intervening in the economy.

Eisenhower had stated his preference for government in this style long before he became a candidate for the presidency but, naturally enough, the most studied expressions of it are found in his White House papers and in the reports of his Council of Economic Advisers. In the *January 1956 Economic Report* (p. 72), for example, there is the following:

"[L]asting prosperity of the Nation depends far more on what individuals do for themselves than on what the Federal Government does or can do for them . . . [thus] the rate of economic advance . . . will depend largely on our ability as a people to preserve an environment that rewards individual initiative and encourages enterprise, innovation, and investment.

And in the *January 1961 Economic Report* (p. 57):

Government makes its basic contribution not through the volume of its own expenditures but by promoting conditions favorable to the exercise of individual initiative and effort.

*   *   *

Why government in this style was so widely regarded in the 1950s as essentially inactivist is one of the mysteries of those years. To be sure, it required that government stand aside in many situations in which the typical activist would have favored intervention. But one would expect it to have been obvious that to keep the economy competitive, and in particular to keep it free of inflation (with what that meant for the management of the nation's finances and the handling of money policy) were not tasks for a government which, in any acceptable sense of the word, could be called inactivist. But the negative effects on the economy of large deficits in the federal budget and rising rates of inflation were not as well understood in the 1950s as later. Nor was it realized how easy it was to slip into them and how difficult to get out. Indeed, in Eisenhower's time the accent in public discourse was more likely to be on the putatively beneficial effects on growth and employment of a budget deficit and some upward tilting of the price trend.

Eisenhower had grave reservations about all of this. Responding to a 1959 news conference question on how he felt about the criticism that he seemed to "worry a little too much about inflation . . . and perhaps not enough about the slow rate of growth of [the] economy," he struck out vigorously at the theory that you could trade inflation for growth:

> [T]he kind of concern you speak of is really not two different problems—inflation or economic growth. I believe that economic growth in the long run cannot be soundly brought about except with stability in your price structure.[1]

In other words, one did not have the option of choosing between inflation and unemployment, in the manner of a "trade off." The danger was that opting for inflation, even where the rate was low, would ultimately lead to higher rates of both inflation and unemployment. "Creeping inflation . . . has a tendency finally to become galloping inflation," Eisenhower warned in a 1965 interview, with his White House years behind him and with the country on the eve of what was soon to be a wrenching experience with double-digit price increases.[2] It was rare even then, however, for the inflation risk to be given the weight it deserved.

*   *   *

It was, of course, no novelty for an administration to make price stability a goal of economic policy. What divides presidents as well as economists on this point is not whether one is for or against inflation, but at what point the inflation danger is taken seriously, and how one goes about overcoming inflation, once it is underway. There was never any doubt about where Eisenhower stood on either point. Inflation was a latent danger against which it was necessary to be constantly alert. And while he reserved the option of using direct controls under emergency conditions to help cope with it (a point on which many would fault him, and in my view deservedly), his philosophical antipathy toward direct intervention into the economy (plus his understanding of what was at the bottom of across-the-board increases in prices) put him squarely on the side of inflation control through the indirect forces of monetary and fiscal restraint. The charter statement of this position is in his first State of the Union Message:

> The great economic strength of our democracy has developed in an atmosphere of freedom. The character of our people resists artificial and arbitrary controls of any kind. Direct controls, except those on credit, deal not with the real causes of inflation but only with its symptoms. In times of national emergency, this kind of control has a role to play. Our whole system, however, is based upon the assumption that, normally, we should combat wide fluctuations in our price structure by relying largely on the effective use of sound fiscal and monetary policy, and upon the natural workings of economic law.[3]

Correct as this position was, there was a certain awkwardness in it for Eisenhower. His need to rely in stabilizing the price level—a central element in his economic program—on a procedure over which he had no control, and which was carried out by the independent Federal Reserve Board in a manner so arcane as often to escape the attention of his critics and perhaps also their understanding, invited the characterization of his administration as nonactivist.

Eisenhower was sensitive to this lack of power on his part and (like all presidents in the same situation) was at times uneasy about it. Indeed, he was tempted once to ask Congress to authorize a fundamental change in the White House-Federal Reserve relationship. But in the end the element in his makeup that distrusted politics (it was a major one) took charge: his considered conclusion was that it was best to keep political considerations out of money policy. His respect and admiration for William McChesney Martin who, initially appointed by President Truman, led the Federal Reserve throughout Eisenhower's presidency, was doubtless also a factor in shaping that final judgment.

Consistent with the position he took on the White House-Federal Reserve relationship, his administration (led aggressively in this by George M. Humphrey as Secretary of the Treasury and W. Randolph Burgess as Under Secretary of the Treasury for Monetary Affairs) sought consistently, in three major ways, to enhance the Federal Reserve's ability to act independently. First, there was an early and unqualified acceptance of the "accord" reached in the latter part of the Truman administration between the Federal Reserve and the Treasury under which the former was released from the commitment it had been under during World War II to hold the prices of government bonds unchanged. This "pegging" of bond prices was widely acknowledged as having helped generate inflationary pressures, and Eisenhower pledged in his first State of the Union Message that the practice would not be repeated:

> Past differences in policy between the Treasury and the Federal Reserve Board have helped to encourage inflation. Henceforth I expect that their single purpose shall be to serve the whole Nation by policies designed to stabilize the economy and encourage the free play of our people's genius for individual initiative."[4]

Second, unlike later administrations, Eisenhower's had no quarrel with the "bills only" policy under which the Federal Reserve confined its open market operations (purchases and sales of Treasury securities) to transactions in obligations of short maturity. "Bills only" made it possible for the system to perform its key task—the management of member bank reserve balances and thus (at a further remove) the management of credit and economic conditions—with a minimum of direct intervention in credit markets. In this way it fitted perfectly, indeed rather elegantly, into Eisenhower's noninterventionism. For all its merits, however, it projected an image of government, of the White House as well as the Federal Reserve, as standoffish and nonactivist.

Third and finally, it was the Treasury's policy, as we will shortly see, to manage the public debt with an eye to strengthening the ability of the Federal Reserve to act freely and flexibly in carrying out its central banking duties. This required that in borrowing new funds and in refinancing outstanding debt it would seek as much as possible to avoid the use of shortterm securities. As we will see in dealing later with the problem of coping with recession, debt management in this manner had at times a counterproductive effect on the economy. But this resulted not so much from defects in the basics of what was being attempted as from miscalculations in the timing and day-to-day execution of policy.

*   *   *

Eisenhower's philosophical leanings were also crucial in shaping what he stood for in fiscal policy. In the end, Congress has the decisive role here, but in Eisenhower's time drawing up an overall fiscal plan was uniquely the president's business. The Joint Economic Committee held hearings on what the White House proposed, but had no authority to modify it. There was no Congressional Budget Office drawing up alternative budget projections, as there is now, and no Gramm-Rudman-Hollings legislation setting budgetary limits to which the president was expected to conform. And when Congress acted on the president's budget it acted on it piecemeal, not in one huge package, put before the president on a "take it or leave it" basis. Effectively, this left overall fiscal leadership in the hands of the president, and Eisenhower exercised it to the full, and with relish. It was no accident that "fiscal responsibility" became the hallmark of what he stood for in economic policy.

At the same time there has been much misunderstanding of what was meant by "fiscal responsibility." Its first requirement was of course that money should be spent prudently. It also meant that budget receipts and outlays should be so matched that, except during recession, they would be in balance, or roughly so. But it did not mean, as was routinely alleged by Eisenhower's critics, that the accounts had to be balanced every year. It would not only be impossible to adhere to such a rule in an economy subject to cyclical fluctuations, but attempting to do so would almost certainly make matters worse. In the current idiom, what fiscal responsibility called for was a budget in "structural balance," the test of which would be that the accounts, though almost certainly in deficit during recession, would return promptly to balance or to surplus when recession was ended. Over time, the budget would thus allow some reduction in the federal debt, some permanent reduction in the tax burden, or some combination of the two.

The goal was put as follows in the *January 1956 Economic Report* (p. 73), "sufficient revenues should be raised to meet the Government's outlays, if not every individual year, then surely over a term of very few years," and by Eisenhower in responding to a 1959 news conference question, "I sometimes wonder whether we shouldn't think of our budget balancing in . . . 5-year terms, or at least to include the length of . . . the ordinary business cycle. . . . One year's budget is not the whole answer. . . ."[5]

But even formulated in this moderate and flexible rule, the notion of fiscal responsibility was not one for which, in the 1950s, there was much approval. At a time when cutting taxes to help get out of recession was the "litmus test" of economic literacy, counseling against undermining the tax system's revenue-raising capability by countercyclical tax reduction for which a fully persuasive case could not be made (as Eisenhower had occasion frequently to do) was no formula for winning either popular or professional acclaim. Nor did it project the positive and activist image so much admired at the time to remind Congress (as he did repeatedly) of the need to maintain a balance between what it proposed to spend and what the tax system was capable of raising. There was such a reminder in a 1960 message to Congress:

> This truth we must take to heart: in good times, we must at the very least pay our way. . . . This simply means that we must adhere to necessary programs and sensible priorities. . . . If the Congress prefers other priorities at greater national cost, responsibility dictates that it accompany them with the additional taxes to pay the bill.[6]

Eisenhower knew that such statements were regarded by many as out of touch with then-current thinking on fiscal matters, but was in no way disposed to retreat from them. When a 1959 news conference question implied that he had "made a fetish" out of balancing the budget he first reminded the gathering that "we didn't have a balanced budget [in fiscal 1959] and we didn't make a fetish about it," and then went on to make a statement which, thirty years later, stands up well against the flood of what in the interim has been spoken and written on the subject of budgets and budget deficits:

> I don't know why suddenly a balanced budget is getting to be a bad word. I think it is rather a good thing to be a bit frugal and say that we can live within our income . . . I do not know what is [in] the future. '. . . I am not a seventh son of a seventh son. [But] I say this . . . if we cannot live within our means as prosperity is growing and developing, when are we going to do it? And if we are going to always live under deficit spending, what is going to happen to our currency?[7]

Most often, the answer at the time would be that the currency was not in danger. For the moment, critics of what fiscal responsibility stood for were in the saddle.

*   *   *

Alongside Eisenhower's goal of having budget income and outgo so matched as to be at least in balance in good times went an even greater heresy—his determination to retard, and if possible ultimately to reverse, the rising trend in the ratio of government spending to national income. The stakes here were high. What was involved was not merely a matter of financial accounting. What was involved was the structure of the American economy, how it would be divided between public and private sectors, and the political and intellectual tides were running strongly against Eisenhower's preference.

But gaining control over the balance between the public and private sectors of the economy was critically important to Eisenhower. First, he shared the view that, as a purely technical matter, the economy would perform better in the production of goods and services the greater the scope given to private initiative. Second, his "connectedness of freedoms" theory posited that a large and vigorous private sector was vital to the maintenance of freedom generally. And third, there was an inflation angle to it. Eisenhower was much impressed by the theory (it was attracting some attention at the time) that the ratio of government spending to national income could become so high, and lead to such a burdensome level of taxation, that attempting to fund additional spending through still higher taxes would provoke so much public resistance that the political solution would be a resort to deficit financing, thereby increasing the danger of inflation. There were grounds for believing that the flashpoint came when government spending reached 25 percent of national income, and Eisenhower frequently pointed out (correctly) that that point had already been passed in the United States.[8]

For all these reasons, putting a check on how the balance was shifting toward the public sector and away from the private sector was a major objective for Eisenhower. As we will see, it was also one in which he had important success.

*   *   *

Temperament, notably his natural distaste for extremism, was also a factor in determining how Eisenhower approached questions of economic policy. In the 1949 paper read to the American Bar Association (already alluded to) he spelled out his preference for "a practicable middle course between too little and too much government;" and at a news conference when only two months into the presidency he stated: "I don't like extremists of any kind." In short, he was basically and from the beginning a moderate and a centrist.

There are many expressions of these leanings in his papers and public statements, personal and official. A 1954 letter to a longtime Army friend, Brigadier-General B. G. Chynoweth (Retired), is a particularly revealing one. Chynoweth had written to take exception to Eisenhower's "philosophy of the Middle Way" and received a lengthy reply, of which the following is part:

"I think that the critical problem of our time is to find and stay on the path that marks the way of logic between conflicting arguments advanced by extremists on both sides of almost every economic, political and international problem. . . . [In] our own day we have those individuals who believe that the

Federal government should enter into every phase and facet of our individual lives, controlling agriculture, industry and education, as well as the development of every natural resource in our country. These people, knowlingly or unknowingly, are trying to put us on the path toward socialism. At the other extreme we have the people—and I know quite a number of them—who want to eliminate everything that the Federal Government has ever done that, in one way or another, represents what is generally classified as social advance. . . . When I refer to the Middle Way, I merely mean the middle way as it represents a practicable working basis between extremists, both of whose doctrines I flatly reject. It seems to me that no great intelligence is required . . . to discern the practical necessity of establishing some kind of security for individuals in a specialized and highly industrialized age. . . . On the other hand, for us to push further and further into the socialisitc experiment is to deny the validity of all those convictions we have held as to the cumulative power of free citizens, exercising their own initiative, inventiveness and desires to provide better living for themselves and their children.[9]

*   *   *

Also bearing on his gradualism, Eisenhower frequently recalled a conversation, shortly after his first election to the presidency, in which ex-President Hoover warned him that, as president, he would be under pressure from both the right and the left, the former looking for a return to the "good old days" and the latter wanting him to "enlarge and increase every welfare program in the country" and charging him with being "the tool of Wall Street" if he resisted.[10] Hoover was making the case for gradualism: it would be unwise, and in any case not possible, to turn the ratio of government spending to national income "sharply downward"; it had been moving up for years and the most any administration could do, or should attempt to do, was to "flatten the curve."

There is no reason to believe that Eisenhower ever felt otherwise. As he noted in his memoirs: "the government cost curve cannot be abruptly turned down; it has to be gradually bent."[11] And as it turned out, that is what happened. The ratio to national income of goverment spending (federal, state and local), which had climbed from 12 percent in 1929 to 23 percent in 1940 and then to 33 percent in 1952, was stabilized at the latter rate in the Eisenhower years. After a time it began to rise again, but that was after Eisenhower, and it is another story.

As Mr. Hoover had forecast, gradualism, centrism and moderation drew criticism from both the right and the left. Eisenhower knew it would, but did not mind. A year or so after leaving the White House, reflecting over that experience, he remarked to Governor Adams: "I feel pretty good when I'm attacked from both sides . . . it makes me more certain I'm on the right track."[12]

*   *   *

So much for the basis in philosophy and temperament of Eisenhower's major goals and methods in economic policy. Like all presidents, he had to apply his philosophy in a world complicated by, among other things, the ups and downs of the business cycle. We will turn in due course to that story, but first to a number of steps taken in 1953 to get government started along new lines.

Notes

1. *Public Papers, DDE*, 1959, p. 125.
2. *Nation's Business*, October 1965, Vol. 53, no. 10, p. 37.
3. *Public Papers, DDE*, 1953, p. 22.
4. *Public Papers, DDE*, 1953, p. 22. This pledge was also made in a September 1953 speech by Secretary George M. Humphrey. See *The Basic Papers of George M. Humphrey, as Secretary of the Treasury, 1953–1957*, edited by Nathaniel R. Howard (The Western Reserve Historical Society, Cleveland, Ohio, 1965), p. 118. (Hereafter cited as *Humphrey Papers*) See also pp. 307–29 of the same collection.
5. *Public Papers, DDE*, 1959, p. 197. To the best of my knowledge, Eisenhower never favored proposals to legislate a balanced budget, by a constitutional amendment or otherwise. A plan for legislative mandating of a balanced budget was discussed within the administration in 1960 but was opposed by the CEA and was abandoned before being presented to the president. On this, see the July 8, 1960 memorandum and attachments in *Abilene Papers*, Administrative Series, Box 34.
6. *Public Papers, DDE*, 1960–61, p. 618.

7. *Public Papers, DDE,* 1959, p. 197.

8. The theory was put forward by Colin Clark, a much respected economist, in an article entitled "Public Finance and Changes in the Value of Money," which appeared in the *Economic Journal,* December 1945, Vol. 55, pp. 371–89 and started considerable controversy. Joseph Pechman and Thomas Mayer challenged Clark's theory in *The Review of Economics and Statistics,* August 1952, Vol. 34, pp. 232–242. Nearly a decade later a theory essentially the same as Clark's was advanced by Simon Kuznets in his monumental study, *Capital in the American Economy: Its Formation and Financing* (Princeton University Press, Princeton, New Jersey, for the National Bureau of Economic Research, 1961), pp. 449–61, in this case without raising serious dissent.

9. *Abilene Papers,* Name Series, Box 5.

10. *The White House Years,* Vol. I, pp. 410–31 and *Abilene Papers,* Ann Whitman File, Box 10, June 1959, [1].

11. *The White House Years,* Vol. I, p. 574.

12. *Public Papers, DDE,* 1953, p. 129 and Adams, *Firsthand Report,* p. 463. Eisenhower also remarked to Adams: "we kept to what I have called a middle-of-the-road course, away from the extremes favored by the reactionary conservatives of our own party and away from the vast spending schemes of the irresponsible elements of the Democratic Party. This is the course that any administration must follow if its policies are to meet the needs of the times."

III. Getting Started

Like every new presidential administration, especially when a change of party is involved, Eisenhower's began with a long list of changes to be made and goals to be reached. But, like all others, his was in many ways conditioned in what it set out to do by the backlog of problems carried over from what had gone before. Things took on a different cast later in the year, when the economy moved into recession, but attention centered at the outset in 1953 on problems that had little or nothing to do with the ups and downs of business. Some of them, such as what to do about the badly arranged and enormously expensive programs to assist agriculture, were too complicated to be acted on without extensive study, and while there was some hesitation about offering the country "a diet of commissions," as Governor Adams had put it, a spate of special groups— cabinet committees, interagency task forces, presidential commissions and such—was set up to examine into them.[1] Other questions, such as what to do about what remained of an apparatus for the direct control of wages and prices, did not need the same depth of study, and in any case were too urgent to be approached in that manner.

We can begin with one of the most urgent problems facing Eisenhower as his presidency began—what to do about the president's economic advisory services.

Reconstituting the Council of Economic Advisers

It is not unusual for there to be extensive reorganization of Executive Branch agencies when there is a transfer of presidential power, and Eisenhower's accession to the presidency in January 1953 was no exception. Changes are usually made at the initiative of the incoming administration, but one of those carried out in 1953—the reconstitution of the Council of Economic Advisers (CEA)—was mainly a response by the newcomers to an action that had already been taken by Congress. It happens that there has been much misunderstanding of it.

The story of how the problem evolved begins with certain actions taken during the closing session of the last Truman Congress. The Democratic Party was in control of both House and Senate. With the legislators in an economizing mood, a floor vote in the House included the CEA with a number of other agencies whose funds for the fiscal 1953 year were to be cut by about 25 percent. Dr. Leon Keyserling, who was CEA chairman at the time, protested the cut and, when the appropriations bill reached the Senate, rallied a bipartisan group of Senators to the Council's support. Robert A. Taft (Ohio), Republican leader in the Senate, was among them.[2] Although the solution devised by the group was open to the interpretation that it was a repudiation of the CEA, it was not that: it was a stratagem (for which there was ample precedent in the conduct of congressional business) intended to make it possible for the Council, despite the cut in its budget, to continue operations, for a time at least, substantially as before. The plan provided that the funds being appropriated for the Council would be available to it only through March 31, 1953. Thus the Council would be able to spend for nine months at the rate originally requested for twelve, and in the process the White House and Congress would have close to five months to decide how presidential economic advisory services would be provided after the March 31, 1953 cutoff point had been passed. On that basis, the CEA's budget for fiscal 1953 was voted by the Senate and acceded to by the House.

The effect of this was to put the ball in the administration's court and to excite debate at both ends of Pennsylvania Avenue. In this, the CEA had many supporters in Congress, Republicans as well as Democrats, all of whom could be counted on to work for the Council's continuation broadly as it had been originally structured—as a three-member body. But there were others in Congress disposed to terminate that format and substitute for it a single adviser, operating in the White House Office as Economic Adviser to the President.

Even in this troubled context, a solution might have been worked out more or less placidly within Congress, and between Congress and the White House, had it not become apparent early in 1953 that the money available to the CEA would be exhausted even before March 31, 1953. Accordingly, as that date approached, in an action widely misunderstood as a repudiation by Eisenhower of the CEA as originally established, it was necessary for the new administration to terminate the employment of all CEA employees under a "reduction in force" requirement (a "riffing," as it is called in federal lingo). Shortly thereafter, additional funds were found (doubtless in an account over which the president had discretionary authority) and a few key Council staff members were recalled to their jobs, but the agency's future remained in question.

There were two principal grounds for the opposition in Congress to the Council. One was that its members under President Truman had not always been able to reach a consensus on policy questions, and sometimes expressed opposing views on them in public.[3] A second was that certain Council members had engaged in what some in Congress regarded as "political" activity, in particular that Dr. Keyserling, first as Vice Chairman and later as Chairman, had been overly aggressive in pressing the case, in Congress and elsewhere, for the Truman administration's policies.[4]

There was merit to the view that Council members should try to reach agreement on policy questions, and certainly that they should avoid any public display of disagreement. But that they were not always of the same mind on these matters, even that there were continuing differences among them, did not constitute an inherent defect in the Council's structure. Certainly it did not constitute grounds for discontinuing the Council.

Nor were there grounds for discontinuance of the three-member Council in the complaint that some of its members engaged at times in what was thought to be "political" activity. Every Council member can be understood to be speaking for the president's program when making a statement in public, and thus what is said necessarily has a political quality. Granted, some Council members have in the past been more aggressive and explicit in this regard than others, as some may well be in the future; but these are differences in personal style and, again, do not constitute an inherent and continuing defect in the Council's structure, or suggest any deficiency in its utility as an advisory body.

To the best of my knowledge there is no documentary evidence on how Eisenhower, as he began in November 1952 to prepare for presidential duties, wished to have his economic advisory services organized. However, based on his already established record for extensive use of professional staff, and considering the importance of the function involved, one can be reasonably sure that there would have been provision, one way or another, for economic advice.[5] And it is also reasonable to assume that had it not been for the questions about the Council's future that were already in the air in 1953 there would have been no question from the White House side about continuing it broadly as provided for in 1946 in the Employment Act. At the same time, considering the Council's identification with Truman administration policies about which Eisenhower had strong reservations, and especially considering his distaste for the interventionism that was at least potential in the "economic budgeting" being advocated by the Truman Council, it is reasonable to surmise that he would have been open to suggestions for changes in the medium through which the economic advisory function would be performed.

Whatever the merit of these assumptions and surmises, Eisenhower came down early in favor of reconstituting the Council broadly as originally structured, and against allowing it to be terminated as it ran out of money and substituting for it the single-adviser format for which there was much support in Congress. In a February 4, 1953 action that should long ago have put to rest the version of these happenings that has Eisenhower opposed to continuation of the CEA, Governor

Adams, in requesting a supplemental appropriation of funds for the Council, notified the legislators that "while the President has not yet completed his plans for the Council of Economic Advisers, he believed it highly important that the Council be continued."[6] The rest of the story, then, is how a reconstituting of the Council was carried out.

*   *   *

It was done promptly. Counseled by Dr. Gabriel Hauge, a trained, experienced and respected economist, and the White House staff member with particular responsibility in economic matters, Eisenhower, having requested the supplemental appropriation from Congress alluded to above which would carry the Council through the unfunded months of April, May, and June, engaged, Dr. Arthur F. Burns (at the time Professor of Economics at Columbia University and Director of Research at the New York-based, privately-supported National Bureau of Economic Research) to study how best to organize the White House economic advisory function.[7]

The request for supplemental funds was followed a few weeks later by Burns's nomination to the Council as a member, and by his confirmation in that post on March 18, 1953, but there having been no action yet on the president's supplemental budget request the Council's future was still uncertain. As the *January 1954 Economic Report* described it, alluding to the early 1953 "riffing" of employees already noted, "the Council had practically exhausted its funds and was obliged to begin to wind up its affairs."[8] Actually, Congress did not act on the request for supplemental funds until March 28, 1953, three days before the Council would otherwise have been "out of business," and when it did act (sparingly) it gave a hint of how it wished to see the organizational problem solved by providing $50,000 for the establishment in the White House of an Office of the Economic Adviser to the President.

There was no choice for Eisenhower but to accede to this, and the office was established, with Dr. Burns designated as its head. At the same time, however, search for a different solution continued. Carried out by Dr. Burns jointly with Dr. Hauge and the Bureau of the Budget, it led to the submission to Congress on June 1, 1953 of Reorganization Plan No. 9, under which the CEA would be continued, but with certain changes in the format laid down in 1946. In effect, it was reconstituted: administrative responsibility would be lodged exclusively in the chairman (it had previously been shared equally by all members); only the chairman would report to the president; and the office of Vice Chairman would be abolished.[9]

The proposal to make these changes doubtless helped persuade Congress to abandon the single-adviser format that had already been legislated and allow the CEA to be continued substantially as provided for in the 1946 act. Thus reconstituted, the CEA was provided with funds for full-scale operations. Dr. Burns was nominated and confirmed again as a member, and named chairman on August 8, 1953. By the end of the year, all three Council members had been appointed, all of them academicians, as were all subsequent Eisenhower appointees.

It can be assumed that the format created by Reorganization Plan No. 9 responded adequately to congressional concerns; certainly it worked fully to Eisenhower's satisfaction. And it has remained unchanged to this date.

*   *   *

The result (a happy one for the economist's position in White House organization and in the federal government generally) can be attributed mainly to the efforts of Hauge and Burns, supported by the president, and of course to the Council's friends in Congress. But in the end the Council's influence in government depends on how the president uses it, and Eisenhower used it completely in the manner that had been the original intent of Congress. As it has under every president to this date, the CEA operated under him as the one fully-staffed and independent economic advisory agency in the federal government, responsible solely to the president and, by virtue of its independence, able to advise the president impartially on plans and proposals originating anywhere in government, as well as those coming from the public.

Functioning in this manner, the CEA under Eisenhower occupied a highly influential position. Its central task was to keep the president and the cabinet posted on developments affecting the economy's outlook, and to plan and monitor the carrying out of measures to promote the economy's growth and stability. It figured prominently in all policymaking activities of the White House having significant economic content and, with the regrettable and unnecessary exception of some debt-management operations conducted by the Treasury, was involved in the planning and carrying out of all Executive Branch actions likely to have a significant economic effect, other than those for which the Federal Reserve Board was responsible. All legislative proposals of an economic nature, whether originating within or outside government, were submitted to the Council for comment directly to the president. The Council's chairman or another of its members attended all cabinet meetings and all meetings of the president with legislative leaders, making presentations at many of them. The CEA chaired or otherwise participated in numerous cabinet-level committees and interagency task forces and represented the United States on the Economic Policy Committee of what is now the Organization for Economic Cooperation and Development (OECD). It participated fully in the shaping of economic and financial proposals that would be part of the president's legislative program and in the preparation of major presidential papers and statements, notably the Economic Report. The chairman participated in all presidential press conference briefings and, in what is indisputably the acid test of his position in the White House complex, had prompt access to the president, as often as needed.

It was, in short, a close client-counsel relationship, with Eisenhower making a deliberate effort to assure the Council a context in which it could work independently. At a 1954 news conference he summarized for the press the substance of the charge he gave to Dr. Burns on his appointment as CEA chairman:

You are never . . . to develop an opinion and bring it . . . to me or to anyone in the Cabinet or the Legislature that supports someone's political view, including mine. You are to dig out the facts of this economy, and present them as honestly as you and your associates can possibly do it, not only to me but to the public.[10]

To my knowledge, the same charge, in much the same words, was given personally by Eisenhower to all his subsequent appointees to the Council.

Finally, in a January 6, 1954 letter to his brother Milton, written in the reflective mood that was typical of these exchanges, Eisenhower had the following to say (doubtless with staff counsel) about the CEA's functioning:

> Maintenance of prosperity is one field of governmental concern that interests me mightily . . . The first task, of course, is the determination of the scope of federal responsibility and authority. This varies with the times.
>
> In these days I am sure that government has to be the principal coordinator and, in many cases, the actual operator for the many things that the approach of depression would demand.
>
> In its overall aspects the matter falls within the advisory responsibility of the Chairman of the Council of Economic Advisers. He does *not* [DDE's italics] have the responsibility of developing all of the government's subsidiary and operational plans. But he does have the responsibility of watching and studying economic portents, and of assuring the President that each of the measures taken by the government is fitted to the problem and is instituted at the proper time."[11]

*   *   *

Eisenhower took a step early in 1953 (again, almost certainly at the suggestion of Hauge and Burns) to help the CEA perform the policy-coordination function alluded to in his January 6, 1954 letter. As part of the Reorganization Plan that reconstituted the Council, an interagency group—the Advisory Board on Economic Growth and Stability (ABEGS)—was created under the leadership of the CEA chairman. Its purpose was "to make the work of the Council . . . more effective at the top level of the executive branch . . . [and to keep the president] closely informed about the state of the national economy and the various measures necessary to aid in maintaining a stable prosperity."[12]

ABEGS was composed of principal officers of all cabinet departments having a major economic mission. It had a link to the White House by having as a regular member the Special Assistant to the President who had responsibilities in the economic area, and a link with the Federal Reserve by having a stated member who was a member of the Federal Reserve's Board of Governors.[13] ABEGS met weekly from the beginning to the end of Eisenhower's two terms, with but one change in format: attendance during the latter part of the second term was expanded at one meeting each month to include the heads of certain agencies not having regular membership (among them the Small Business Administration, the Veterans Administration, the Housing and Home Finance Agency, the Federal Farm Credit Administration and the Federal Home Loan Bank Board). Their participation would give greater reach to the group's policy-coordinating efforts and make all its members more promptly and fully sensitive to shifts in the economy's tempo.

*   *   *

The ABEGS formula worked well, but when a danger of recession was sensed in 1957 a smaller group was organized at the suggestion of Robert B. Anderson, at the time Secretary of the Treasury, in which both the president and the chairman of the Federal Reserve Board participated directly. Other regular members were the Secretary of the Treasury, the CEA chairman, the Director of the Budget Bureau and the Special Assistant to the President for Economic Affairs.

The Anderson Group, as I will call it, was one of a series of arrangements, quite possibly the first of its kind, that has fascinated students of White House organization. It was nothing more, however, than a straightforward way of meeting two needs that all presidents have: how to be involved more regularly and deeply in the discussion of fiscal and monetary affairs than is possible in meetings of the cabinet, especially when there is a particular need for this involvement; and how to bridge the organizational gap that separates the White House from the Federal Reserve Board.

The group worked well, but oddly enough has had relatively little attention in the literature on the Eisenhower administration or in the large volume of writing on the presidency generally. This could be because it did its work with a minimum of publicity. Also, it never occurred to anyone to give it a name (Triad, Quadriad) such as in later administrations lent a certain mystique to arrangements that were essentially the same in purpose and composition.

*   *   *

Other presidents have had other arrangements to assist them in shaping, coordinating and monitoring economic policies, with an increasing tendency for the activity to be centered in the White House Office rather than at the CEA, and to be headed by a member of the president's cabinet or personal staff rather than by the CEA chairman.

No one can say that Eisenhower's formula was demonstrably the best. It can be said, however, that it worked well. It kept the development and coordination of economic policies continuously under study. It had the merit of involving the president personally in the discussion of policy when his involvement was most important. And, happily for the role of economics and the economist in the governmental process, it had the CEA at the center of things.

Eliminating Wage and Price Controls

Nothing could have been a more natural target for elimination by an administration committed to dealing with inflation by the orthodox methods of monetary and fiscal restraint than the still large but limping wage and price control apparatus to which Eisenhower fell heir in January 1953. The system had been set up in 1950 when war broke out in Korea, but support for it in Congress had virtually ended by 1952.[14] The Defense Production Act of that year had stripped away most of the control authority, including the president's power to impose selective

credit controls. The chairman and all members of the Wage
Stabilization Board had resigned in 1952 (and were not replaced) when President Truman intervened in a coal strike and
awarded the miners a larger wage increase than the board
thought was justified. At the same time, whatever wartime
justification there had been for direct controls was rapidly
eroding: upward pressure of demand on wages and prices had
lessened; supplies of most commodities were greatly improved;
and prices were in most cases already below their permitted
ceilings. After rising 8.6 percent in 1951, the index of wholesale
prices (predecessor of the present index of producer prices) fell
3.5 percent in 1952; and the index of consumer prices, which
had risen 7.9 percent in 1951, rose only 2.2 percent in the
following year.

It is remarkable, given these circumstances and the new
administration's distaste for direct controls, that it took as long
as it did to deliberate over the schedule on which they would be
ended. Congress had already set deadlines for their termination
(April 30, 1953 for some; June 30, 1953 for the rest) and
Eisenhower's first State of the Union Message had said there
would be no request to extend them. But no position had been
taken on whether the system might be ended before the deadlines were reached, which the law allowed the president to do.

On that question there was a strong letter to the president
from Senator Robert A. Taft urging prompt, predeadline termination. Eisenhower replied in general affirmatively, but cau-
tiously:

> [T]he point of view . . . you outline is . . , very close to my
> own. . . . While we must consider a great number of factors in a
> decision of this sort, my own thinking for some time has been
> evolving in the direction of prompt removal.[15]

It was the first test of where Eisenhower and his cabinet
stood on direct versus indirect methods of controlling inflation,
and the cabinet proved to be divided. A hard line favoring
prompt termination was taken by George Humphrey (Treasury)
and Charles E. Wilson (Defense) at the preinauguration meeting held in New York City. Taking the other side, Harold

Stassen (slated to be a member of the White House staff) and Henry Cabot Lodge, Jr. (slated to represent the United States at the United Nations) cautioned against acting "too quickly," fearing a surge of price increases.[16]

Eisenhower did not commit himself then or at the cabinet's first meeting following inauguration, when the subject was again discussed extensively, but shortly after this second meeting (the question having been studied by staff in the interim) he came down firmly on the side of what he had all along been saying: reliance for inflation-control would be on monetary and fiscal restraint; direct controls would be terminated promptly.

An Executive Order to that effect was issued on February 6, 1953 and on that date, or within a few days of it, all controls except those on rents were ended. Rent controls were allowed to remain until July 31, 1953 (to give states time to deal with local problems raised by the ending of federal controls), but within about six months they, too, were ended and authority to reimpose them expired, all without White House complaint.

*   *   *

Not everyone was happy with the way the problem was handled (no decision made until the issue had been adequately "staffed out"), notably those whose ideological convictions regarding direct controls were sufficiently fixed to rule out any need for deliberation. And it may well have been some discomfort in those quarters that inspired a letter to the president from a friend and fairly frequent correspondent noting (delicately) that some legislative leaders thought he took too much time "announcing a decision."

One cannot be sure, but the phrasing of Eisenhower's response suggests that he not only expected but desired that his reaction would be conveyed (as it probably was) to the malcontents. It could well be an example of Eisenhower's use of what has been called "the hidden hand." In any case, he replied (somewhat loftily, perhaps):

> I have the grave fault of always wanting to know what is right in any case; if it were simply a matter of determining what was politically expedient, I could operate much more rapidly.[17]

Actually, there were more than just a few on the right wing of
the Republican Party who were never reconciled to
Eisenhower's deliberative style, or to what they regarded as his
liberal views. Among them was his brother Edgar (a Tacoma,
Washington, lawyer), who wrote (toward the end of
Eisenhower's first year in the White House) to register a general complaint to the effect that there were many (obviously
including himself) who thought the new administration was
unduly timorous in dealing with certain policy issues on which
conservatives felt deeply.

Eisenhower replied:

> You say that these critics complain about the continuance of
> "controls," presumably over our economy. There is nothing in
> your letter that shows such complete ignorance as to what has
> actually happened as does this term. When we came into office
> there were Federal controls exercised over prices, wages, rents
> as well as over the allocation and use of raw materials. The first
> thing this administration did was to set about the elimination of
> those controls. This it did amid the most dire predictions of
> disaster, "run away" inflation, and so on and so on. We were
> proved right, but I must say that if the people of the United
> States do not even remember what took place, one is almost
> tempted to regret the agony of study, analysis and decision that
> was then our daily ration.[18]

Not fully persuaded, Edgar would return later with substantially the same complaint.

*   *   *

One more scene remained to be played out in this one-and-only
encounter with wage and price controls—a sequel that fortunately came to nothing. But it illustrates something of what
Eisenhower had to contend with in sustaining a noninterven-
tionist position. It involved a prominent Republican—Senator
Homer Capeheart of Indiana—who introduced a bill that would
give the president authority to invoke direct controls in an
emergency.

The initiative had considerable support. Liberal economists
testified readily in its favor. So did a representative of the U.S.

Chamber of Commerce and several businessmen and financiers, including the redoubtable Bernard Baruch. An official of one of the large trade unions supported a version of the bill that would authorize limits on price increases but (not surprisingly) opposed the same for wages as "based on false economic reasoning."[19]

Overreacting to the support the bill was receiving, the Eisenhower administration expressed a willingness to accept what it would provide—standby authority to impose a 90-day freeze on wages and prices—but made a point of stating that it was not asking for it. Eisenhower was in favor of direct controls in an emergency, such as during war, but not to the extent of wanting to have discretionary authority positioned in the wings, ready in the event there should be an emergency.

The proposal fared poorly in the Senate, and its counterpart in the House did even less well. In the end it died in a dispute over a totally unrelated matter—a provision appended to it that would establish an agency to make loans to small businesses.

*   *   *

So, the first test of the new administration on a basic economic policy question was concluded; not as resolutely as was warranted and as some would have liked, but leaving no doubt as to the difference between how Eisenhower would proceed in controlling inflation and how it had previously been dealt with. Boom times in 1956, helped by a sharp liberalizing of terms on consumer installment credit, led to some speeding-up of price increases and again provoked an interest in direct controls. But, as the economy slowed in 1957, proposals to revive direct control authority lost their appeal.[20] Confidence grew that fiscal and monetary restraint could do what direct controls had failed to do, confirming the strategy that Eisenhower favored.

Redrawing the Line Between Public and Private Activities: Terminating the Reconstruction Finance Corporation

Circumstances made it possible early in 1953 to move with broad support toward another of the administration's major objectives: withdrawing the federal government from private business activities. "Redraw[ing] the line separating public from private activities" was how the *January 1954 Economic Report* described it.[21]

There had been for some time a lively interest in Congress, as well as in the business community, in "getting the federal government out of business," but other than ending certain lending operations there was not a great deal of this to do—not as much, obviously, as has confronted governments in countries where a number of basic industries have been nationalized. There were, however, a few public enterprises of fair size that could be sold, among them a barge line operating mainly on the Mississippi River, and certain plants producing synthetic rubber that had been set up during World War II. In addition, there were numerous small production and service units located on or near military posts and naval bases that could be sold or simply closed down. And there was one major undertaking to be completed: liquidating the Reconstruction Finance Corporation (RFC), at the time a gravely troubled agency.

What was at stake in these sales or liquidations varied greatly from case to case. Abandoning a dry-cleaning establishment near a military post, or selling it to a private operator, could be of considerable local interest but was obviously not of national moment. Nor would be the liquidation of several hundred such enterprises. But discontinuing the RFC was another matter. Benefiting over a long period from able and colorful leadership, it had wielded immense financial power in its time, but charges of "influence peddling" in its lending operations had generated demands on all sides that it be discontinued, and by the time Eisenhower became president it was already on the defensive.[22]

There were three major phases in RFC's 25-year history. In the first of these, following the corporation's establishment in 1932 (at the bidding of President Hoover), its business was to lend to (or buy assets from) large financial institutions (mainly, insurance companies, commercial banks, and mortgage banking companies) whose capital resources had been impaired by loan defaults and by declines in the value of their assets, and to make loans to nonfinancial companies (railroads, in the main) that were having difficulty servicing what was in many cases an unsupportable burden of debt. It was hoped that keeping these companies from failing would forestall other cases of bankruptcy or insolvency that could lead to a general financial and economic collapse. It was a kind of anti-financial-domino strategy.

In the second phase of RFC's existence, as depression eased, the agency's powers were extended to give it a more lasting function—in this case, lending to enterprises that were solvent but for one reason or another were unable to obtain financing on what were judged to be "reasonable" terms. Not everyone felt that this species of loan facility was needed. Some argued that any applicant with a justifiable claim to credit could get it from private sources and, considering the circumstances, get it on reasonable terms. But the RFC continued in this new function on a basis that in effect assumed these alternatives were not available.

But World War II quickly settled any argument over RFC's functioning. Suddenly an agency was needed that would help finance war production where conventional tests of creditworthiness were not applicable and where speed in making funds available was essential. The RFC could do this, and private lending institutions were for the most part content to let it do so; in turn, they bought the Treasury bonds that were (in effect) issued to fund the RFC's lending operations.[23]

It was in this third phase that RFC developed the flaws that were ultimately its undoing. Charges of political influence in the making of loans inspired Congress to look deeply into the corporation's affairs, and evidence was turned up that led quickly to demands for its liquidation. The issue was defused in part when President Truman succeeded (by a narrow margin) in gaining approval of a plan that would save the corporation by reorganizing it, but opposition continued. Formulas for handling the situation varied greatly: some would terminate it altogether; some would continue it in the format proposed by President Truman; others would end all of its functions except lending to small businesses, but would give that to another agency.[24]

It was the last of these formulas that prevailed. Legislation was enacted in 1953 (with the White House and both parties in Congress supporting it) that transferred the function of lending to small businesses to a new agency—the Small Business Administration (SBA)—and terminated all remaining activities of the RFC.

*   *   *

That was as far as the redrawing of lines between public and private activities was carried under Eisenhower. It was by no means an inconsequential exercise, but it left the federal government still deeply involved in a number of essentially business-type operations, notably in the financing of agriculture and housing. And what was done under Eisenhower was not only narrower in scope but different in concept from the deregulation of finance, industry and transportation that began in the 1970s. But what the administration did in this connection pointed in the direction of what would nowadays be termed "privitization," and went at least a short distance on that path.

Confronting a Larger-than-Expected Budget Deficit: First Test of Fiscal Responsibility

Ending wage and price controls, even liquidating the RFC, were relatively simple undertakings compared to what the new administration faced in January 1953 in seeking to bring the federal budget under control. True, the problem pales in comparison with the budgetary imbalances of the 1980s, but it was large for its time and far larger than the newcomers had anticipated.

President Truman's final budget projected a deficit of $5.9 billion for the 1953 fiscal year, the term of which was half completed when the message presenting the proposals was sent to Congress. The question, however, was not what to do about the fiscal 1953 year but what to do about fiscal 1954, for which the Truman administration had projected a deficit of $9.9 billion. Compounding the problem, it was concluded early that the outgoing administration had overestimated fiscal 1954 revenues by $1.2 billion and that over and above the expenditures that the Budget Bureau estimated would reach $78.6 billion there was an overhang of unused spending authorizations of $81 billion.[25]

Some overhang had to be expected, even a large one, but $81 billion was something of a shock: "This whole matter," said Eisenhower, in a May 19, 1953 radio address, "is rather like buying C.O.D. . . . you do not need any money until the items you ordered come to your front doors—and then it is Cash on Delivery. This administration faces payment on just such an 81 billion dollar C.O.D. over the next several years."[26]

To remedy the situation, work began at once on both sides of the budget—on spending and taxes—and was pressed vigorously. Even so, the size of the task was initially underestimated. A diary item shows that as late as April 1, 1953 Eisenhower was viewing the budget imbalance—indeed, the whole range of his administration's problems—with unwarranted optimism. Prompted by the good relations that had been established between the White House and the Republican leadership in Congress ("Senator Taft and I are becoming right good friends"), and in a burst of high spirits, he wrote in his personal diary on April 1, 1953:

> "I think we should be able to build a splendid progressive record, including substantial balancing of the 1954 budget, greater achievements in our whole security program, a stronger position in Asia, real progress in the NATO concept, and possibly a real prospect of lowering taxes by the end of the 1954 fiscal year. If we can have the [Republican] solidarity that will accomplish these things then the chances for the Republicans retaining control of the House and Senate . . . shall be very bright.
>
> If that comes about, the only remaining great problem will be the date of my announcement that I am through with politics."[27]

Unhappily, it proved not to be that easy. On May 20, 1953 it had to be reported to Congress that even though fiscal 1954 outlays could be held to $74.1 billion ($4.5 billion under what President Truman had projected), and $8.5 billion could be trimmed from the recommended requests for new appropriations, there would be a deficit of $6.6 billion in fiscal 1954 unless something was done to forestall certain already-legislated tax reductions. Accordingly, Congress was asked to (1) defer for six months the expiration of an excess profits tax that had been imposed to help finance the Korean Conflict and was scheduled to end on June 30, 1953, (2) rescind a cut in the corporate income tax (from 52 to 47 percent) that would otherwise take place on April 1, 1954, and (3) cancel the scheduled expiration of certain excise taxes "pending the development of a better system." The one bright spot in this otherwise dark prospect was that the social security system's reserves justified deferring for a year a payroll tax increase that had been scheduled to take effect January 1, 1954.

The tax decisions were bitter ones for Eisenhower to make. Having made all the economies in nondefense areas he thought were fair and prudent, further savings would have to be found in the defense budget; but large reductions had already been made in defense and to make additional cuts, he told Congress, "would require more drastic curtailment of our national security programs than we can safely afford in today's troubled world." Despite the newfound economies, if the tax rollbacks were allowed to stand, the fiscal 1954 budget would be in deficit by an estimated $6.6 billion; even if the tax reduction were deferred, the shortfall would come to $5.6 billion. As Eisenhower told the Business Advisory Council (a group of corporate executives selected to advise the Department of Commerce), this ruled out tax reduction:

> We must have a balanced budget in sight, a proved capability, before we can begin to lower revenues—which doesn't mean you may not reform taxes, but you must never lower revenues.[28]

And on May 20, 1953 he told Congress:

> I have come to the conclusion that no reductions in tax rates should become effective during this [1953] calendar year. I

regret this conclusion because I share the widespread feeling that our taxes are generally too high and that some of our tax laws are inherently defective. But facts are facts and I propose to face them. It seems to me that under the conditions stated here and regardless of the origination of the tax reductions now written into the law, no Administration could acquiesce in their taking place as scheduled unless it was willing to take vigorous action to reduce expenditures sufficiently to bring outlays within available revenues.

The problem of fiscal readjustment is one of timing. Under present conditions of high business activity, coupled with a budget deficit, a tax reduction would not be consistent with attaining the vital financial objective of a sound dollar. I want to see a tax reduction carried out; I want it very much. But I want even more to stop the deterioration of the currency which has been going on for so many years under the unsound fiscal and monetary policies of the past Administration.

As a matter of basic long-term policy, we must look forward to reducing tax revenues as Government expenditures are curtailed. But it is also wise under existing conditions not to reduce receipts any faster than we can cut back on expenditures.[29]

There were those who felt that this put too much stress on budget deficits, arguing that, in the circumstances, a deficit would not be inflationary and, in any case, inflation could be handled adequately by management of the money supply. But Eisenhower saw (correctly, in my view) a linkage between a budget deficit and the money supply (certainly when the deficit was large), and between the both of these and inflation. And, as stated in the following 1953 letter, he was determined to act firmly against anything arising out of these relationships that could have inflationary consequences:

I believe . . . that by avoiding unwarranted increase in the supply of money—which, of course, also means avoiding great deficits in the federal budget—we can establish the stability that will keep people saving their money and anxious to indulge in longterm investment.[30]

And to a retired Army friend who wrote to protest the tax decisions, he replied:

"Suppose we reduce taxes and so increase the deficit, what is going to be the value then of your retired pay? There are millions of people living on pensions or on income from investments, or payment from insurance companies, or on interest. Everyone of these individuals will be ruined if we do not stop the deflation in the value of the dollar. Indeed . . . there is no such thing as tax reduction as long as your dollar is continuously decreased in value, because you cannot bring to the individual enough benefit (by) reducing taxes . . . to compensate for the constant lowering of the purchasing power of the dollar.

Of course, the budgetary deficit is only one of the items that makes inflation, but . . . when it is present all the others work with particular emphasis . . . I have always maintained . . . that the annual deficit must be eliminated in order that tax reduction can begin. Reverse this order and you will never have tax reduction.

All this seems so simple that no one ever quarrels with me when I lay it out in front of them face to face. But I get letters such as yours daily. People apparently think they can *reduce* taxes regardless of how much is owed by the federal government, or how much the federal government spends. So I spend my life trying to cut expenditures, balance the budget, and then get at the *popular* business of lowering taxes [Eisenhower's italics].[31]

It happened that the recommendation to defer tax reduction had to be defended also before two titans of the Republican Party's conservative wing: Senator Taft and Congressman Daniel A. Reed (R N.Y.), the latter a longtime party stalwart, newly installed as chairman of the House Ways and Means Committee, where debate on tax legislation would have to begin. The two took essentially the same position: the Republican Party had pledged itself to reduce taxes and it should make good on that pledge; it could do that if the White House would only bear down hard enough on spending, including defense spending.

The disagreement with Taft surfaced during one of the president's first meetings (April 10, 1953) with the Republican legislative leaders, and in a manner that was particularly painful to

Eisenhower. The dispute was not, however, over cutting taxes in the face of a budget deficit; it had to do with the possibility and merits of funding a taxcut by reducing defense expenditures.

Eisenhower described the incident in a May 1, 1953 diary entry as "one of the worst days I have experienced since January 20," noting that "not once did he [Taft] mention the security of the United States or the need for strength either at home or among our allies. He simply wanted expenditures reduced, regardless." Eisenhower closed the entry: "If this thing ever has to be dragged out into the open, we at least have the right to stand firmly upon the platform of taking no unnecessary chances with our country's safety, but at the same time doing everything we can to protect its solvency and its economic health."[32]

The quarrel with Reed was no less painful: not only was he opposed to any delay in reducing business taxes, he had introduced a bill (HR 1) that would accelerate by six months a reduction in the individual income tax that was scheduled to take effect January 1, 1954. And he supported his proposals with a formidable economic argument that was laid out early in a press interview. It went as follows: (1) revenue losses from tax reductions had been overestimated; (2) lower taxes would stimulate the economy and lift revenues (to prove this he invoked the record of Secretary of the Treasury Andrew W. Mellon who, under three Republican presidents—Harding, Coolidge, and Hoover—presided over three tax cuts, each followed by an increase in revenues); (3) there were already signs of impending recession (a view the administration mistakenly did not share) and accelerating the reduction of personal income taxes (as his HR 1 would do) would help prevent it ("If we oppose tax reductions until the slide begins it will be too late. . . . One must act in advance and that is what I propose to do"); (4) the excess profits tax was a "bad, vicious, and immoral" levy (which the administration did not deny) and what it sought to do could in any case be done better by the renegotiation of war contracts, under arrangements already in place; and (5) "the Republican Party [had] pledged to reduce [taxes]" and if this were not done as scheduled "there [would] be a Democratic

Congress next time." Finally, in a thrust at the administration
that was clearly undeserved, he asserted that (6) "the more I
keep driving for tax reductions the more they [the White
House] will try to reduce expenditures . . . but if you ever let
up . . . they would just not try to cut expenditures at all."[33]

Against this assault the administration retorted that bringing
expenditures and revenues closer to balance had to come before cutting taxes, that expenditures had been cut as much as
was possible without reducing domestic programs unduly and
without impairing the country's security, and that the revenue
that would be lost through enacting Reed's proposals would
delay reaching the point at which taxes could be cut within the
context of a balanced budget. It was the argument of financial
prudence, opting for the longterm benefits of fiscal balance,
nearterm political disadvantage notwithstanding, and (un-
wisely) giving no weight to Reed's recession forecast.[34]

In the end, the administration's tax proposals were accepted
by Congress. Taft dropped his opposition once the administration's proposals were before Congress, but not Reed: the White
House plan was accepted in the House only after parliamentary
maneuvers so offensive to him that he threatened to resign.
Fortunately he did not do so.

The fracas was a bruising one and a serious embarrassment
to the White House, not the least because Reed proved to be
right about the recession danger. But it put a stamp of total
authenticity on a principle on which Eisenhower laid great
stress; to have an adequate and sustainable defense establishment one needed to operate from a strong economic foundation, especially from a strong fiscal position, and that the administration was serious in seeking to achieve that posture. As
Eisenhower put it, the budget's condition in 1953 put the administration "between the Scylla of a deep deficit and the
Charybdis of an inadequate military budget." It was with the
idea of escaping from this condition and reconciling the requirements of fiscal soundness and defense adequacy that,
when the Reed affair was over, the Secretary of the Treasury
was added to the National Security Council as a regular member ("to recognize the relationship between military and eco-

nomic strength") and Eisenhower launched his "New Look" campaign at the Pentagon, aimed at modernizing the nation's military forces at the lowest possible budgetary cost.[35]

Restructuring the Federal Debt

While the unhappy incidents involving Senator Taft and Congressman Reed were unfolding, the new team at the Treasury was engaged in an operation which, although not much noticed by the public at large, was followed closely by the financial community and had important implications for the economy. Its object was to lengthen the average maturity of the outstanding federal debt. Eisenhower's first State of the Union Message had given notice that the program would have a high priority, saying: "Too great a part of the national debt comes due in too short a time."

Though not as widely recognized as it should have been, there was the possibility of a disruptive effect on the economy in what the Treasury proposed to do; but there was also a logic behind it. When the Treasury borrowed on a short term basis, there was a tendency for a large share of the funds raised to come from the commercial banking system. This, in turn, tended to enlarge the money supply and increase the danger of inflation. Also, frequent trips by the Treasury to the credit markets, which a pileup of short term public debt made inevitable, jeopardized the tactical independence of the Federal Reserve System. Whenever the Treasury "went to the market" the Reserve system was under some obligation to do what it could to assure the success of the financing. It did that by buying government securities for its own account, which increased the capability of the system's member banks to acquire the securities being issued by the Treasury. But this could mean that it was increasing member bank reserves at a time when, absent the Treasury financing, it might have preferred to be taking a neutral stance, even moving to tighten credit conditions. Accordingly, the Treasury Department, with the enthusiastic support of the Federal Reserve and of the banking community generally, threw itself into the task of doing as much as possible of its financing through the issuance of long-dated securities.

The first move to this end was a probing action. In February 1953, holders of $9 billion in Treasury certificates of indebtedness having a bit less than a year to run were offered a choice between a one-year certificate, which would leave average maturity roughly unchanged, and a 5- to 6-year security, which would increase it.

This went off well enough to suggest a bolder step, which the Treasury took in June by offering $1 billion in bonds having a maturity of 30 years and bearing an interest rate of 3.25 percent. The issue was designed to attract funds from longterm investors: purchases by commercial banks were limited to not more than 5 percent of their time deposits; no Federal Reserve support was expected, and none was given.

The second of these moves raised two questions: Did the Treasury offer too high an interest rate, and did the sale of the bonds, by drawing funds out of the mortgage market, raise the cost of borrowing by homebuyers, suppress homebuilding, and contribute in this way to the economic downturn which, following on the heels of the Treasury operation, began in August 1953? The answer to the first question is that the "coupon" on the bonds (the stated interest rate) probably was a trifle high. The issue was oversubscribed about five to one and went quickly to a small premium. But a degree of overpricing (setting the interest rate on the high side) is typical, even essential, when securities are being issued to which the market is not accustomed, as was the case here.[36] And the answer to the second question is that the issue almost certainly did help bring on recession in 1953: mortgage borrowing costs rose and housing starts fell.

What the Treasury was doing was fully in accord with the financial orthodoxy of the time, but it became the subject of a rather prickly exchange of letters between Elliot V. Bell, a prominent Republican and widely respected financial economist and journalist (at the time editor and publisher of *Business Week* magazine), and Under Secretary of the Treasury W. Randolph Burgess, who was orchestrating the exercise.[37] Bell's criticism elicited from Burgess (a longtime advocate of aggressive measures to lengthen the debt) a response that was a mixture of apology and defense for what the Treasury had done. In Burgess's account, the Treasury in mid-1953 had been "sitting on the preceding boom" (it was this to which Bell was mainly objecting!) and while it had not seen evidence of a turn toward recession when it decided to put out the 3.25 percent issue it was prompt in urging the Federal Reserve to relax its policy once the situation changed.

As we will see as we trace the developments leading to recession in 1953, the Treasury's decision to issue the longterm bond was by no means entirely without support in what was known at the time about the cyclical condition of the economy. Production was rising and employment was high and steady. But those who gave special weight to monetary factors and to the trend of credit costs (as Bell did) read the evidence differently. "There were plenty of signs early in '53," Bell wrote, "that the 'hard money policy' was being overdone."

Examining the question now, it is clear that the Treasury's move took more chances with the economy's stability than it was prudent to take. Indeed, a September 1953 speech by Secretary Humphrey suggested that the Treasury had itself come to that conclusion. "We will use care," he promised, "not to press the market in competition with state, municipal and private financing."[38]

For the moment, however, the deed was done. It illustrates how difficult it is after a prolonged period of heavy use of short-term financing to withdraw from it without disruptive effect. It also illustrates how narrow the margin is between what will work and what will not work in economic stabilization policy, and how difficult it is to distinguish between the two. It was several years before another aggressive maturity-stretching exercise was undertaken; unfortunately, with not dissimilar results.

Reviewing Antitrust

Those who expected Eisenhower to be soft on antitrust, as many did, either did not understand the importance of competition to the performance of the market-directed enterprise system he espoused, or underestimated the depth of his commitment to making such a system work. But if it was not apparent a priori that it would be an active period for antitrust, an address given early in 1953 by Herbert Brownell, Eisenhower's first Attorney General, was notice that it would be.

For the antitrust laws, Brownell's speech promised "equity of enforcement, a simplification of administration, assistance to companies wishing to act within the law, [and] no wholesale dismissing of pending suits." To help give effect to these pledges, a panel of experts would be appointed (the Attorney General's National Committee to Study the Antitrust Laws) to make a "thorough and comprehensive study of [the] antitrust laws," to give guidance to the administration on what changes in them, if any, it should seek, and to make recommendations on how best to proceed with enforcement.[39] The composition of the panel (fifty-three experts from outside government and four from within) made it obvious that it would do its work independently and report its findings candidly, as it did.[40]

There were numerous dissents from what the majority finally agreed to report (a statement by one panel member, Professor Louis S. Schwartz of the University of Pennsylvania Law School, was an almost total rejection of the majority's conclusions) but considering the controversial nature of the subject matter, and the disputatious manner in which it is commonly discussed, it is something of a miracle that the consensus was as broad as it proved to be.[41] Summarizing the nearly 400-page legal paper that was delivered to the Attorney General (as briefly as only a nonlawyer would undertake to do), what it came to was this.

- The antitrust laws were not in need of major change.

- There were no serious defects in how the laws were being interpreted by the courts.

- Without rejecting altogether the merits of *"per se* illegality" as a standard in applying the laws, the "rule of reason" should be followed as "the general rule of construction in Sherman Act cases."

- The size of the business unit involved, or the extent of any particular company's market share, was not what determined whether monopoly existed; the evidence of monopoly was power to control market prices and exclude competition, and the exercise of these powers; monopoly due to superior skill or superior products, or to natural advantages or special efficiencies, was not in itself illegal when these advantages were used within the law.

- Finally, although existing law was adequate on the whole, Congress should repeal legislation that sanctioned price maintenance (the Miller-Tydings amendment to the Sherman Act and the McGuire amendment to the Federal Trade Commission Act); and (except where this had already been accomplished by the Taft-Hartley law or by the antitrust laws as written) it should prohibit labor unions from taking actions which had as their effect the direct control of markets, such as fixing the kind or amount of products which could be used, produced, or sold, their market price, the geographical area in which they could be sold, or the number of firms that could engage in their production or distribution.[42]

The panel's conclusion that no overhauling of antitrust laws or of their enforcement was needed conformed not only with the administration's views but with the prevailing sentiment in Congress. Accordingly, except for legislation that extended federal regulation to all mergers of banks, and required federal approval for the acquisition of banks by holding companies (areas not covered explicitly in the committee's report), what the administration sought and obtained from Congress was mainly legislation that would help the Justice Department and the Federal Trade Commission (FTC) enforce laws already on the books. Legislation was obtained that increased the fines for violations of the Sherman Act (Congress raised them more than the administration requested), gave the federal government the right to sue for damages sustained as a result of Sherman Act violations, and set a four-year statute of limitations in private antitrust suits.

Had Congress been willing to enact more of what the administration asked for, there would have been legislation (as there is now) requiring companies of significant size to give advance notice of plans to merge, giving the FTC authority to seek preliminary injunctions in mergers viewed as likely to violate the antitrust laws, and authorizing the Attorney General to issue civil investigative demands to obtain necessary facts when civil proceedings were contemplated in antitrust suits.[43] But Congress was not yet willing.

As we will see, considerable strengthening of the limitations on secondary boycotts, which the Advisory Committee proposed, was achieved in the 1959 amendments of the Taft-Hartly law, but in another area, on which the panel had taken a particularly bold stand—proposing repeal of the price-maintenance laws—the administration made no proposals and Congress took no independent action.[44] The Republican leadership in Congress was apparently willing to follow the panel's suggestion, but a legislative proposal to that end would have encountered stiff opposition in Congress and the same from many business and labor groups. Eisenhower was not alone among presidents in choosing not to undertake that struggle.

*   *   *

Granted, there was little in this record of legislative change that met Professor Schwartz's notions of what was needed. But in line with the administration's accent on enforcement of law already on the books it acted vigorously in that area. Commenting on this, former Attorney General Brownell has noted (in a Columbia University Oral History interview) that the administration's principal effort was to enforce "the antimerger law that had been passed in 1950 [the Celler-Kefauver amendment to the Clayton Act] and not really enforced [until 1953]" and to start "widespread and vigorous enforcement of . . . Section 7 [of the Clayton Act]." Recalling what was done, he cited cases that tested "how far [oil companies] could cooperate in foreign countries in the production and transportation of oil," the administration's studies of whether to seek a breakup of AT&T and "whether Eastman Kodak had the right to tie up the development of [photographic] film," the prosecution of

General Motors ("when one of the cabinet members was its former president"), and prosecution of the Bethlehem-Youngstown merger case ("the first big test of mergers in the steel industry").[45]

In addition, an antitrust action was brought by the Justice Department against the Continental Can Company, notwithstanding close personal and political connections between the president of the company (General Lucius Clay [Retired]) and both Brownell and Eisenhower. The case was handled, said Brownell, "exactly as it would have been handled if [Clay] hadn't been a friend." Cases that involved especially flagrant anticompetitive practices by employees of several large manufacturers of electrical equipment were prosecuted vigorously, as were a number of cases that introduced antitrust considerations into areas of business (agricultural cooperatives, broadcasting, communications, airlines, and labor unions) which had traditionally been regarded as exempt from such challenges (mainly because they were subject to regulation by some federal agency). Finally, the "consent settlement" method that had been endorsed in the majority report of the Advisory Committee, but previously had not been much used, was employed to resolve a number of cases, setting a precedent that has since been followed extensively and usefully.[46]

* * *

Thus, in the enforcement of existing law, and to a degree in legislation enacted, the administration's antitrust record (separating it from the record of the bipartisan FTC, for which it had no direct responsibility) was a good one.[47] In the end, however, what counts in determining success and failure in these matters is what happened to the competitive quality of markets during the Eisenhower period and for as long thereafter as its policies had a significant influence on market structure and behavior. Was the economy as receptive as previously to the formation of new businesses, or less so? Did competition become keener, or did it weaken? What happened to concentration in industry?

It is easier to ask these questions than to answer them, in part because data that bear significantly on them are so scarce, but mainly because it is impossible to disentangle the impact on market structure and behavior of the administration's actions from the impact that must be assigned to everything else that affected them. What can be said, however, supports the rating given above to the administration's efforts.

- The number of businesses formed rose faster between 1953 and 1960 than previously, especially in the last year or two of that period.[48]

- There was no surge of mergers at any time in the 1950s, such as occurred in the second half of the 1960s; actually, there was a slowing.[49]

- A carefully researched study of changes in the competitive structure of industry in the United States concluded that "average market concentration of manufacturing industries [showed] no marked tendency to increase or decrease between 1947 and 1966."[50]

*   *   *

Although there was clearly no parallel in the Eisenhower years to the wave of deregulation that began in the 1970s and continued in the 1980s, greatly enhancing competition in a number of industries (notably in banking and finance and in transportation), antitrust as a means for promoting greater and more vigorous competition is a strongly positive chapter in the story of Eisenhower's presidency, and considering the needs of the day and the mood of Congress and of the country at the time it is doubtful that more could have been achieved than was actually accomplished. Finally, it is not amiss to note that by compiling a strong antitrust record the Eisenhower administration performed entirely contrary to the image constructed for it by those who, at the administration's beginning, were sure it would be partial to "big business" and soft generally on anticompetitive practices.

Notes

1. Governor Sherman Adams's warning was issued at the pre-inaugural cabinet meeting held at the Commodore Hotel in New York

City, January 13, 1953 (*Adams Papers,* Box 7). The Adams papers are in the George F. Baker Library at Dartmouth College, Hanover, New Hampshire.

2. Included with Senator Taft were Senators Leverett Saltonstall (R Ma.), Allen Ellender (D La.), and Burnet R. Maybank (D S.C.), all of them highly influential in the Senate. The incident was described in detail by Dr. Keyserling in May 13, 1953 and December 31, 1965 letters to the editor of *The Journal of Commerce* and in correspondence with me.

3. Testimony to that effect was given on July 14 and 17, 1953 by Senator Ralph A. Flanders (R Vt.), Representative Jesse P. Walcott (R Mich.) and George D. Riley (representing the American Federation of Labor) to a subcommittee of the Special House Committee on Reorganization, chaired by Margaret Stitt Chase (R Maine).

4. It is not clear what Mrs. Chase meant by this, but she stated during her subcommittee hearings that she hoped "we would never again find a Council taking an active part in politics" (Chase Hearings, July 14, 1953, p. 13). Congressional dissatisfaction with the CEA was noted also in the Columbia University Oral History Project interview given by Dr. Neil H. Jacoby, a member of the council during a major part of the first Eisenhower term. Columbia Oral History papers are in the university's Butler Library, New York City, New York.

5. Adams wrote in his memoirs that "among the Republican leaders in Congress the Council of Economic Advisers had fallen into disrepute as a guide for executive action. . . . indeed, some of them would have been happy to have [it] abolished" (*Firsthand Report,* p. 155).

6. *Economic Report,* January 1954, p. 119.

7. The circumstances in which these steps were taken were described by Dr. Hauge in his Columbia University Oral History interview, especially p. 51.

8. *Economic Report,* January 1954, p. 119.

9. *Economic Report,* January 1954, pp. 120–21 and 135–38.

10. *Public Papers, DDE,* 1954, p. 530.

11. The letter continued:

In one way or another, practically every Department and Agency of the government is involved [in combatting recession]. Means available to the government include revision of tax laws to promote consumption; extension of credit and assuring of low interest rates; vigorous liberalization of all social security measures; extension of all kinds of reinsurance plans, as well as direct loans and grants; acceleration of construction programs involving everything from multipurpose dams, irrigation projects, military equipment and public buildings on the one hand to increased expenditure for soil conservation, upstream water storage and public housing on the other. . . .

Certain of these things . . . could be done promptly in an emergency. The Federal Reserve Board could promptly lower reserve requirements in member banks to ease credit and make money available for industrial and

58   THE US ECONOMY UNDER EISENHOWER

consumer purposes. On the other hand, everything that touches public
works . . . requires a vast degree of advance planning. . . .

In view of the complexity and continuing nature of this problem, I
sometimes wonder whether we should not have an office in government that
in the economic field would parallel the Office of Defense Mobilization in
the military field (*Abilene Papers,* Name Series, Box 12, Milton
Eisenhower, 1954, Folder [3]).

The CEA's perception of its function, circa 1953–54, was described in
a memorandum entitled "The Economic Policy of this Administration" (*Abilene Papers,* Subject Series, Box 12, October 1953) and in
Neil H. Jacoby's Columbia University Oral History interview, pp. 11–
12 and 50.

12. Economic Report, January 1954, p. 137. There were numerous
interagency groups dealing with economic and financial questions, but
none with a mandate as broad as that of ABEGS. Others included the
Council on Foreign Economic Policy, the Defense Mobilization Board,
the National Advisory Council on Monetary and Financial Problems,
the Cabinet Committee on Small Business, the Coordinator of Public
Works Planning, the Federal Council on Aging, the Committee on the
Rural Development Program and (in 1959–60) the Committee on Government Activities Affecting Costs and Prices and the Cabinet Committee on Price Stability for Economic Growth (the last chaired by
Vice president Nixon and commonly referred to as the Nixon Committee). The CEA was represented on all of these, in several cases
supplying the chairman. Also, while CEA chairman I served on the
Board of Directors of the Federal National Mortgage Association
(Fanny Mae) and, as indicated, as a member of the Economic Policy
Committee of the OECD. CEA activities are described in an appendix
to each of the *Economic Reports.*

13. The roster of ABEGS members is given in an appendix to each
of Eisenhower's *Economic Reports.*

14. Crauford D. Goodwin, ed., *Exhortation and Controls; The
Search For a Wage-Price Policy, 1945–71,* (Brookings Institution,
Washington, D.C., 1975), pp. 89 and 108–13.

15. *Abilene Papers,* Official File, Box 564.

16. *Adams Papers,* Box 7 and Adams, *Firsthand Report,* pp. 157–
58. Also, *Abilene Papers,* Cabinet Series, minutes of cabinet meetings
on January 13, March 13, and March 20, 1953.

17. *Abilene Papers,* Name Series, Box 31. The reference here is to
Professor Fred I. Greenstein's book, *The Hidden-Hand Presidency,
Eisenhower as Leader,* Basic Books, 1982.

18. *Abilene Papers,* Administrative Series, Box 11, Edgar
Eisenhower Folder, 1954, [2].

19. *Congressional Quarterly Almanac,* 1953, pp. 400–404. (Hereafter, cited as *CQ Almanac.*)

20. Cabinet discussions of the possible need for executive authority to control extensions of consumer installment credit are reported in Adams, *Firsthand Report*, p. 362, and in minutes of cabinet meetings on March 13 and 20, 1953 (*Abilene Papers*, Cabinet Series).

21. *Economic Report*, January 1954, page 35. A January 1961 report by the Budget Bureau stated that, in the nondefense area alone, 1400 "activities" that were competitive with private business had been discontinued, that there were plans to discontinue another 100, and that in 400 additional cases competitive activity had been, or was planned to be, curtailed (*Abilene Papers*, Administrative Series, Box 34).

22. Jesse H. Jones, who was the central figure in RFC's early history as chairman of the Corporation, wrote (with Edward Angley) an interesting and informative book on his tenure there, entitled *Fifty Billion Dollars: My Thirteen Years With The RFC (1932–1945)*, (Macmillan: New York, 1951).

23. I have elsewhere (*Federal Lending and Loan Insurance*, National Bureau of Economic Research, 1958) dealt at length (in collaboration with Harold G. Halcrow and Neil H. Jacoby) with the history, functioning and lending experience of all federal loan-insuring agencies active through the 1950s, including the RFC.

24. The 1951 issue of the *CQ Almanac* (pp. 339–40 and 498–507) describes the rigorous investigation of the RFC by a Senate committee chaired by J. William Fulbright (D Ark.) and President Truman's proposals for reorganization of the corporation. The same source (1953, pp. 428–30) describes how the RFC was ended and how SBA began.

25. The Truman messages are in *Public Papers of the President, Harry S. Truman*, 1952–1953, pp. 63–117 and 1128–64.

26. *Public Papers, DDE*, 1953, p. 309.

27. *Eisenhower Diaries*, p. 234.

28. *Public Papers, DDE*, 1953, p. 101.

29. Special Message to the Congress Recommending Tax Legislation, May 20, 1953, *Public Papers, DDE*, pp. 318–26.

30. A June 23, 1953 letter to George Whitney, a friend and frequent correspondent (*Abilene Papers*, DDE Diary Series, Ann Whitman File, Box 3). The connection running from federal budget deficits to money supply and from there to inflation is alluded to also in Eisenhower's February 25, 1959 speech to the U.S. Savings Bond Conference (*Public Papers, DDE*, 1959, pp. 219–22) and in his August 25, 1959 Special Message to Congress Urging Action on Debt Management Legislation (*Public Papers, DDE*, 1959, pp. 602–6).

31. A letter to Brigadier General B. F. Caffey (Retired), *Abilene Papers*, DDE Diary Series, Ann Whitman File, Box 3, December 1953–July 1953, Folder [2].

32. *Eisenhower Diaries*, pp. 235–36. The Taft incident and related matters are dealt with in *The White House Years,* Vol. I, pp. 125–33 and 201–3, in Adams, *Firsthand Report,* pp. 20–22, and in the *Humphrey Papers,* pp. 37–47, 63–76, and 79–99.

33. *U.S. News and World Report,* June 19, 1953, pp. 44–53.

34. The Reed imbroglio was naturally of great interest to the media, and Eisenhower was hard pressed to maintain the position he had taken in it. Asked during the March 19, 1953 news conference about his reaction to Reed's HR 1, his reply was: "I want the revenue. As a matter of fact . . . I think we must have it." Apparently sensing that the answer was a bit brusk, he went on: "I am not trying to take an arbitrary position on this. I merely say that as long as you have got almost an incentive to cheapen and cheapen your money, then next year taxes will be higher and higher. Finally you cannot catch yourself as you chase your tail around the tree. And that is just exactly what I am trying to prevent . . . things just going in a spiral until it is hopeless" *Public Papers, DDE,* 1953, pp. 115–16.

35. *The White House Years,* Vol. I, pp. 126–33.

36. *The Wall Street Journal,* April 22 and June 12, 1953.

37. *Abilene Papers,* Arthur F. Burns Papers, Box 7, Department of the Treasury, Folder 1953–1955.

38. *Humphrey Papers,* pp. 123–24. Eisenhower must have approved of the Treasury's plans since he wrote to Secretary Humphrey in January 1954 when a maturity-extending move was being made that he was pleased that investors were being given a choice of maturities (*Abilene Papers,* DDE Diary Series, Box 4). But in *The White House Years* (Vol. I, p. 304), he included the 1953 maturity-stretching exercise among factors that "may have" contributed to the onset of recession in 1953–54.

39. See the address to the Fourth Circuit Judicial Conference, June 26, 1953, cited (p. 18) in Theodore P. Kovaleff's book, *Business and Government in the Eisenhower Administration,* (Ohio University Press, 1980), on which I have drawn heavily.

40. There is a short account of the committee's history and a roster of its members in *The Report of the Attorney General's Committee to Study the Antitrust Laws* (U.S. Government Printing Office, Washington, D.C., March 31, 1955).

41. Professor Schwartz's dissent was reproduced in *The Antitrust Bulletin,* Vol. 1, no. 1. The panel was the Attorney General's committee, appointed by him and reporting to him, not a presidential commission, as were most other study groups established in 1953. On Eisenhower's determination to distance himself from antitrust proceedings (of which the manner of this panel's organization is an example) see entries in *Eisenhower Diaries,* March 20, 1957 and February 28 and March 8, 1958.

42. My summary borrows language from Attorney General Brownell's paper, which presented the Advisory Committee's findings to the cabinet (*Abilene Papers,* Cabinet Secretarial Records, 1953–60, Box 1. "Preview of the Antitrust Report," March 18, 1955). I have relied also on the summary by Professor S. Chesterfield Oppenheimer (School of Law, University of Michigan), who was co-chairman of the panel with Judge Stanley N. Barnes, Assistant Attorney General, in charge of antitrust. Professor Oppenheimer's paper is also in *The Antitrust Bulletin,* Vol. 1, no. 1.

43. Administration proposals that remained unenacted in January 1961 were listed in the *January 1961 Economic Report,* p. 67.

44. Minutes of the March 18 and 24, 1955 meetings of the cabinet (*Abilene Papers,* Cabinet Series, Box 5) report presentations by Attorney General Brownell on the committee's proposals.

45. Pertinent comments are in Brownell's Columbia University Oral History interview, Vol. 2, pp. 338–41 and vol. 3, pp. 15–16.

46. The enforcement history is told in detail in Kovaleff, *Business and Government in the Eisenhower Administration,* Chapters III and VII.

47. There are appraisals of the FTC record in *The Federal Trade Commission: a fiftieth-anniversary symposium,* Milton Handler and others, (DaCapo Press, New York, 1971).

48. There are data on new business formations in all *Economic Reports,* in *Historical Statistics,* Vol. 2, p. 911, and in *Business Conditions Digest,* Series 10. Publication of the last-named of these sources (referred to hereafter as *BCD*) was terminated by the Department of Commerce with the April 1990 issue.

49. *Historical Statistics,* Vol. 2, p. 914.

50. *Studies of the Staff of the Cabinet Committee on Price Stability* (U.S. Government Printing Office, Washington, D.C., January 1969), p. 58).

IV. Promoting the Economy's Stability and Growth: Encounters with the Business Cycle

Next to its history of trending to higher levels of production, employment, and income, nothing has characterized the American economy more than its tendency to swing through alternating periods of recession and recovery. Yet, except during the recession phase, when the economy's troubles quickly take charge of policy, presidential administrations tend to make their plans and go about their affairs much as if the business cycle did not exist. The impact of its ups and downs is so great, however, and diffuses itself so widely, that most of what there is to say about economic policies, and about how and why they are adjusted from time to time, can be said best, indeed must be said, within a format set by the cycle.

The Eisenhower years are a case in point. They divide into four cyclical periods, each (it happens) of two years' length: 1953–54, in which the economy skidded unexpectedly into recession and stayed there for about ten months, forcing a reversal of tax policy; 1955–56, which were years of rapid expansion, raising difficult questions about the management of prosperity; 1957–58, in which there was a second recession, brought on in large part by the exuberance of expansion in the preceding two years; and 1959–60, during which there was an industrywide steel strike, a troublesome outflow of gold and, toward the end of 1960, a mild but politically untimely recession.

The story of the eight years will be told in that format.

*   *   *

An Early and Unexpected Recession: 1953–54

Recessions never approach without giving some notice, and never without inspiring some forecasts that in the end turn out to be right; but, as 1953–54 and practically every other cyclical downturn in America's history demonstrates, they have a way of taking government by surprise.

The surprise in 1953 was all the more remarkable because Eisenhower's administration was notable from the beginning for a more-than-usual sensitivity to the cyclical risk. The appointment of Arthur F. Burns, the country's leading student of the business cycle, to head the reconstituted Council of Economic Advisers was assurance that cyclical changes would be monitored closely, as they were. And, at the president's explicit direction, the CEA had been at work well in advance of the 1953 downturn developing contingency plans to combat recession, should one occur.[1] Also, Gabriel Hauge, Special Assistant to the President, was warning Treasury Secretary Humphrey as early as March 1953, obviously with the recession risk in mind, that "we are going to have to shift our mental gears on the preoccupation with inflation sometime before too long."[2]

But as we have seen in the quarrel with Congressman Reed, and in the Treasury's mid-1953 floating of a longterm bond, there was little in the administration's policy moves during the first half of 1953 that showed significant weight being given to the recession danger. Nor was there anything in the public remarks of leading administration spokesmen that reflected concern about recession as an early possibility, notably not in those of Secretary Humphrey. "There will be readjustments of course," said the secretary in an April 1953 speech, referring to the cutbacks in defense spending that were then under way, "but depression, no."[3]

It was, of course, an unwarrantedly complacent view, but it must be said in Humphrey's defense, and in defense of all the presidential administrations that over the years have been victimized by the business cycle (there are no exceptions), it is easier to see the signs of oncoming recession after the affair has begun than when it is shaping up.

Moreover, the White House was not alone in 1953 in failing to anticipate a downturn. The last of the *Economic Reports* prepared under President Truman had warned, wisely, that "there are always new problems to be solved . . . (and) it is none too early to begin improving our defenses against the forces of deflation." All the same, it concluded that "1953 commences with the economy in better shape than at the beginning of any year since our work was started 6 years ago."[4] And in December 1952, at an annual event sponsored by the National Industrial Conference Board that brought together eighteen private forecasters, all in good standing, it was the consensus that "1953 would be entered in business annals as a year of sustained high-level activity."[5] As these forecasters saw it, the problem faced by the country was transitional not cyclical—how to make a smooth transition from the wartime economy that had prevailed during the Korean Conflict. Some bumpiness had to be expected, but not a cumulative, recessionary downturn.

Eisenhower was of the same mind. In his February 3, 1954 news conference, five months after what is nowadays accepted as the beginning of the 1953–54 downturn, he described the economy as "going through, inescapably, a transition from a semiwar economy, or even a [war] economy . . . into a freer economy not supported by great munitions expenditures of all kinds." Responding to a questioner who (goading him a bit) noted that "several top Republicans have suggested that there is something unethical, almost un-American, about using this word 'recession' in connection with the present business conditions," he remarked that, while everyone was free to use whatever words they wished and "we have receded from something because not everything is at its peak today," the situation could be characterized as one in which "we are going through a readjustment [such as] we have had to [go through] every time we have been in one of these (war to peace) emergencies."

The *Economic Reports* took the same view. The January 1954 report, which was much on the president's mind when he made the foregoing comment ("I . . . put in many hours of hard work with my advisers on [it]"), had referred to "periods of readjustment;" and the January 1956 report described what had happened in 1953–54 as "the general economic readjustment that followed the close of hostilities in Korea."[6]

It is true of course that there were transitional adjustments that put the economy under heavy downward pressure. From an annual rate of nearly $11 billion in the first quarter of 1952, the volume of military contract awards for work to be done in the United States was cut in one year to $8.4 billion, and by the fourth quarter of 1953 it had been cut further to $1.6 billion (the numbers look small now but they were large relative to the economy's size at the time).[7] Defense Department personnel (military and civilian) were reduced in number by 479,000 in the two years ending in the fourth quarter of 1954.[8] Federal spending for "major national security programs" was cut 20 percent, nearly $10 billion, between the fiscal years 1953 and 1955.[9] And farm prices, which had been lifted sharply by wartime demand during the Korean Conflict, fell about 20 percent from early 1951 through 1953, depressing farm income.[10]

But there were also cyclical forces at work.[11] New orders for machinery and equipment peaked early in 1951 and, except for increases in the first half of 1953 that gave a misleading clue as to what was actually happening in the economy, declined until March 1954. What had been a $15 billion stimulus in 1951 from additions to business inventories had been reduced virtually to zero by the time the recession began. Exports (excluding military items) dropped sharply from an early 1952 peak while imports rose, cutting to zero by the end of 1952 what had been a large trade surplus and a strong expansionary force in the economy.

Although the effect of these developments was to retard the economy, there was still in 1952 and during the first six months of 1953 a strong upward momentum. Data available at the time showed industrial production 10 percent higher in January 1953 than twelve months earlier, with all the increase in the last six months of that period. Gross national product in inflation-adjusted (real GNP) terms rose 4.6 percent between the fourth quarter of 1951 and 1952 and (as we know now and doubtless surmised at the time) was increasing in the final quarter of 1952 at an explosive 8.7 percent. In the first quarter of 1953 the increase in national output, at a 6.5 percent annual rate, was still well above a sustainable pace.

Naturally enough, there was a resurgence of inflation. The annualized rate of change in the GNP implicit price deflator (a useful broad measure of price changes) rose to 5.8 percent in the fourth quarter of 1952, the highest since the 11 percent reached briefly during the Korean Conflict. Also naturally enough, there was a sharp increase in the demand for credit. Augmented by a shift from surplus to deficit in the federal budget (a $6.1 billion surplus in fiscal 1951 and deficits of $1.5 and $6.5 billion in the fiscal years 1952 and 1953, respectively), total funds raised in U.S. credit markets rose 36 percent between 1951 and 1952.[12]

Reacting to these conditions, the Federal Reserve bent itself to the task of slowing the economy's expansion and bringing down the inflation rate. As the Federal Reserve Bank of New York described it, the object was to "prevent a bubble on the boom" which it would do by allowing the demand for credit to "exert (its) full tightening effect on the money and credit markets."[13] To accomplish this, the net reserves of member banks (we will have many occasions to refer to these as a measure of the ease or tightness of credit conditions) were allowed or caused to drop from a plus $723 million (exceptional ease) in January 1952 to a minus $870 million (exceptional tightness) in December 1952. (Net reserves are positive, and credit is easy, relatively speaking, when member-bank borrowings from the Federal Reserve Banks are less than the excess of reserves which the member banks hold over and above what they are required to hold; conversely, net reserves are negative, and credit is tight, again relatively speaking, when reserves held by member banks over and above what they are required to hold are less than the volume of their borrowings from the Reserve Banks.) In addition, the rate charged member banks for borrowing at their respective district Reserve Banks (the discount rate), which the member banks do when they need additional reserve balances, was raised in January 1953 from 1.75 to 2 percent.[14]

The impact of these moves was strongly restrictive on both the credit markets and the economy generally. With nominal GNP (which bears directly on the demand for credit) increasing at nearly 15 percent a year, and what we will call the narrowly-defined money supply (demand deposits at commercial banks plus currency in circulation) rising at an annual rate of only 3.4 percent, the monetary jacket into which the economy had to fit itself (a useful simile, I hope) was a tight one, and getting tighter.[15]

Interest rates were affected as one might have expected. Rates were astonishingly low by present standards, and their bit-by-bit increases were small, but they moved up quickly in 1953 to levels that were high for the times. The rate on 90-day Treasury bills, for example, was only 2 percent in early 1953, but this was the highest it had been in twenty years; it went in less than six months to 2.33 percent. And when the prime rate (the rate charged by banks in the major lending centers to borrowers of highest quality) was raised in April 1953 from 3 to 3.25 percent it was (at the new level) higher than at any time since the "bank holiday" of the early 1930s.[16]

It was in this context that the Treasury issued the $1 billion of 3.25 percent longterm bonds already commented on. The plan to float that issue, of which the Federal Reserve would routinely be informed in advance, put a difficult problem to the authorities there. Should they help the Treasury, or should they abstain from doing so? To withhold help would handicap the Treasury; beyond that, it might tighten credit to a degree that would turn the economy down. On the other hand, some members of the Federal Reserve's Open Market Committee (where the decision would be made) felt that a "cooling" of the economy was much needed, and that to stand aside would not only accomplish that purpose but would be an appropriate and not overly risky exercise of the independence only recently won under the Reserve System's accord with the Treasury.[17]

In the end (and not surprisingly) the decision was to aid the Treasury. Securities were bought in the open market for the system's account between early May and early June 1953 in amounts that added substantially to member-bank reserve balances. And on June 24 a cut in reserve requirements (reducing the volume of reserves that member banks were required to hold at their respective Federal Reserve Banks) was announced, with the same reserve-bolstering and credit-easing effects.

It speaks instructively of the mood at the Federal Reserve Board and at the White House at the time that, accompanying these actions, care was taken in both quarters to calm any fear that what was being done would blunt the antiinflation effort. The Federal Reserve stated that it had acted not to ease credit but to prevent it from getting tighter; and the Treasury noted that the cut in reserve requirements was "entirely consistent with the policy of restraint of inflation without too drastic credit restriction."[18] But, perhaps to distance itself from measures that some in the financial community viewed as a greater easing of credit than was justified, the Treasury added that, while the actions had been taken after "full consultation with the Treasury," the Federal Reserve had "acted on its own responsibility." On both sides—at the Treasury and at the Federal Reserve—there was clearly more concern about inflation than about a possible downturn in the economy.

It was not long, however, before signs of a downturn took charge of policy. From early in 1953 through June, the "leading indicators" (the series to which one looked for clues as to the economy's upcoming condition) had been giving mixed signals, but in August (reporting data for July) the negatives began to predominate. And what the leaders said was soon confirmed by the "coincident indicators" (which show the economy's current condition).[19] The credit tightening that had been designed to "prevent a bubble on the boom" had done its work. Indeed, it had done more than its work: the economy had begun to slide into recession.

*   *   *

The *January 1954 Economic Report* resisted a cyclical interpretation of what was happening, arguing that the business and
financial communities had simply overreacted to the changes in
Federal Reserve policy.[20] In retrospect, however, it is clear that
while there was some overreaction, the credit restraint was
more abrupt and more severe than was warranted. In any event,
it was quickly evident that measures were needed to check
what was obviously a cyclical downturn, whatever might have
caused it, and to the credit of all concerned they were taken
promptly.

The first adjustments were system-generated. As the economy slowed, the demand for credit declined and member banks
reduced their indebtedness to their respective Reserve Banks.
At the same time the Reserve Board authorities purchased
securities in the open market, reduced member-bank reserve
requirements, and cut the discount rate in February and
March. The result was that the exceptional credit market tightness of November–December 1952 (negative net reserves of
nearly $900 million) was transformed by mid-1954 into excep-
tional ease (positive net reserves of $750 million). The shift
from minus to plus did not come, however, until just before the
economy passed into recession, regarded now as having occurred in August 1953.

Credit market interest rates did not react at once, but when
they started down, they dropped sharply. By October 1953 the
increases in yields on 90-day Treasury bills that had occurred
during the period of credit tightness had been erased; and by
mid-1954 the yield on longterm Treasury securities had been
cut by about one quarter. Interest rates charged by commercial
banks were slower to move. The prime rate was not reduced
until March 17, 1954, by which time the economy had been in
recession roughly eight months and the downturn was within
two to three months of its end. And the quarterly average of
rates charged to the run of commercial borrowers did not
decline to any significant degree until the second quarter of
1954, by which time the recession was nearly over.

*   *   *

Crucial as money policy is to counteracting recession, it was recognized early that steps were needed to supplement its effect. First, there was a reversal of the administration's position on tax reduction. It was announced in September 1953 that there would be no further opposition from the White House to the scheduled expiration on January 1, 1954 of the excess profits tax, and that the administration would no longer oppose the similarly-scheduled reduction (to their pre-Korea level) of individual income tax rates. Shortly thereafter, Eisenhower signed a bill he had previously opposed that cut certain excise taxes, effective April 1, 1954, expressing the hope that the cuts would help promote recovery. And on August 16, 1954 he signed an omnibus tax bill (it had been developed jointly by the House Ways and Means Committee and the Treasury) which was, as he correctly described it, "the . . . first complete revision (of the tax code) in seventy-five years." It was estimated that the joint revenue loss of these cuts and tax code adjustments would come to $7.4 billion on a full-year basis, warranting the president's description of the result as "the largest dollar tax cut in any year in the nation's history."[21] There were, however, some varieties of tax reduction that he would not accept, even in recession. In August 1953, a bill that would have repealed the 20 percent tax on motion-picture theater admissions was rejected at the White House on the grounds that "we cannot afford the loss of revenue involved" (estimated at between $100 and $120 million a year) and that it was "unfair to single out one industry for relief."[22] A July 31, 1953 diary item shows that he might have accepted a two-thirds cut but thought the movie industry had "overreached" in seeking full elimination of the tax.[23] He was concerned also that a cut in one tax might "start a general rush" for the elimination of excises, which he believed the country could not afford and which would jeopardize the chances of achieving at some later date a more general and better-thought-out tax reform.

Second, the Treasury abandoned, for the time at least, its efforts to place longterm securities with nonbank investors. For the Treasury, the June 1953 experience with maturity-stretching had been educational and (as we have seen) even a bit chastening.[24] It was obvious that the fall of 1953 was no time for a repeat performance.

Third, sooner than had been expected, there was occasion to draw on the work done at the CEA on counterrecessionary contingency plans.[25] As part of this, a group was set up in the Executive Office to expedite work on federal and federally-assisted construction projects already planned and funded and either under way or in a position to be started promptly. The terms under which home mortgage loans would be insured or guaranteed by the Federal Housing Administration (FHA) or the Veterans Administration (VA) were liberalized to help speed private homebuilding. The Commodity Credit Corporation (CCC) more than doubled its lending on farm crops in 1953, increased it by another 58 percent in 1954, and its outlays for commodities purchased under farm price support programs tripled to $1.6 billion in 1953 and by 50 percent more in 1954. Tax refunds were accelerated. Finally, steps were taken through a variety of federal activities (construction, stockpiling, and procurement) to aid economically hardpressed regions and industries. Eisenhower would like to have been able to expedite construction under the administration's proposed Interstate Highway System, but legislation authorizing a start on it had not yet been enacted; it was possible only to speed up the processing of grants to states for the financing of roadbuilding under other federally-assisted programs.

*   *   *

Recession was over by mid-1954, ten months after it had started.[26] Compared to other cyclical declines between World War II and the present it was by no means the most severe. Nor was it the longest. But it was all the same a serious setback. Real GNP dropped 3 percent; industrial production fell nearly 10 percent; employment was down 3.5 percent; and the overall unemployment rate went from 2.5 to 6.1 percent.

If there were gains from the experience, they were that the administration's alertness to the recession risk was raised, that there could no longer be any question of its readiness to act promptly and vigorously to counteract a downturn, and that public confidence in the ability of the economy to make adjustments to recession and to overcome it was heightened.

Like much of what happens in the economy, how recovery came about in 1954 remains in part something of a mystery. The Federal Reserve's shift from restraint to ease was a major assist. So also was the shift in tax policy. And it was helpful that the Western European economies were expanding strongly at the time. What was done through the special White House task force to accelerate procurement and spur the housing industry was almost certainly helpful (housing starts recovered early). Whether there was a useful effect from the program to accelerate federal spending on construction is less clear. Outlays in this category were lower in 1954 than in 1953 by 17 percent in current dollars, but they might have been still lower in the program's absence. Taking the budget as a whole, however, federal spending was clearly a negative. Federal purchases of goods and services (adjusted for price changes) dropped by nearly 18 percent from cyclical peak to cyclical trough, more than five times the percentage decline in aggregate physical output; and in absolute amounts, the decline in real federal spending was roughly equal to the decline in the economy as a whole. Whatever else was demonstrated by the 1953–54 recession, it showed that recovery could begin and proceed vigorously in the face of even large declines in federal spending.

Finally, if a shift from one budget deficit to a larger one is stimulative to the economy, as it is commonly thought to be, there was a boost to recovery in calendar 1954 when a boost was needed. And then, as recovery began, and private credit demand increased, there was (in my view) a positive effect for the economy as the deficit turned to surplus and supplied savings to the credit markets, helping resist the tendency for interest rates to rise. In short, there are grounds for concluding that we had in the period from 1953 to 1955 a case of the federal budget acting as a positive force in both recession and recovery, first when it was in deficit and later when it was in surplus.

*   *   *

But an even greater mystery than how recovery got started is how Eisenhower could have played the role he did in 1953–54 (and in other cyclical downturns) in helping initiate and orchestrate the counteractive measures that helped turn the economy around and yet have been so widely regarded as having taken a basically hands-off attitude toward such efforts.

Part of the reason for this failure to understand Eisenhower's role was undoubtedly his style of working with little publicity, and his habit of keeping his own efforts in the background. There were times when special measures had to be taken to correct misstatements about what was happening in the economy and in government policy, but Eisenhower's was not a media-oriented presidency. As he reminded his cabinet on June 4, 1954, it was important that there be "visibility" to what was being done, but in the end it was substance that counted. Another factor that helped project an essentially hands-off image of Eisenhower, when the reality was that his presidency was very much a hands-on affair, was almost certainly his bluntness in turning aside proposals that in his view would be more harmful over the longrun than beneficial in the short-term.

And it was frequently necessary for him to do just that. The business cycle's recession phase is typically so short that counteractive proposals rarely appear until well after they might be of any value. On February 17, 1954, for example, when the economy was close to where it could be expected to be turning into recovery, and when there were already indications that such a process was under way, Eisenhower had to protest at a news conference that it would be a mistake "until you know what you are doing" to "throw the government wildly into all sorts of actions, lashing around everywhere."[27] And a month later, when, despite additional encouraging signs in the economic statistics, demands for crash programs were still being pressed on him, he observed (correctly) that "there is nothing that has developed that would call for a slambang emergency program," pointing out that "many things have been done . . . but we just don't believe this is the time to move on an emergency basis."[28]

Within government, however, Eisenhower was always for action where he thought there were chances of constructive effect. This is evident in the mandate given early in 1953 to the CEA to prepare antirecession contingency plans, and in the steps taken, also early in 1953, and beyond anything any previous administration had done, to put the planning of federal construction programs on a basis that would make them usable for countercyclical purposes. And although Eisenhower's interest in having authority to develop an Interstate Highway System was primarily for what it would accomplish toward improving the nation's infrastructure, he viewed it from the beginning (as he viewed all construction over which the Executive Branch had control) as a program that could be used to help stabilize the economy.

This readiness to act firmly to counter recession is evident also in the September 1953 reversal of what earlier had been a determined opposition to tax reduction. But most of all, Eisenhower's activism in economic stabilization matters is evident in minutes of Cabinet meetings that show him, session after session during the 1953–54 downturn (as he was in later recessions), supporting the CEA in what it was doing and pushing cabinet members for additional and more vigorous counteractive measures.[29] Although a good deal had been done by March 19, 1954, the CEA was on that date urged to "proceed with its studies and determine what (further) actions should be taken." On April 9, 1954 the cabinet was reminded that there was "more risk in doing nothing than in doing something." And on June 4, 1954, with the economy beginning to move out of recession, the cabinet was again admonished that "government must do everything, even though it jar[s] the sense of logic of Cabinet members, to get out of the present situation and restore vigor to the economy."

*　　*　　*

In the end, results did speak for themselves, and if it is something of a mystery how recovery begins it is something of a miracle how quickly, once the corner is turned, media attention can shift from the need for crash programs to an absorption in other interests. There was just such a shift in mid-1954, as the economy moved into what proved to be three years of remarkably good times. With production, employment and income up strongly, the federal budget shifted quickly to surplus (showing that it was by then in structural balance) and stayed in surplus for nearly three years. The price stability for which a good basis had already been established by the end of the Truman administration was set firmly in place, also lasting nearly three years. In an atmosphere of confidence higher than had been felt at any time since the 1920s, consumer spending increased briskly. In capital goods spending, a boom began for which there are few parallels in the country's history.

All of this was, of course, a welcome change. As we will see, however, it was in good part the vigor in 1955–56 of these responses to better times that was ultimately their undoing. To that subject we turn next.

Managing Prosperity: 1955–1956

Vigorous recovery and growth are gratifying experiences, not least of all to those who (in a way) preside over them, and there was much to be gratified about in the recovery that began in June 1954. What had been lost in output and employment in close to a year of recession was made up in six months of recovery. And by the time the advance was interrupted, three years and three months after it had started, nearly 10 percent had been added to what was the previous (1953) high in the nation's production. In the end, however, and illustrating how easy it is for there to be "too much of a good thing" in the upphase of a business cycle, the vigor of the advance, leading to a resurgence of price increases that prompted a spell of stiff monetary restraint, had a large part in bringing the good times to an end.

This last comment is not made as a rebuke to the monetary authorities. There were aspects of money policy in 1955–56 to which it is fair to take objection, but what the period exemplifies is not so much a fault in money policy as the difficulty one confronts in attempting to avoid excesses in an economy that, largely because of its natural tendency to exuberance, is prone to generate them, and how difficult it is to make policy adjustments that will moderate their destabilizing effects.

*   *   *

The story begins with how the recovery came to be so rapid. It was the work in part of forces normal to the upphase of the business cycle, but in this case there was exceptional strength in the advance, due to certain underlying conditions that, until the mid-fifties, had been prevented (mainly by war in Korea and recession in 1953–54) from having their full stimulating effect on the economy.

First were the demographic factors. In an addition in seven years equivalent to what it had taken the previous ten to achieve, a population that had numbered 152 million in 1950 increased by 1957 to nearly 172 million, from which followed certain other developments of great economic significance.[30] In a characteristic reaction to war and its ending, there were (on a yearly average basis) 42 percent more marriages in 1946 than in the first six years of the 1940s. Births were also more numerous, exceeding again by 42 percent the average for the previous ten years. And, following from this, the number of "household formations" began again to increase, rising to between 900,000 and 1,000,000 annually after a virtual standstill in 1954. Adding to the effect of these changes, the population was qualitatively different—more urbanized and more given to moving around. While aggregate population rose by about 17 million between 1950 and 1956, farm population dropped by 4.3 million; and the shifting of residence by persons in the 25-to-30 age group appears to have been twice as high between 1955 and 1960 as between 1935 and 1940.

Second, it was decisive for the tone of the economy that the buying power of this larger, younger, more urbanized and more mobile population was rising. The aggregate of real disposable personal income (income payments less personal tax and certain nontax payments, corrected for inflation) increased between 1947 and 1957 by 3.8 percent a year, and by 2.1 percent annually on a per capita basis.[31] These were exceptionally high rates of income improvement—strikingly higher than the historical norms—and they justified the ambitious plans for consumption that quickly made themselves felt. There was an early and large increase in homebuying, giving (as usual) a broadly spread stimulus to the economy. Sustained by the easy availability of mortgage credit at declining interest rates, housing starts had dropped only moderately during the 1953–54 recession; by May 1955 they had recovered to an annual rate of 1.7 million, nearly 30 percent above their August 1953 low.

The impetus from homebuilding started to wane in 1955 but its role was taken over by nonresidential construction, the expansion of which had the merit of lasting longer. The joint effect was a thrust to the economy from the construction industry that was both powerful and lasting.

In addition, sales to consumers of "big-ticket" items rose dramatically, with automobiles the star performer. Cars were bigger, more colorful, more fully equipped, and (for better or worse) more prodigal in the use of gasoline than ever before. And they were immensely attractive to the consumer. Sales rose to a high of 6.1 million units in 1953, dropped back to 5.6 million in the 1954 recession year, and then surged to an unprecedented 7.9 million in 1955, a volume not achieved again for ten years.[32]

Also, there were large increases in purchases of radios, TV sets, furniture, and household appliances. Spending on all consumer durables, including cars, which had accounted for 7 percent of real GNP in the second quarter of 1954, accounted over the next year for nearly 25 percent of the increase in real national product. In 1955 especially, the increases were explosive.

Third, it was a period of rapidly increasing use of credit by households, invited in part by a liberalization of credit terms. For homebuyers, mortgage interest rates moved down in 1953 and 1954—not sharply, but noticeably; the maximum repayment period allowed on FHA-insured and VA-guaranteed home mortgages was lengthened, first from 20 to 25 years and then to 30; and downpayment requirements were reduced.[33] There was a parallel easing of terms on consumer installment credit.[34] In

1955 alone, consumers added $5.3 billion to their installment indebtedness, nearly ten times as much as in 1954.[35]

Lacking impetus from another quarter, the advance might well have faltered in 1956, when homebuilding and new car sales dropped sharply; but there are times when the economy operates a little like a variety show, kept going by one act following another in close succession, and the mid-fifties was one such period. The advance was kept alive by a fourth force—a capital goods boom of exceptional strength.

All conditions were "go" for this to happen. When recovery began in 1954, utilization of manufacturing capacity was at 80 percent, an unusually high rate for a recession trough, and it rose over the following two years to 88 percent, an intensity of use not exceeded until 1965–66. This, plus the rapid rate at which consumer demand was rising, justified large increases in productive facilities. And ample financing was available for the capital investments this required. Corporate retained earnings were high, and in credit markets the real rate of interest was low and declining.[36] A bull market in stocks (prices 2.4 times higher in 1957 than in 1950) facilitated the raising of equity funds.[37]

In this context, spending on machinery and equipment rose between the first quarters of 1955 and 1956 by close to 30 percent, a boom-time rate. As usual, increases in spending on plant and other nonresidential structures lagged behind and were less rapid than increases in spending on equipment, but they continued longer. The two together rose for nearly three years at a rate two-thirds again as fast, on the average, as their longterm trend of increase.[38]

Fifth and finally, the period from 1953 to 1957 was preeminently the era of "economic miracles" abroad. In Western Europe the increase in industrial production averaged 12 percent a year, and in Japan nearly 15 percent, with the American economy drawn rapidly into the stream of things. Imports to the United States increased strongly, but it was especially a period of rapidly rising U.S. exports. These grew 16 percent a year in real terms in the three years following the first quarter of 1954, and their excess over imports accounted for roughly 10 percent of the increase in real GNP. Caught up in these advances, an increasing number of American companies began operations abroad. It was the beginning of the true internationalizing of American industry and finance.

*   *   *

It was inevitable that in these circumstances there would be large increases in U.S. production, employment and income. In the three years following the second quarter of 1954, annual percentage increases averaged 6.6 in industrial production, 2.2 in employment, 4.7 in real disposable personal income and 4.0 in real GNP, well above the long-term trends of increase.[39] It was inevitable also that growth at these rates would present tests to economic policy by putting upward pressure on wages and prices. The *Economic Report* called it "the delicate task of preventing inflation without impeding economic growth."[40] And the Chairman of the Federal Reserve Board—William McChesney Martin, Jr., throughout the Eisenhower presidency—is reported in the minutes of the system's Open Market Committee to have remarked at the January 1955 meeting that, "what we are dealing with . . . is the possibility that inflationary seeds are germinating and when they come to full bloom it will be exceedingly difficult to restrain them."[41]

The inflation danger continued through 1955 to command attention—by the White House no less than by the Federal Reserve; but there was at the same time a danger of overreacting to it, and Eisenhower was alert to that risk. After having remarked at his August 4, 1955 news conference that "America is today enjoying almost unprecedented prosperity," he was asked whether there was "a serious threat of inflation." Threading his way through a response that recognized the inflation danger but at the same time acknowledged the risk of overreacting to it, he replied:

> I wouldn't say "serious threat," but let us remember that any free economy is always in a situation of balance, even though it is going forward in its expansion . . . There are always present the . . . twin dangers of deflation and inflation, and the function

of government so far as it affects this matter at all is to be watchful, to be vigilant and alert, and to take measures from time to time that tend to move in one direction if the signs are [that] we are moving in the other. . . . As of this moment we have . . . activity . . . that is almost beyond calculation, measured by former standards. So, the time is here to be watchful, but I wouldn't say there was serious danger, no.[42]

*   *   *

Success in confronting such danger as there was in the situation depended in large part, of course, on what the Federal Reserve did. And it went quickly into action. Its first big move came in 1954 when, around midyear, it began to reverse the credit ease that had helped turn the economy into recovery. Between mid-1954 and mid-1955 the net reserve balances of member banks swung from a positive $730 million (a high degree of ease) to a negative $500 million (a high degree of tightness). The latter condition was relaxed briefly in the second half of 1956 to aid a Treasury financing operation, but restraint was resumed quickly when that exercise was finished, and net reserves fell again to a negative $500 million. At the same time, and helping make the credit firmness more effective, the discount rate was raised in seven closely-spaced steps from 1.5 to 3.5 percent. It was a policy designed to keep the member banks on a short leash; indeed, nearly as short a leash as under the restraint that preceded recession in 1953.

An inflow of gold to the United States between mid-1954 and mid-1957 worked against what the Reserve System was seeking to accomplish by increasing member-bank reserves; at the same time its purposes were aided by a drain of currency out of the member banks into domestic circulation, depleting their reserves. But the effects of these developments were not exactly offsetting, and to hold their reserve balances at the required amount, member banks had to increase their borrowing at the discount windows of their respective Federal Reserve Banks by about $800 million.

It was of course this increase in member bank borrowing that was the cutting edge of the restraint. Whether the banks were forced into it by the Federal Reserve's open market sales of securities ($1.4 billion), or the Reserve System was forced into the open market sales to offset member bank borrowing, is neither here nor there. What matters is that, with member bank reserve balances roughly constant (down an inconsequential $35 million), and with required reserves up fairly substantially ($226 million), if the banking community had abstained from increasing its indebtedness to the Reserve System it would have had a reserve deficiency of roughly $280 million. The result was a marked swing from credit ease to credit tightness.

Inevitably, this had impacts on money supply and interest rates. Money supply (demand deposits and currency) had risen at an annual rate close to 4.5 percent while the ground lost during recession was being made up, but under the Reserve System's subsequent restraint the increase slowed to just under 1.0 percent a year. It remained at that low figure from mid-1955 to mid-1957, literally (as in 1953) to the threshold of recession. True, deposits were being worked harder (i.e., deposit turnover was increasing), which lessened the impact on business liquidity of the reduced rate of increase in money supply, but because the volume of business being transacted was rising significantly faster than the increase in money supply the economy was again (as in 1953) in the position of having to fit itself into a monetary jacket that was tight and getting tighter.[43]

Reflecting what was happening in the economy and in money policy, interest rates moved up with little interruption from mid-1954 until recession began in 1957. Indeed, rates at the cyclical peak were at levels nearly half again as high as had been reached at the peak in 1953. The prime rate, for example, which was 3.5 percent at the 1953 peak was 4.5 in August 1957, the highest it had been in twenty-six years.

There were differences within the Federal Reserve over the merits of this policy. Some Open Market Committee members were more or less continuously urging a stiffer stand against what they judged to be a serious inflation danger. Others were concerned that tight money would slow the economy too much. To call the latter "doves" regarding the inflation danger would not be altogether correct; but the colleagues in the committee against whom they were aligned could quite correctly be called "hawks."[44] From time to time there were intrusions into the debate of the question whether, and in what way, the system should ease the credit market when funds were being raised in large amounts by the Treasury, but discussion centered mainly on the inflation danger versus the need to sustain the economy's expansion. The outcome was unequivocally a victory for the hawks: net reserve balances were held in negative territory, between minus $250 and minus $500 million, in all but a few months of 1955 and 1956.

*   *   *

For most of 1955, sentiment at the White House was strongly supportive of what the Federal Reserve was doing. Secretary Humphrey remarked at a March 4, 1955 cabinet meeting that the job was to avoid a "1955 boom" that could end in a "1956 bust"[45] And, in this mood, policies over which there was White House control were geared to reinforce the Fed.[46] The Treasury, always eager for such an opportunity, returned to the longterm credit market with a $2 billion issue of 40-year, 3 percent bonds, and followed this quickly with another $800 million. Under a program devised at the CEA, steps were taken to cool the home mortgage market. The permitted maximum on "time to repay" on FHA-insured and VA-guaranteed home mortgage loans was reduced from 30 to 25 years, and the minimum acceptable downpayment was raised two percentage points. A regulation was issued that ended what was called (familiarly) the "no-no-downpayment" mortgage loan, under which a homebuyer using a federally-guaranteed loan was permitted to make the purchase not only with no downpayment but with the closing costs on the transaction included in the face amount of the mortgage, thus achieving longterm, 100 percent financing of legal fees as well as housing. The Federal National Mortgage Association (Fanny Mae) sold loans out of its holdings into the credit market to sop up funds, and the Federal Home Loan Bank Board tightened the limits on loans to member institutions (mostly savings and loan associations) by the regional Federal Home Loan Banks.

In related actions, supplies of certain key materials scheduled for delivery to federal stockpiles (copper, aluminum, nickel) were diverted to civilian uses deemed to be essential. There was some discussion also of the possible need for presidential authority to control the terms on which consumer installment credit was being extended. The administration was philosophically disposed, however, to avoid such measures, and because it was not clear either that the control authority was necessary (in view of the overall restraint on credit) or that it would work constructively, Congress was not asked for it. But other steps were taken. With the thought that it might inspire lenders to be more cautious in their credit practices, arrangements were made to have all federal bank examination agencies, as they examined individual lending institutions, ask for a special schedule of information on the amount of installment credit being extended to customers and on what terms.[47] There is no direct evidence to corroborate this, but there is reason to believe that the inquiries had the desired deterrent effect on the banks. At the same time, the Federal Reserve was asked to make a study of the installment credit problem.

*   *   *

Illustrating how stabilization policy can be pulled by opposing forces, while the Federal Reserve was striving with White House support to restrain the economy there was political pressure for a tax policy that would stimulate it. The Republican leader in the House (Charles Halleck of Indiana) believed that a tax cut in 1955 would be essential to Republican success at the polls in 1956; and, in Governor Adams' account, Secretary Humphrey was at the time "as anxious for tax reduction as the President was for a balanced budget."[48] According to Adams, Eisenhower's response, turning aside the entreaties, was to tell his Republican congressional allies ("sternly") that "he would cut no more taxes until the budget was balanced" and to remark (rather tartly) to his friend the Secretary of the Treasury that he (Humphrey) was "too quick to recommend tax reductions on the basis of anticipated savings in expenditures that might not necessarily materialize." Accordingly, the fiscal

1956 budget, as presented to Congress in January 1955, proposed a small reduction in spending (to $62.4 billion, from the $63.5 billion expected to be spent in fiscal 1955) and recommended that tax reductions scheduled to take place on April 1, 1955 (in the corporate income tax and in certain excises) be deferred for a year. Relying on acceptance by Congress of its proposals, the White House projected a deficit in fiscal 1956 that would be smaller, at $2.4 billion, than the $4.5 billion expected at the time in fiscal 1955, but expressed a hope that tax reduction would be possible "next year."

It was one thing for Eisenhower to resist the tax-reduction urgings of Republican colleagues, but doing the same against his political opposition was another matter. Early in 1955 a move started in Congress from the Democratic side that presented a formidable challenge. The proposal was to give every taxpayer, every taxpayer's spouse, and every taxpayer's dependent—in effect, every living American—a tax reduction of $20 by increasing the personal tax exemption. It was not a large item, put in that per capita form, but the Treasury estimated it would remove 5 million people from the tax rolls and cost $2.3 billion annually in lost revenue.[49] Senator Lyndon B. Johnson (D Tex.) was prominent among its advocates, arguing that it was needed to spur the economy (the Federal Reserve was trying to restrain it!) and that it would correct inequities introduced into the tax code by the 1954 changes.

Eisenhower was deeply annoyed. Writing to his friend George Allen—an influential Democrat, who was at the time advising him on the development of a homestead in Gettysburg, Pennsylvania—and perhaps surmising that what he said would be passed on to the measure's architects (the "hidden hand" again?)—he denounced the bill as ill-structured and not affordable, and as a political maneuver designed to embarrass him and help defeat Republicans in the 1956 elections:

> These are the things that make one grow old and look with longing eyes to life on a farm. . . . I don't care how much these demagogues are gunning for me, but I get riled when I find them playing fast and loose with the soundness of our economy and the future of 163 million Americans.[50]

Although the letter indicated that Eisenhower understood the proposal to be the work of House Speaker Rayburn (D Tex.) and "some of his close cronies," and hinted broadly that he (Eisenhower) would retaliate when he could ("you would wonder what cooperation he [Rayburn] expects when it comes to legislation in which he will be vitally interested"), his public comments on the tax proposal were devoid of any mention of personalities, as was his manner in such things. At a news conference on the day following the dispatch of his letter to Allen, he described the bill, without mentioning its sponsors, as "some kind of height in fiscal irresponsibility." And when it was defeated (it died in the Senate, after passing the House by only a small margin) his reply to a question on how he felt about its demise was to ask, rather dryly, "Would it be allowable just to say hurrah?"[51]

*   *   *

All the while, and on the whole unexpectedly, it was becoming apparent that the budget would be in balance in fiscal 1956, rather than in the red, as had first been expected. It was a welcome development for what it would do to help cool an expansion that threatened to run to excess. Indeed, speaking for the CEA, Dr. Burns's advice to the cabinet was that the administration should work, through expenditure reduction, for a budget surplus. As it turned out, a surplus of $1.6 billion was achieved, but stabilization policy is an on-again, off-again thing, and by mid-1956 it was apparent that the problem had become less how to moderate a potentially too-rapid expansion than how to prevent an economic slowdown.[52]

The evidence on what was happening was mixed, to be sure, but negative on balance. Retail sales continued to rise strongly through 1956, but elsewhere there were opposite signs. The average length of the manufacturing workweek (a particularly sensitive "early warning" indicator) ceased rising in 1955, began to decline late in that year, and dropped sharply through 1956. Employment continued to rise, but at a reduced rate. And by yearend 1955 the drop in the unemployment rate had stalled between 4.0 and 4.5 percent, suggesting (correctly, as it turned out) that the unemployment problem was becoming more severe as the economy moved from one cycle to the next. Confirming these clues, real GNP increased at a noticeably reduced rate in 1955's fourth quarter and fell a bit in the first quarter of 1956. Industrial production turned from a rising to a roughly flat trend.

The administration's response to these unsettling developments was quickly to reverse the steps it had taken earlier to moderate the economy's advance. In December 1955 and January 1956 the Federal Home Loan Bank Board, at the CEA's urging, relaxed its limits on borrowing by member institutions, and the maximum permitted maturity on FHA-insured and VA-guaranteed home mortgage loans was restored to 30 years.[53] To the same end, efforts were intensified to obtain passage of a bill that had been previously requested but not enacted which would authorize the start of construction on what would later be the Interstate Highway System.[54] At the same time, convictions grew within the administration that credit was too tight and hardened when the Federal Reserve Board, on April 13, 1956, as part of what it was doing to "manage the expansion," raised the discount rate to 2.75 percent, the fifth in a series of increases that started at 1.5 in April 1955.

The effect of these moves by the Federal Reserve was to raise a storm. It is apparent from the record that Humphrey, Burns, and Hauge knew in advance that the discount rate increase was being considered (it was entirely proper that they should) and that all of them (in varying degrees) opposed it. But Chairman Martin at the Federal Reserve was sufficiently persuaded of the need for an increase that, according to Humphrey, he would have resigned if "violently opposed by the administration."[55] Eisenhower also thought credit was too tight and encouraged his colleagues in their efforts to dissuade the Fed from what it was proposing to do. But he abstained from involving himself directly in the effort, on the ground that to get into it would violate his known commitment to respect the system's independence. Cabinet minutes report him as having stated, one week after the discount rate was increased, that he might have phoned Chairman Martin prior to the increase but decided against it, believing that to have done so "would have constituted an overruling of the financial experts with a purely political judgment, which [he] had not felt to be in order."[56]

It was otherwise with his associates. They had made no public statements prior to the April 13 discount rate increase, but reticence was abandoned once the increase was announced. Responding to an inquiry from Congressman Wright Patman (D Tex.), Chairman of the Joint Economic Committee, Dr. Burns and Secretary Weeks called the increase "untimely," Secretary Humphrey told the Senate Finance Committee that he "would not have made it," and, in a press statement, Secretary James Mitchell (Labor) called it "unnecessary."[57]

It was the first real test of Eisenhower's convictions regarding Federal Reserve independence. Without taking sides on the question, he acknowledged at news conferences on April 25 and May 4, 1956 that there were grounds for debate over how much credit restraint was needed, but when he was questioned explicitly at the April 25 session on the possibility of making the Federal Reserve responsible to the president his answer was unequivocal: "I really personally believe it would be a mistake to make it definitely and directly responsible to the political head of the state."[58] There were occasions, however, when Eisenhower's resolve on the issue of Federal Reserve independence was tried nearly to the breaking point. He is reported to have remarked in a telephone conversation with Secretary Humphrey shortly after the April 13, 1956 rate increase that "if they [the Federal Reserve] don't do something (toward easing credit), we ought to go to Congress."[59] And about a month after the increase his response to a suggestion from Harold Stassen that greater credit ease was needed was that "we are working on it."

But feelings cooled soon thereafter. At the June 1, 1956 cabinet meeting, at which there were calls again for easier credit from Wilson, Summerfield, Burns and Stassen, and to a degree also from Humphrey, Eisenhower concurred with the Treasury Secretary's ultimately softened view that they should "bear with and help the [Federal Reserve] Board in getting to

an easier credit position," and warned against "any infringe-
ment of the prerogatives of the Board." To a suggestion that he
"might profitably confer with . . . Martin on this problem,"
Eisenhower responded that "his beliefs were already known
and . . . he would not want to be in the position of seeming to
pressure the Federal Reserve Board."[60] And by September
1956, in a less agitated context, he had reached a conclusion
fully supportive of Federal Reserve independence. He wrote a
letter at that time to Lewis W. Douglas, a friend and frequent
correspondent, and later U.S. Ambassador to Great Britain,
that can be taken to represent his considered view on the White
House–Federal Reserve relationship:

> We are, of course, suffering some of the pains of prosperity.
> The supply of savings and money generally has never been
> greater but the demand is greater still. The confidence people
> have in the future has produced plans in a surging volume and
> the result is so-called "tight money."
> While the System's policy of restraint has been rightly di-
> rected toward the goal of stability at these high levels of activity,
> among us here we have had for some time reservations about
> the timing and extent of the policy. These opinions have been
> made clear to the Federal Reserve Board chairman and I am
> sure he has accorded them full weight. But he feels strongly
> about his responsibility under the law, as he should.
> The general public, of course, makes no differentiation be-
> tween the Administration and the fully independent Federal
> Reserve Board. We are continuing to explore ways both of
> making this (differentiation) clear and of securing further provi-
> sion for the legitimate credit needs of small business and agri-
> culture, and I have some reason to hope that the Federal Re-
> serve Board will loosen some of their restrictions within the
> next few weeks.
> We must find a way to foster a healthily growing, high-
> employment, peacetime economy while containing inflation. It
> is a new and challenging task.[61]

As a final observation on this incident, it must be remarked
that the Federal Reserve appears to have been right in its April
1956 decision to raise the discount rate, and the White House to

have been wrong in opposing it. To have had a somewhat firmer restraint in 1956 might have obviated the need for the still greater restrictiveness that was imposed on the economy in 1957. Chairman Martin, who managed the Federal Reserve's side of the affair with great skill and tact, later testified that he thought restraint should have been greater in 1956 than it was.[62]

*   *   *

While the Federal Reserve was "flexing" money policy in 1955–56, Eisenhower was striving to hold fiscal policy to a steady course. As noted, the budget put before Congress in January 1955 for fiscal 1956 was designed to that end. So was the budget proposed in January 1956 for fiscal 1957. In contrast to the expenditure reduction that had been recommended the year before, there was provision in the fiscal 1957 plan for a small increase in outlays ($65.9 billion recommended, following the $64.3 billion expected in fiscal 1956), but Congress was asked to defer for another year the tax reductions scheduled to take place during the 1957 calendar year. The small surpluses which this was expected to produce ($200 million in fiscal 1956 and $400 million in fiscal 1957) would be applied against the public debt.

The strategy was outlined in the January 1956 Budget Message:

> It is unquestionably true that our present tax level is very burdensome and, in the interest of longterm and continuous economic growth, should be reduced when we prudently can. It is essential, in the sound management of the Government's finances, that we be mindful of our enormous national debt and of the obligations we have toward future Americans to reduce that debt whenever we can appropriately do so. Under conditions of high peacetime prosperity, such as now exist, we can never justify going further into debt to give ourselves a tax cut at the expense of our children. So, in the present state of our financial affairs, I earnestly believe that a tax cut can be deemed justifiable only when it will not unbalance the budget, a budget that makes provision for some reduction, even though modest, in our national debt. In this way we can best maintain fiscal integrity.[63]

The same position was taken three months later when Eisenhower was queried at his April 25, 1956 news conference on the prospects for a tax cut. He replied:

> I see, so far, no logical reason for reducing taxes, and I really believe it would be not to the good interests of America to reduce them at the moment. . . . We are in a time of very high income. We certainly must be able to run our government now without going into debt to do it or we never will.[64]

*   *   *

In another two weeks, however, fiscal policy was again in dispute. A slowing of the economy's advance prompted interest within the administration in a tax reduction. A June 1, 1956 presentation to the cabinet by Dr. Burns took the position that it was "time to reconsider tax policy," and proposed that, with a surplus in prospect for fiscal 1957 ($4.5 billion in the cash consolidated budget), a tax cut of $3 billion might be possible.[65]

But Eisenhower was not persuaded. As recorded in the June 1 minutes, he remarked, looking at longrun prospects, that while he was ". . . not taking an irrevocable stand against a tax cut . . . [he] did not believe it possible to reduce expenditures markedly over the next ten years and . . . did not want a huge national debt hanging forever over the Government's head." Illustrating his sensitivity to the political context, he also emphasized the need for some reduction of the public debt to avoid having to go every now and then to Congress for a temporary debt-ceiling increase and having to make a concession on one thing or another (often of some consequence) in order to get it, and his "doubts about the nature of any tax-reduction legislation that might be passed by an opposition majority in an election year."

*   *   *

Showing still again how quickly a change in the economic climate can transform the debates on policy, it was not long after these discussions of a possible need (or opportunity) to cut taxes that the case for giving some stimulus to the economy was out and once more the case for restraint was in. Following settlement of a strike in the steel industry, industrial production rose sharply (8.0 percent between July and December 1956) and aggregate real output spurted, rising to an annualized rate close to 5.0 percent in the final quarter of that year. At the same time, increases in labor costs and in prices became suddenly more visible, underlined by a poststrike increase of 6.5 percent in the basic price of steel. Complicating matters and pointing to a more widespread upward pressure on prices, productivity improvement fell from close to 3.0 percent in 1955 to under 1 percent in 1956, and labor cost per unit of output rose 6.0 percent.[66]

Normally, developments of this nature would be reflected fairly promptly in the inflation indexes; in this case, however, the effect was shrouded for a time by a technical complication. When the prices of industrial products at wholesale began to move up in 1955, farm prices (also a component of the index of wholesale prices) were still moving down, leaving the overall index for a time roughly stable. But when farm prices stopped dropping (around yearend 1955), the overall index was soon rising at between 3.0 and 3.5 percent a year. Similarly, the consumer price index, which had been broadly flat for three years, thanks in part to declining food prices, began around April 1956 to increase when food prices started moving up. In other words, an upward trend in prices that had, so to speak, been underground suddenly came to the surface. By the end of 1956 the overall index of consumer prices was rising at close to 4 percent a year.

Although inflation at that rate is low by comparison with what afflicted the United States in the 1970s, it was high for the 1950s, and it tended to validate what commentators were saying about "living in an age of inflation." The danger was exaggerated in many cases, but there was all the same the possibility that, unless resisted, inflation at 4 percent would rise to 5, and after 5 to 6, and so on.

There were obvious implications in this for money policy. Credit restraint seemed called for and the Federal Reserve took steps to provide it. The discount rate was increased to 3 percent on August 24, 1956, in this case with no protest from the administration, and (except for a brief period around the end of the year) net reserves were kept at sizeable negative figures (between $250 and $500 million). Increases in money supply (demand deposits and currency) were held under 1 percent a year through 1956 and well into 1957. In this context, bond prices tumbled. Longterm interest rates had risen by yearend 1956 to heights not reached previously for twenty years. The prime rate was boosted on August 21, 1956 to 4 percent, the highest since 1933.

There were implications in these events for fiscal policy as well. The Budget Message sent to Congress in January 1957 (for fiscal 1958) extended the "hold the line" policy on taxes for still another year, arguing that it "would be neither fair nor appropriate to allow excise and corporate tax reductions to be made [as was scheduled under legislation then on the books] when a general tax reduction [could not] be undertaken." Rather, the surpluses expected in fiscal 1957 and projected for fiscal 1958 ($1.7 and $1.8 billion, respectively) should be used to reduce the public debt.

> At a time like the present (the Message reasoned), when the economy is operating at a very high rate and is subject to inflationary pressures, Government clearly should seek to alleviate rather than aggravate those pressures. . . . For the Government to do its part in the coming year, taxes must be retained at the present rates so that receipts will exceed budget expenditures and the public debt can be further reduced. The prospective budget surplus in the fiscal year 1958 will reinforce the restraining effect of present credit and monetary policies. The present situation also requires that less pressing expenditure programs must be held back and some meritorious proposals postponed.[67]

*   *   *

This combination of fiscal forbearance and monetary restraint, tending to moderate the upward pressure on prices of aggregate demand, would in most situations be sufficient to overcome inflationary tendencies, but as 1956 ended it was clear that an additional force was complicating things. It was the tendency, not unusual when the economy is moving up briskly, for wage and benefit costs to rise faster than productivity, causing labor cost per unit of output to rise and putting further upward pressure on prices. Attempting to forestall this effect by fiscal and monetary restraint alone ran the risk of requiring that the restraint be so severe as to turn the economy into a decline. Thus the question became: How could this push of costs on prices be suppressed without increasing the recession risk?

Eisenhower's answer was to add a third dimension to the defenses against inflation—an appeal to the leadership of labor and business for "responsibility" in setting the wage-increase terms agreed upon in labor contracts and in posting increases in prices. It was put as follows in the *January 1957 Economic Report:*

> [B]usiness and labor leadership have the responsibility to reach agreements on wages and other labor benefits that are fair to the rest of the community as well as to those persons immediately involved. Negotiated wage increases and benefits should be consistent with productivity prospects and with the maintenance of a stable dollar. And businesses must recognize the broad public interest in the prices set on their products and services.
>
> The full burden of avoiding price inflation . . . cannot be successfully carried by fiscal and monetary restraint alone. To place this burden on them would invite the risk of producing effects on the structure and functioning of our economy which might, in the years ahead, impair the vitality of competitive enterprise. And failure to accept the responsibilities inherent in a free economy could lead to demands that they be assumed by Government, with the increasing intervention and loss of freedom that such an approach inevitably entails. The successful extension of prosperity with price stability must be a cooperative effort in which the policies of individuals and economic groups and of all levels of Government are consistent with one another and mutually reinforcing.[68]

It was not the first time an American president had made such an appeal, nor would it be the last, but there were numerous complaints. It was anathema to the leaders of labor, who asserted that wage increases were innocent of any significant influence on prices. As they saw it, inflation was mainly an "administered price" phenomenon, caused by companies that, by virtue of doing a large share of their industry's business, were able arbitrarily to fix prices at higher and higher levels, without necessarily having a basis in cost increases for doing so.[69] On different grounds, but no less vigorously, conservatives deplored the appeal as an unwise interference with market processes, with the monetarists among them warning that money policy not only did not need the help such an initiative promised but might actually be weakened by it. Nor did Eisenhower have the support of everyone in his official family. Several cabinet members, invoking a variety of reasons, were opposed to including the appeal in the State of the Union Message and in the *Economic Report:* Humphrey on the ground that the relationships among wages, productivity and prices were too complicated to be dealt with "in a paragraph;" Weeks asserting that the appeal presupposed "too much correlation" between wage increases and productivity; and the Labor Department protesting (to the CEA) that it was neither good economics nor good politics.[70]

Eisenhower was familiar with these dissents but dismissed them all, persisting in his wish to have the matter dealt with firmly in the yearend messages. As cabinet minutes show, and as my conversations with him at the time and later repeatedly confirmed (I had become CEA chairman in December 1956, just as the problem was emerging), the issue involved fundamentals on which he was not about to be shaken. One was that the leaders of business and labor, because of their discretionary power in a free economy, had to act responsibly if the system was to perform as it should; indeed, he would insist with great stress that they had to do so if the system was to survive. There was no confidence here that somehow "the market" would produce the right result. The other fundamental was that when such a question arose the president had a duty to give the public an indication of what constituted responsible action, though he should do it in a way that would not in the end invite direct governmental intervention. The problem was to put the appeal in words sufficiently plain to inspire the desired reactions, but not so specifically as to invite direct intervention by government into the bargaining process.

Accordingly, complaints of critics and colleagues notwithstanding, and in terms that many thought insufficiently specific but was deliberately so, the appeal was put before Congress and the nation as follows in the January 1957 State of the Union Message:

> I have often spoken of the purpose of this Administration to serve the national interest of 170 million people. The national interest must take precedence over temporary advantages which may be secured by particular groups at the expense of all the people.
>
> In this regard I call on leaders in business and in labor to think well on their responsibility to the American people. With all elements of our society, they owe the Nation a vigilant guard against the inflationary tendencies that are always at work in a dynamic economy operating at today's high levels. They can powerfully help counteract or accentuate such tendencies by their wage and price policies.
>
> Business in its pricing policies should avoid unnecessary price increases, especially at a time like the present when demand in so many areas presses hard on short supplies. A reasonable profit is essential to the new investments that provide more jobs in an expanding economy. But business leaders must, in the national interest, studiously avoid those price rises that are possible only because of vital or unusual needs of the whole nation.
>
> If our economy is to remain healthy, increases in wages and other labor benefits, negotiated by labor and management, must be reasonably related to improvements in productivity. Such increases are beneficial, for they provide wage earners with greater purchasing power. Except where necessary to correct obvious injustices, wage increases that outrun productivity, however, are an inflationary factor. They make for higher prices for the public generally and impose a particular hardship on those whose welfare depends on the purchasing power of

retirement income and savings. Wage negotiations should also take cognizance of the right of the public generally to share in the benefits of improvements in technology.

Freedom has been defined as the opportunity for self-discipline. This definition has a special application to the areas of wage and price policy in a free economy. Should we persistently fail to discipline ourselves, eventually there will be increasing pressure on government to redress the failure. By that process freedom will step by step disappear. No subject on the domestic scene should more attract the concern of the friends of American working men and women and of free business enterprise than the forces that threaten a steady depreciation of the value of our money."[71]

We were alert to the risk that an appeal couched in broad qualitative terms might be transformed as it passed through the legislative process into a quantitative and unacceptable version, and the reality of that danger was quickly demonstrated by the reaction of the Democratic majority on the Joint Economic Committee (JEC). It held that the proposal went in the right direction but was deficient in not providing the "standards" and "workable machinery" that business and labor needed "in accepting responsibility for maintaining a stable price level."[72] But "machinery" was precisely what Eisenhower wanted to avoid: it might not start as a system of direct wage and price controls, but it could easily become that.

As it turned out, there was little support in Congress or in the country for what the JEC majority thought was needed. On the other hand, Eisenhower's appeal, while it had no identifiable impact on the movement of either wage rates or prices, had a broadly favorable public reception. We believed it had the useful effect of promoting a better public understanding of a matter that was critical in determining how well a free economy could operate.

*   *   *

Thus, going into 1957 there was a threefold strategy at the White House for carrying out "the delicate task of preventing inflation without impeding economic growth"; the Federal Reserve was supported in a money policy that would be adequately antiinflationary without (it was hoped) overdoing that virtue; the budget was kept as close as possible to balance by restraint on spending and a "hold the line" policy on taxes; and the leadership of labor and management was urged to have regard for the community's interest in making wage demands and setting prices.

The test of this strategy did not come until after mid-1957 and (getting ahead of the story a bit) it must be acknowledged that it failed in its purpose of avoiding recession. What 1957 illustrates, however, is not that the essentials of the strategy were faulty, though exception can be taken (as I will) to aspects of its execution, but how easy it is for there to be "too much of a good thing" in the expansion phase of the cycle, and how difficult it is to cope with this exuberance. We turn, then, to how the economy's advance was interrupted in 1957, and the administration's response to that distressful result.

A Second Recession: 1957–58

The chances of avoiding recession are slim enough when homebuilding is down, are still less when a housing decline is joined by a slump in the auto industry, and are next to nil when, adding to these misfortunes, there is a collapse of capital-goods spending, typically the last support of a boom. It happened that the economy was hit by all three in 1957, but its fate in the end was sealed by a ratcheting up of interest rates, brought on by good times and a spell of exceptionally tight credit.

Homebuilding was the first to decline. It is characteristic of that industry to move in surges followed by deep reverses, with the periods of greatest activity separated by four to five years and never lasting more than a few months; in this case the move from high to low followed the usual pattern. Reflecting favorable demographic factors and the drop in interest rates that helped reverse recession in 1954, housing starts rose to an annual rate of 1.8 million in December of that year, a volume not reached again until the 1970s. It stayed at that level for a few months and then, as interest rates began to rise, went into a decline that lasted two years and brought the rate of housing starts to around 1.2 million in early 1957, a drop of about a third.

New car sales had much the same history. They reached nearly 8 million in 1955, a volume not attained again for ten years, then dropped to below 6 million in 1956. There was a recovery of sorts in 1957 (to 6.1 million), then a drop to 4.3 million in 1958, the latter made all the more damaging by the conspicuous failure in the 1957–58 model year of the Ford Motor Company's much-touted Edsel.[73] The number of cars sold in 1955 was so much greater than the 5 to 6 million that was more or less normal at the time that, like the early 1955 peaking of housing starts, it was clearly a surge that couldn't last.[74] But the automobile industry somehow always manages to believe that good times, however extravagant, will last forever, and the eventual collapse of the sales boom, disappointing these hopes, had a chilling effect on Detroit and on the economy generally.

Finally, there was the ending of the capital-goods boom. The retreat began in 1956 with a decline in appropriations for the replacement and expansion of manufacturing facilities. This was followed early in 1957 by a drop in new orders to equipment producers. Then, late in 1957 and continuing into 1958, there was a decline in actual spending on plant and equipment. The latter seems to have reflected principally the operation of the "acceleration principle," which has it that the demand for capital goods depends not on the level of the economy's output of final goods but on whether that output is rising or falling, and by how much.[75] At the time, the course of final output was turning from rapid increases to no growth at all, bringing the principle into play negatively and forcefully.

Given these reverses there was a certain inevitability to the downturn of the economy, and Eisenhower was undoubtedly right in remarking, as he did some years later, that "the prior boom had a lot to do with the [1957–58] recession."[76] But policy cannot be absolved from having had a hand in the result; indeed, it had a heavy hand in it.

*   *   *

The involvement of money policy was clearly the deepest. How it evolved in the initial and middle phases of the 1954–56 upturn has already been told: first, a vigorous easing of credit to promote recovery; then, beginning in mid-1954 and continuing until mid-1955, a retreat from ease, designed to prevent the economy's advance from proceeding too rapidly; and, following that, a third phase, lasting to the threshold of recession in the fall of 1957, during which credit markets were kept tightly restrained (except for a brief period toward the end of 1956, to accommodate a Treasury financing operation), with net reserves of member banks of the Federal Reserve System held at negative amounts varying between $250 and $500 million.

It was an unmistakably restrictive credit policy and, because restraint is increasingly effective the longer it is continued, its restrictiveness increased as 1957 progressed. Then, on what proved to be literally the eve of the economy's decline into recession (September is now identified as the first down month), restraint was intensified by a spate of interest rate advances, including increases in the Federal Reserve's discount rate and in the prime rate.

There was firm support for the policy within the Federal Reserve System, but there was opposition, too. One member of the Open Market Committee (Governor James K. Vardaman) is reported to have observed as early as May 7 (correctly, as it turned out) that "the bloom was off the rose"; and Alfred Hayes, who by midyear 1957 had succeeded Alan Sproul as head of the New York Federal Reserve Bank, was advising with some regularity (along with some others) against a discount rate increase. Hayes was worried about the consequences for the economy and for some soon-to-be-conducted Treasury financing if the discount rate was raised, but he was also concerned about the public posture of the Reserve System if its policy should prove to have been too tight. The committee's minutes report him warning his colleagues at the July 9, 1957 meeting that "We must give serious thought to the consequences to the System if we are later blamed for recession."

There were differences also among the economists. It would go too far to say that the CEA and the staff of the Federal

Reserve System were miles apart, but the differences between them were wide enough to imply significantly different views on policy. The CEA's opinion, which I put regularly before Chairman Martin and Vice Chairman C. Canby Balderston, was that, given the prevailing policies, the economy would expand less rapidly in 1957 than in 1956; beyond that, there could be a "general retrenchment" toward the end of 1957 if the capital goods boom were to fail (as it did). On this view, which was received respectfully by the Fed's leadership but (necessarily) without comment, there was not only no need for a further tightening of policy (the narrowly-defined money supply had been growing for two years at less than 1 percent a year) but a fairly obvious need for some easing.[77] Reflecting that state of mind, the *January 1957 Economic Report*'s comment on nearterm prospects had been cautious: after much reflection over the outlook, all it would venture to say was that "How economic activity will move in the coming months cannot be confidently foreseen."[78]

Contrasting with this concern at the CEA, the staff advising the Open Market Committee was continuing as before to advocate restraint. A senior adviser observed at the July 9, 1957 meeting that "a worldwide atmosphere of ebullience and the tendency to accept inflation as inevitable seem to call for continued restraint, through whatever monetary and fiscal measures may be available"; and at the same meeting one member of the committee (Governor Balderston) was reported to have warned that the "time had come for the System to take action" (presumably to increase the discount rate, but possibly also to raise reserve requirements), noting that "if it continued to wait for the Treasury to be in the clear or to refrain from action just before or just after a Treasury [debt management] operation . . . it might well be that (it) would not act at all."

With views within the policymaking establishment divided along these lines, the economy and the credit markets continued for some months in the summer of 1957 on a broadly flat trend. Net reserves fluctuated around the minus $500 million level (at times less negative, but not greatly so), and the discount rate was held a bit above the federal funds rate (the rate at which member banks could borrow reserves in the open market), in this way imposing a penalty on banks that chose to use the discount window to correct reserve deficiencies. In short, a steady and fairly severe restraint was continued in a period that, on the surface at least, was one of calm.

The calm was broken, however, on August 6, when the prime rate was raised by money-center banks by one half a percentage point to 4.5 percent. It was an increase twice the size of the four that had preceded it, and put the rate at its highest level since 1931. The effect of this untimely move (it came exactly as the economy was turning from up to down, though that was not visible in the data available at the time) was to create a gap between the prime rate and the discount rate that the Federal Reserve authorities could not ignore. After what was clearly a tense debate in the Open Market Committee, and doubtless also among the Board of Governors, the system's response, beginning on August 9 at four Reserve Banks, was to raise the discount rate also by half a percentage point.[79] This increase (twice the size of the six that preceded it) brought the rate (at 3.5 percent) to its highest level since 1933.

The discount rate increase was strictly in the character of what, in the universal language of central banking, is routinely called "an adjustment to market conditions," and it is true that the prime rate increase did force the Federal Reserve's hand. To have allowed a gap of one-and-a-half percentage points to persist between the prime rate and the discount rate might well have been too great an incentive to member banks to borrow at the discount window, with potentially unwanted consequences for credit expansion, for the increase of money supply, and (ultimately) for the inflation rate. Some argued, however, that, regardless of what the prime rate happened to be, the discount rate increase was needed to break the inflation psychology then prevailing. But with the money supply growing at less than 1 percent a year, as it had been since mid-1955, it would seem that inflation was being suppressed strongly enough without requiring the shock that was delivered by these rate increases, and without the economy having to pass (as it soon did) through recession. In any case, a heavily repressive effect was imposed on the economy precisely when, to borrow Sproul's phrase again, the economy was at the brink of a downturn. Perhaps even a bit over the brink.[80]

One must conclude from the Federal Reserve's relatively quick reversal of the August 9, 1957 discount rate increase (it came within ninety days) that its effect was more repressive than they either wished or expected it to be.[81] However inspired, the reversal was a welcome development. But ninety days is a lifetime at a cyclical turning point, and in that short span the economy turned clearly into recession. Worse still, it took nearly six months for the commercial banks to undo their prime rate increase. Recession gathered momentum quickly and deepened. It lasted eight months.

*   *   *

It is entirely possible that recession might have occurred in 1957 solely as a reaction to the exhaustion of the forces that propelled the economy upward in 1955 and 1956, reinforced as it was by the repressive effect of a persistently tight money policy. But the recession risk was heightened, and the downturn that began in the second half of 1957 was almost certainly deepened, by a development for which the administration itself must take full responsibility.

It began with a press conference called on January 15, 1957 by Secretary Humphrey to discuss the fiscal 1958 budget, due to be delivered to Congress the following day. Drawn up in an atmosphere of concern over the recently-surfaced inflationary tendencies in the economy and "continuing threats to world peace" (uprisings in Poland and Hungary in October of 1956, and the Suez incident in October–November of that year), the budget continued the policy of the two that had preceded it by proposing to "hold the line" on taxes. Adjustments involving a minimum loss of revenue would be made in taxes affecting small businesses, but it was proposed that reductions in the corporate income tax and in certain excise taxes that were due to be made on April 1, 1957 be deferred for another year. There would be a small ($2.8 billion) increase in spending.

There had been little or no argument in the Executive

Branch over the tax proposals. The Treasury was unhappy but not obdurate about the rate reductions for small business, but it was deeply aroused by the proposed spending increase. Coming after increases of $1.9 billion in fiscal 1956 and an expected $2.4 billion in fiscal 1957, it would reverse by nearly three-quarters the economies achieved in the 1954 and 1955 fiscal years. It did not appease Secretary Humphrey that there had been a $1.6 billion surplus in fiscal 1956, that a $1.7 billion surplus was expected in fiscal 1957, or that, despite the proposed spending increase in fiscal 1958, a surplus of $1.8 billion was projected for that period. Spending increases per se were the problem, or so it appeared.

The secretary began his news conference by reading a statement that deplored the trend to higher spending, and in a colloquy with the press that followed was asked: "Who do you blame for this increase?" His answer was that "everybody" was to blame—the administration, Congress, and the public—and that while the budget was the best that could be had at the time "there are a lot of economies . . . we ought to be able to make [and we] ought to improve it [the budget] as time goes on." When asked to reconcile these economizing possibilities with the budget's proposed spending increases, Secretary Humphrey made a remark that became instantly a news sensation: "If we don't over a long period of time [reduce spending], I will predict that you will have a depression that will curl your hair."[82]

This avidly repeated and still memorable pronouncement had three negative effects. First, it suggested, incorrectly, that there was a rift between Humphrey and the president and Eisenhower had to move quickly to squelch that inference. Speaking to the press about Humphrey's prepared statement he said: "I not only went over every word of it, I edited it, and it expresses my convictions very thoroughly."[83] All the same, there was a disturbing effect on public sentiment. Second, although Humphrey was referring to a distant danger his remarks, naturally enough, were applied to nearterm prospects, with a further disturbing effect on public sentiment. And third, in what was the most damaging consequence of all, both the

White House and Congress were provoked into an ultimately fruitless budget-cutting exercise that not only helped produce and deepen recession in 1957 but may well have contributed to the downturn that occurred in 1960. Specifically, a resolution was proposed in Congress by fifty-seven Republicans calling for an upper limit of $65 billion on fiscal 1958 spending—a draconian measure that would have required a cut of 5.7 percent from what was currently estimated to be spent in fiscal 1957 (already half finished) and nearly 10 percent from the fiscal 1958 spending which the president had proposed to Congress as a "rockbottom" amount.

Mercifully, the Republican resolution was not adopted, but a second one, sponsored by the Democratic majority in the House, succeeded. With a transparent show of innocence, it called on the president to "indicate the places and amounts in his budget where he thinks substantial reductions may best be made."[84] It was not clear how best to respond to the congressional request. Consideration was given to the preparation of a new budget, but that course was quickly (and wisely) rejected. Instead, a letter went from Eisenhower to Speaker Rayburn making suggestions for the reduction of outlays but pointing out that in two large areas of the budget (the 24 percent of spending "rigidly prescribed by law" and the 63 percent for defense) expenditures either could not or should not be reduced.[85] The president took an adamant stand on defense: "I most solemnly advise the House," he wrote to Speaker Rayburn, "that in these times a cut of any appreciable consequence in current expenditures for national security and related programs would endanger our country and the peace of the world." It followed that reductions would have to be made in the remaining 13 percent of the budget, but the president pointed out that to make cuts in those areas "would destroy or cripple many essential programs." As an alternative, he proposed a reduction in spending authority, as distinct from current spending, but reminded Speaker Rayburn that of the $1.3 billion of such reductions and postponements that were possible "less than half . . . can be reflected in reductions in expenditures during the next [1958] fiscal year, and even a part of these . . . will have to be restored in the future."

Despite reservations about what could be done, a vigorous effort was launched to find economies. No department or agency was spared, but the major stress, necessarily, was on "military functions," which accounted for two thirds of the $2.9 billion increase that had been proposed for all spending combined.

The first result of these efforts was a reduction in Defense Department commitments to spend. "Awards to prime contractors for work to be done in the United States" were cut nearly 50 percent in the first six months of 1957, and a more inclusive category—the gross volume of "obligations incurred"—was cut about 25 percent. The immediate impact was to cause defense contractors to make fewer commitments to suppliers and to cut back their plans for capital expansion. The impact on spending came only with some lag, owing to the length of the Defense Department's "pipeline," but what had been a sharply rising curve of purchases since early 1956 turned flat in the first half of 1957, precisely when an increase would have been helpful in stabilizing the economy.

Complicating matters further, late in the summer of 1957, with the business community already concerned about a downturn in the economy, the Air Force (at the urging of the Treasury, where a congressionally-imposed limit on the amount of public debt that could be outstanding had caused cash to be drawn down to a perilously low level) notified its suppliers that "progress payments" were being scaled back. The availability of these advances reduced the need that defense contractors had for working capital and, lacking them, many contractors were forced to seek bank financing at a time when credit was tight. The result was something close to panic in the defense community, with cries that "Uncle Sam is going broke." Alternative financing arrangements that involved access to credit at the Federal Reserve Banks for qualifying contractors were quickly improvised, but not without there having been another shock to business sentiment.[86]

Large as defense programs were in 1957 in the national scheme of things, it would be a mistake to attribute to them the power to move the economy by themselves from up to down, but whatever the merits of that year's economizing exercise may have been it could hardly have been more awkwardly timed. The 1957 cutback in Defense Department commitments to buy, coming when other forces were increasing the recession risk, was particularly damaging. And then, in 1959, when a steady volume of Defense Department purchases would have been helpful, there began a two-year decline that had an adverse effect at a second time of cyclical sensitivity. In short, the budget-cutting exercise that started in January 1957 appears to have been implicated in not one but two recessions, in different ways but in both cases unhelpfully.

In addition it is remarkable, not to say ironic, that, despite the clamor for budget-cutting that was provoked in Congress, and despite the extent to which economizing was actually accomplished in several key areas of the budget, total spending by the federal government in fiscal 1958 came in the end to marginally more ($100 million) than the $71.8 billion first proposed, and $2.5 billion more than was spent in fiscal 1957. In that sense it was an ultimately fruitless exercise.

*   *   *

If money policy and the budget were administered in the first half of 1957 less favorably for the avoidance of recession than one would have wished, as they were, it must be conceded that the signs of cyclical trouble were not apparent until the year was well advanced. As already noted, September is now accepted as the month in which recession began, and some of the "leading indicators" had by that time been declining for several months (some since early 1956). Yet real GNP rose fairly strongly in the first and third quarters of 1957, and several of the series that are relied on most heavily for gauging the economy's nearterm prospects were strong well into 1957's third quarter.[87] During the summer, however, the balance of evidence turned negative, and in September it became clear that for the second time in the Eisenhower administration it would be necessary to mount a program to counteract recession.[88]

One looked for help first from money policy, and help eventually came in some force from that quarter, but not as soon as we on the White House side would have liked. It was not until November that the need for a shift away from restraint was put strongly in the Open Market Committee, and not until December 17, three months after recession was clearly under way, that the Reserve Board's staff was sufficiently impressed by what was happening to substitute "recession" for "downsettling" in their descriptions of events.[89] Also, it was not until December that the committee provided a new directive for the New York Bank's open-market desk; even then the orders were put softly, calling for purchases of securities in a volume that would have the effect of "cushioning adjustments and mitigating recessionary tendencies."

Acting under this directive, it was not until January 1958, when the economy was within a few months of its cyclical trough, that the net reserves of member banks reached a small positive amount. From that point, however, they moved rapidly to the plus $500 million reached in March 1958. Helping to produce this result, reserve requirements were cut in February and April 1958; and the discount rate was reduced in four closely-spaced steps, reversing by April 1958 all but one quarter of a percentage point of the increases that had started in 1955.

These were moves in the right direction, but with the economy in a kind of "free fall" (employment dropped in January 1958 by nearly 2 million; the unemployment rate jumped from 5 to 5.8 percent; and new car sales were 30 to 40 percent below their year-ago totals), and with the White House besieged by pleas to "do something," they came at an agonizingly slow pace. And there was again no help from the money-center banks. Interest rates determined in the open market (e.g., commercial paper rates) moved down as the economy receded, but the prime rate, which is set by management decision, was not cut until January 22, 1958, close to the bottom of the recession.

Rates charged generally to commercial customers (for which only quarterly data were available) showed no decline of consequence until the first quarter of 1958. And reflecting the credit contraction that was by that time proceeding apace, the narrowly-defined money supply fell from September 1957 through January 1958 at about 2 percent a year. It began to rise again as the economy recovered, and beginning in February 1958 moved up for a year and a half at around 4.7 percent a year (a rapid rate for the time), but the crucial fact is that in both the down and up phases of the 1957–58 cycle money supply ran with the tide of the economy, not against it.

*　　*　　*

Where the White House could move on its own, action came more swiftly. A task force to plan and implement corrective measures was formed in September 1957 to supplement what was being done at the Federal Reserve, and it was soon producing useful results. The cutback in Defense Department contract awards was reversed; by January 1958 they were rising again fairly strongly. Steps were taken to accelerate nondefense procurement by the federal government. Work was speeded up on federal and federally-sponsored construction projects that were already under way, and others that were already planned and funded were initiated promptly. Building projects already authorized by the Federal Housing Administration and by the Department of Agriculture (college housing, urban renewal, public facilities, water resource projects and projects of the Rural Electrification Administration) were accelerated. On the same day (April 2, 1958), the Department of Health, Education and Welfare announced that it would give priority in its grant programs to projects that could be started promptly, and the Post Office Department announced that it would accelerate work on facilities being built under its lease-purchase program. To give a boost to homebuilding, the April 1955 ban on "no-no-downpayment" home mortgage loans was revoked, rules applying to allowable discounts on VA-guaranteed mortgages were eased, and Fanny Mae raised the prices it paid for mortgages, hoping to nudge credit markets toward lower interest rates, as it did.[90]

As these steps were being taken, Congress was urged by the White House to act on a measure which, while it would have a demand-enhancing, counter-recessionary effect, was inspired mainly by a desire to lessen the impact of recession on the individuals and families most directly affected. It would help the states make unemployment compensation payments to qualifying persons for an additional period equal to one-half the duration of regular payments.[91] Then as now, these payments were made by the states, with the federal government in a supportive role, and Eisenhower wished to keep it that way. To that end, the White House had already urged those states that were not already doing so to bring regular benefits up to at least one-half the compensation of the individuals involved and to make the payments for not less than 26 weeks. Now, Congress was asked for legislation that would, as a temporary measure, allow a longer duration of eligibility.

The proposal was put before Congress on March 25, 1958 and was debated alongside a bill favored by the Democratic side that would have accomplished much the same end but under a more nearly federalized payment system. Tardily, but still usefully, a bill preserving the federal-state partnership character of the system was passed, substantially as Eisenhower wished. It was signed into law on June 4 and established a pattern of federal support to state systems that has been followed to this day.

*   *   *

Eisenhower supported all these measures, keeping in touch with developments literally day by day, but there were proposals made that he refused to endorse. For one thing, he was determined not to be drawn into public works projects that could not be expected to materialize in actual construction until the recession was over and that, through the spending they would ultimately require, might block progress toward long-term tax reduction and reform.[92] He took the occasion of a

1958 speech to Republican women to describe the public works projects that qualified for inclusion in a countercyclical program:

> All of the [construction] projects being accelerated and being presently readied as a reserve have one thing in common: they are useful and needed in themselves. Moreover, they are generally projects that start quickly and provide employment quickly. They will not drag out so long that they compete with the needs of private enterprise when resurgence comes.[93]

And a few months later, when the corner had already been turned into recovery but proposals for public works spending were still being spawned on all sides, there was this statement to a group of businessmen:

> I am determined not to get bogged down in a slow-starting, emergency public works program, which would provide a minimum of jobs now and a maximum of budgetary deficits in the years ahead.[94]

Congress had fewer qualms. It passed in 1958 a River and Harbor and Flood Control Works Bill authorizing expenditure of $1.7 billion that failed White House tests by a wide margin. Eisenhower vetoed it on April 15, 1958, noting that it was the judgment of the Chief of (Army) Engineers that some of the projects it would authorize had "no economic justification," that there were others for which adequate reports had not been submitted to Congress, and that on some of the larger projects "it would be many months, even years . . . before the necessary plans could be completed and actual construction started. . . ." Also, the bill contemplated a sharing of costs which in Eisenhower's opinion did not adequately reflect the extent of the benefits that would accrue to local communities. As the veto message put it, the bill lacked "the best test yet devised for insuring that a project is sound—the willingness of local people to invest their own money in a joint enterprise with the Federal Government."[95] Suggesting something that Congress could do that would have quick and constructive effect, the message proposed that Congress supply funds for river-basin projects already under way and for which expenditures in 1958 and 1959 would exceed what had already been authorized.

There was no vote on the veto. It was obviated by the passage of a substitute bill which met most of Eisenhower's objections, and he signed it on July 3, 1958.[96] By that time, however, the economy had turned the corner into recovery, illustrating again the near futility of using public works effectively for countercyclical purposes in what is typically a relatively brief downturn.

*   *   *

Proposals to increase spending on public projects got extensive press coverage, but throughout the 1957–58 recession and well into the recovery that followed it the most insistent and most dwelt-upon test of Eisenhower's readiness to act against recession was his willingness to propose a tax cut. It is doubtful that legislation could have been obtained from Congress in this form, but what the tax-reduction advocates typically wanted was a temporary cut that would be withdrawn when the recovery it was expected to help stimulate had restored the economy's growth. In some versions, the cut would expire at a scheduled date.

There is no single point in the tactics of acting against recession on which Eisenhower has been more frequently misunderstood than his attitude toward proposals of this character. He is pictured often as a consistent, even arbitrary opponent of them, when the reality is that (as we have seen) he supported tax reduction in 1953 when it was clear that it could help reverse a downturn and (as we will soon see) was prepared to propose a cut in 1958 once certain prefatory legislative steps had been taken.

That is not to say, however, that there were no differences of consequence between Eisenhower and the typical antirecession-taxcut advocate. There were immense differences. What set him apart was that he had more confidence in the ability of the economic system (given an appropriate money policy) to turn, independently of any new fiscal stimulus, from recession to recovery, that he was readier than most to give the monetary stimulus time to work its effect, that he had more exacting tests for deciding when the time was right for counterrecessionary tax reduction, and that he regularly opposed reducing the long-term revenue-raising capability of the tax system when the case for doing so for shortterm counterrecessionary purposes was not persuasive.

These reservations notwithstanding, the tax reduction option was kept open in 1958 even after it had become clear that a recovery process was under way. Asked at his February 5 news conference if a tax cut would be one of his reserve weapons, "even at the expense of a bigger deficit," his answer was: "It could be, it could be." And some six weeks later (March 26, 1958), confronted with essentially the same question, he replied at greater length, and in a manner that can still be read with profit:

> I have never excluded the possibility that there might come a situation where a [countercyclical] tax reduction would seem desirable.
> At the same time, I think that every thoughtful person . . . views this step . . . with such seriousness that they are not going to be stampeded into doing it. . . . All sorts of difficulties arise . . . [defense] appropriations by '59 will be very considerably greater than they are now [and] there have been all sorts of other proposals . . . that will swell national budgets if all of them are approved.
> Now, if you recognize that any tax cut is bound to increase the gap between revenues and expenditures, [and realize] the seriousness of large and continuing deficits upon our whole fiscal and financial system, then you will see that this is not something to do lightly.
> . . . [W]e are watching every development as closely as we know how . . . and we are certainly going to do those things we think should be done; but we are not going into a tax cut or any other [program] we believe to be unwise [and] can hurt us badly in the future. We have got to think of the years to come as well as the immediate month in which we are living.[97]

Reinforcing the prudential bent that was a prominent element in Eisenhower's makeup were a number of tactical reasons why no tax-cut proposal was made in 1958. To begin with, although no one could be sure in the early months of that year how the economy would move over the nearterm, the administration was more confident of the prospects than were the advocates of emergency tax reduction. As 1957 drew to a close, and despite the trials through which the economy was passing at the time, we at the CEA were sufficiently encouraged by what was beginning to be visible in the economic indicators to write in the *January 1958 Economic Report* that "the decline in business activity need not be prolonged and . . . economic growth can be resumed without extended interruption."[98] And by early February 1958, when calls for emergency action were at a peak, there was enough confidence at the White House to warrant the president issuing a statement which said there was "every indication" that a pickup of job opportunities in March would "mark the beginning of the end of the downturn."[99]

Second, Eisenhower's reservations about the wisdom of cutting into the tax system's long-term revenue-raising capabilities were being hardened by the implications for the future of federal spending of the intransigence of the Russians in the matter of arms control and by their launching in October 1957 of Sputnik, the first of the space vehicles. With defense spending and total budget outlays already on the rise and clearly destined to rise further, with the prospect of large expenditures for space-vehicle development beginning to loom up, and with the case for a countercyclical tax reduction marginal at best, it was not surprising that he reacted with some impatience at his April 23, 1958 news conference to yet another question about a tax cut:

[P]eople come in and blithely say, "Have a tax cut." No one stops to think about this: defense is expensive, and is growing more expensive, and we have got to be ready to pay those defense costs for the next 40–50 years, possibly. It isn't an emergency thing that we meet here. We are meeting [in the recession] a minor emergency internally, but let us not forget the grave international emergency as we are preoccupied with our immediate sources of income. . . . So, I say: you have got to look down the road. . . ."[100]

Letters written by Eisenhower earlier in April 1958 reflect the same reservations:

> When I contemplate the minimum size of the Federal budget that we are now certain to have about 1961, I am alarmed by the amount of deficit spending we shall probably have to do. As I try to peer just a bit down the road into the future, I cannot fail but be impressed by the inflationary factors that we shall likely have to combat. A sizable tax reduction may become one of these; I have not yet been convinced of . . . its necessity. And if it is not needed at the moment then I am quite sure its future effect would be inflationary.[101]

Third, there were questions of legislative tactics to be considered. With a congressional election to be held in a few months, there was more than the usual possibility in 1958 that a tax-cut proposal would have a spate of constituency-pleasing provisions attached to it (get a "Christmas tree" treatment) and would end up costing more in lost revenue than anyone could reasonably justify.

Fourth, certain tax reductions were scheduled to take place on April 1, 1958 (a cut in the corporate income tax and reductions in a broad range of excise taxes) that it was not easy to justify on grounds either of equity or possible countercyclical effect but would almost certainly go ahead on schedule if it was proposed to have at the same time a cut in the personal income tax. Accordingly, it was decided not to ask Congress to cut the personal income tax until it had acted on the extension (for another year) of the corporate income tax and the excises. Then, as it turned out, by the time Congress had acted on a tax-extension measure (Eisenhower had to remind Congress on May 20, 1958 that it had not done so), the signs of recovery were so obvious that the case for countercyclical reduction of the personal income tax had vanished.[102]

Fifth and finally, and illustrating how it may be necessary to carry out tax policy in a quite adverse and sometimes unpredictable legislative context, rumors began to circulate in 1958 that a proposal for emergency-type tax reduction might be made either by a group of Republicans in Congress, acting independently of the White House and contrary to its wishes, or by a group on the Democratic side, similarly without support from their party leadership. To stifle these possibilities, which the leadership on both sides wished to do, a pact was made between the White House and the Democratic congressional leadership under which both agreed to refrain from proposing an emergency-type tax cut without giving prior notice to the other. It was a kind of "no first strike" agreement and, while no guarantee against insurgency, it doubtless worked in that direction. In any case, under the umbrella of this hastily-devised mutual assistance pact evidence that recovery was starting without the help of tax reduction appeared soon enough and in sufficient volume to deter action by either set of dissidents, causing the incipient revolts to die a natural death.

*   *   *

As signs of economic recovery in the making became more and more promising, there was some lessening in calls for emergency action. In this context, Eisenhower opened his April 2, 1958 press conference by recommending to those present that they seek out and read verses 11 and 12 of the second chapter of the Song of Solomon. They would have found the following: ". . . lo, the winter is past . . . the time of the singing of birds is come . . . and the voice of the turtledove is heard in our land."[103] The president may have been merely celebrating the arrival of spring, after what had been a long, cold and trying Washington winter, but the improvement in the economic climate was almost certainly also on his mind, possibly in the front of it.

The economic news could not have been more welcome, especially to those of us who had helped draft the president's February statement that March "would mark the beginning of the end of the downturn" (it tried to say something without saying too much). There was, however, still a risk that the good beginning would falter and, with the president working closely with the CEA, particular care was taken to keep the tax-cut option open. As it happened, there was no need to exercise the option. Recovery flourished, and when the June 18, 1958 news conference passed without a question on either recession or tax cuts, it was obvious that both issues were certifiably dead. As Eisenhower later recalled it, "the storm was over."[104]

Steel, Gold, Recession, and Politics: 1959–60

As 1959 began, recovery from recession was still not complete but the economy was on an upward trend and its momentum was strong. There was no thought that the advance would go on forever, but there were grounds for believing that the cycle's ups and downs could be kept within narrower limits than in the past. If possible, interruptions would be held to short pauses between periods of normally rapid growth. The economy might be flat or only moderately rising during these pauses; ideally there would be no appreciable loss of ground, if any loss at all. I thought of it as an "advance-pause-advance" pattern, and we were determined that policy would be directed explicitly to achieving at least that result. One hoped to avoid even a pause.

The nature of the economy, open as it is to external as well as internal shocks, made this an ambitious goal. But uninterrupted growth is always the object of stabilization policy and we proceeded with the idea of achieving it. One thing was certain: the most important of the keys to success would be to avoid surges such as the one in 1955–56, which had invited an early relapse.

As it turned out, the effort failed, but the margin separating success from failure was narrow, and traceable in good part to two special circumstances. The first of these was a steel strike that started in mid-1959, closed down the whole steel industry, lasted 116 days, had an effect much like that of a small, sharp recession, and for several months after it was over made the trend of the economy hard to decipher.

At the center of the dispute was the question of workrules, typically the least negotiable of all strike issues. At one point in Eisenhower's involvement in it he remarked that there seemed to be something "mysterious" about the workrules problem, as indeed there was.[105] But the mystery was only in how the parties to the dispute could be so far apart on the factual basis of a question that one would think should be amenable to objective analysis. The question was whether workrules were a significant obstacle to keeping costs down and keeping the industry in the forefront of technological development. On the one side, the industry maintained that workrules as they stood were just such an obstacle, and that an easing of them was crucial to improving its competitiveness and profitability. On the other side, labor claimed that the rules were not a problem at all. As it turned out, they were enough of a problem to require Supreme Court intervention to bring the dispute to an end.

There was a series of destabilizing side effects from the strike. The first was a speeding up of the economy in the first half of 1959 as inventories of steel and related materials were built up in anticipation of a shutdown. Then, during the roughly four months that work was stopped, there was a drop in production and employment that, in the economy's overall statistics, looks much like a small, sharp recession. And as work was resumed following the strike's settlement there was a period reaching well into 1960 in which inventories were again built up rapidly, causing a surge of activity that complicated the task of assessing the underlying trend of the economy and had a broadly depressing effect when it subsided. From the CEA's viewpoint the whole affair was an out-and-out misfortune.

There were unhelpful impacts also on economic policy. For one thing, the strike's effect on production and employment was so disruptive that, as a practical matter, it ruled out for a period of six to nine months in 1959–60 any broad Executive Branch economic initiatives other than those aimed at bringing the dispute to an end as soon as possible. In addition, the surging of activity immediately after the strike ended, and the possibility that that surging, plus the terms of the settlement, might start a new wave of price increases, intensified and prolonged the monetary restraint that was having a broadly suppressive effect on the economy and that, absent the strike, would almost certainly have been eased sooner.

Eisenhower was drawn into the dispute at an early date. His first State of the Union Message had asserted that "American labor and American business can best resolve their wage problems across the bargaining table" but conceded that it might be necessary to intervene "in extreme cases, [where] the public welfare require[d] protection," and the 1959 affair was quickly judged to be such a case.[106] In the end, the settlement (reached in January 1960 after the Supreme Court upheld a Taft-Hartley injunction requiring a return to work) included wage and benefit increases close to what the companies had originally offered (variously estimated as costing between 3.2 and 3.7 percent a year) but made no provision of any significance for changes in workrules, which had been at the bottom of the clash.[107] In short, the steel industry failed to win what it had sought—a better posture for keeping abreast of technological change—and the strike must be judged to have been unreservedly a failure from its viewpoint.

And it is hard to see how it was anything but a failure from the public's viewpoint. Naturally, the administration was anxious to have a dispute ended which, in addition to its disruptive economic effects, could be a political embarrassment if continued into 1960, a presidential election year, and left for settlement by some method that Congress would stipulate (almost certainly by compulsory arbitration). But it was also important, as the president had underlined in his 1957–58 appeal for responsible action in settling such disputes, that it be resolved in such a way as not to require an increase in the price of steel.[108]

As it happened, there was no post-settlement increase in the price of steel, but this was mainly because the demand for it was too slack in 1960 to sustain an increase. At the same time there was almost certainly a cost-increasing effect. How much that was is hard to say, but considering the low rate at which productivity was improving at the time in the categories of industry in which steel would be included it was quite likely between 1 and 1.5 percent per unit of steel produced. It is therefore a reasonable surmise that, there being no increase in the price of steel, the nearterm result was to narrow the steel industry's profit margins by some such amount and, in the longer term, to weaken its competitive capability in world markets.

Eisenhower later wrote that he thought at the time that the money settlement "probably would not be inflationary" but that "the effort to modernize workrules should not have been dropped."[109] That was my view, too. The desirability of an early settlement was never in doubt, but the Council was also concerned about the longrun consequences for the competitive capability of American industry in world markets of strike settlements in which the additional labor costs contracted for exceeded the prospects for productivity improvement. And because the settlement failed to make provision for the work-rule changes that would offer the needed opportunities for productivity improvement, I viewed it as a failure from a public-interest viewpoint. It took a few decades, however, and serious difficulties in the steel industry, to reveal the importance to the United States of staying competitive in steelmaking in the world economy and the importance of achieving that posture of wage increases that kept reasonably in step with changes in manufacturing technology.

Yet it must be acknowledged that to have insisted on a meaningful relaxation of workrules would have forced the dispute into Congress, from which it would almost certainly have been sent next to compulsory arbitration. There could have been no assurance that compulsory arbitration would have yielded a constructive resolution of the workrules question, but it could well have had an adverse political effect for the administration in 1960. The question, accordingly, was whether to accept the potentially negative political fallout. Wisely or not, the decision was not to risk it.

* * *

Opinions could differ on how much, if at all, the steel strike should have influenced the direction of economic policy in 1959–60, but there was never any doubt about what response was needed to the second of the special circumstances affecting the economy in that period—a large and persistent outflow of gold. One of its major effects, as with the steel strike, was to support the case for a firmly and visibly antiinflationary money policy. Unfortunately, the side effects of this were, again, to hold the economy's growth rate below what, absent the monetary restraint, it might have been.

The gold drain began in the closing years of Eisenhower's second term, when the results of U.S. trade with the rest of the world were abruptly and in the main unexpectedly reversed.[110] Earlier, trade had been heavily in surplus. With exports surging ahead at nearly 10 percent a year in real terms, twice as fast as imports, payments to the United States for goods and services sold overseas produced a surplus of $5.2 billion in 1957, draining dollars in large amounts from the rest of the world.[111]

The British were among the hardest hit, and clearly the most articulate on the dangers posed by what was quickly dubbed the "dollar shortage." To the extent that economic policy could correct what was happening, it would be by easing domestic economic policies, but the case for this normally attractive response was not an easy one to make before an administration and a Federal Reserve deeply concerned by the 1956 acceleration of price increases. It was put forward vigorously, all the same, by officials of the British Treasury.

Suddenly, however, and again in the main unexpectedly, the situation was once more reversed. Instead of surging ahead, as in the past, exports dropped nearly 20 percent in real terms in the twelve months ending January 1958 and remained at that level for a year and a half; imports rose sharply, reducing what had been a large goods and services surplus to an excess of only $147 million. And the "basic balance" in U.S. international payments, which took account of government grants and flows of longterm capital funds as well as trade, dropped to a deficit of $3.5 billion after having been close to a balance in 1957.[112] Foreigners, previously starved for dollars, began now to pile them up in huge amounts, and before long they were being used to claim gold. By the end of 1959 our gold holdings were down $3.4 billion (15 percent), and with liquid liabilities to foreigners $3.6 billion greater than at the end of 1957 further drains were threatened.[113] Conceivably, a devaluation of the U.S. dollar might have checked this process, at least in the short run; but devaluation as a way of dealing with the problem was not only instinctively and intuitively unpalatable to

Eisenhower but was uncalled for when judged analytically by the financial situation in the United States and elsewhere in the world. It was uncalled for also judged by the relationship between prices here and abroad. True, there was a residual inflationary psychology in the United States in 1959, but price level trends were close to flat and there was reason to believe they could be kept that way. And it was reasonable to expect that in the end, and presumably before too long, the experience of living under stable prices would govern psychology.

There was thus no reason to doubt that the dollar's strength would in time win the respect in the world that it warranted, and that this would staunch the outflow of gold. Moreover, meeting the problem within the context of an unchanged gold value of the dollar would be consistent with America's position as keeper of the world's "key currency," a responsibility on which Eisenhower, the U.S. Treasury, the Federal Reserve and the international financial community laid heavy stress. With no significant dissent at home or abroad, indeed with general approval, it was a solution without devaluation that was sought.

The main thrust of the effort had to be delivered by the Federal Reserve, but there were things for other agencies of the Executive Branch and for American businesses to do. The need was to increase exports. The post-World War II world in which American companies could sell abroad without great effort had ended. Better governmental support services were needed to help US companies do business in overseas markets; at the same time there were things business could do to help itself. To help promote the needed increase in exports, a National Export Expansion Program was launched in 1959 under which U.S. commercial representation was strengthened at our embassies abroad (it had been neglected in the early postwar years), resources of the Export-Import Bank were increased, and seminars and conferences were held in Washington with trade associations and individual businesses to determine how the federal government could help U.S. exporting companies.[114] Also, efforts were made to have other countries reduce the restrictions they placed on the import of U.S.-produced goods and services, and steps were taken to reduce the foreign exchange cost of carrying out U.S. military commitments in Western Europe and extending aid to less-developed countries.

It is easy to overestimate the influence government can have on an economy as large as ours and organized as it is, but an improvement in U.S. foreign trade performance did follow soon after these efforts began. The export-promotion program doubtless helped produce that result; so did the resumption of rapid growth in Western Europe and Japan. In any case, there was success in mending the trade figures: the U.S. balance on goods and services rose to a $4 billion surplus in 1960 and the deficit in the nation's basic balance in international payments was cut to $1.2 billion.

Still, the gold outflow continued. Due principally to movements of shortterm capital, liquid liabilities to foreigners increased by $1.6 billion in 1960, bringing the total to $21 billion, roughly double what it had been when the Eisenhower administration began. And in November and December 1960 gold losses rose to what were widely regarded as crisis proportions, causing Treasury Secretary Anderson to report to the president on November 9, 1960 that "by now we have almost a gold panic situation."[115] The result was to force consideration of a redeployment of the U.S. troops stationed in Western Europe, at least to impose limits on the maintenance overseas of their dependents. These efforts came to little, however, forcing heavier reliance on what could be done through money policy. The result was that monetary restraint was applied almost certainly beyond what, absent the gold outflow, would have been deemed appropriate.[116]

The adjustments in money policy came in three phases. The first was a retreat from the aggressive ease that had helped reverse recession in 1957–58. There was some apprehension in the Open Market Committee that credit tightening would be carried too far but, on the whole, it was viewed as essential, and the Federal Reserve moved aggressively into it. In the January 6, 1959 meeting of the committee, for example, one member warned that "the time [had] come to make restraint a reality," and another warned that the Reserve System had to be careful not to repeat what he viewed as the 1954–55 mistake of not moving soon enough and firmly enough to block inflationary developments. Acting on these concerns, and to put teeth into the tightening of reserve balances (net reserves were reduced from plus $500 million in July 1958 to a small minus by year's end), the discount rate was raised in two steps (September and November 1958) to 2.5 percent.

The second phase extended from early 1959 to February 1960, by which time net reserves had fallen to a negative $350 million and the discount rate had been raised to 4 percent, the highest level reached since 1929. Under this increasingly restrictive policy, interest rates moved steadily upward: in February 1960 the prime rate was lifted to 5.0 percent, the highest it had been since 1930.

In the third phase, beginning early in 1960 and lasting through the remainder of the year, money policy was affected by two sharply conflicting influences: the first was a combination of concern that the steel settlement might spark a renewal of inflationary pressures and desire to check the outflow of gold, suggesting a need for credit restraint; the other was a recognition that the economy was hardly more than flat, pointing to a need for credit easing.

Considering the size of the gold losses, and how heavily these weighed in deciding what course should be taken, it is perhaps remarkable that credit conditions were relaxed to the extent that they were. Net reserves of member banks were allowed (and helped) to rise from the February 1960 minus of about $350 million to a plus $720 million in December of that year, a swing of more than a billion dollars. But the move came slowly from the viewpoint of those of us who were canvassing all ways to spur the economy to a faster pace. And, notwithstanding the steepness of the swing, net reserves did not cross into plus territory until after midyear 1960. Interest rates declined, though not as rapidly as the president and we at the CEA would have liked. The federal funds rate ceased rising in November 1959, but did not begin a sharp retreat until June 1960. The discount rate was held at 4 percent until June 10, 1960. And the prime rate was not cut until August 23.

One would like to have had the shift from restraint to ease started earlier and executed more aggressively, but money policy is made in a world of uncertain signs, conflicting influences, and competing priorities; and it is not easy to see how, with the steel strike's impact not completely absorbed until March 1960, and the gold outflow intensifying throughout 1960, it could have been greatly different than it was. Clearly, however, it would have been helpful, and not too much to have expected, to have had an earlier response by the commercial banking system to the easing of bank reserves, in particular a prompter reduction of the prime rate.

*   *   *

As these adjustments in money policy were being made, changes were taking place also in the fiscal sphere. With budget outlays expected to drop to $77 billion in fiscal 1960 from the $80.9 billion expected for fiscal 1959 (if the president's recommendations were accepted), and with revenues expected to rise to $77.1 billion (boosted by recovery and supported by another "hold the line" year on taxes), a surplus of $100 million was projected in the Budget Message put before Congress on January 19, 1959. But following the $12.9 billion deficit which was at the time expected in fiscal 1959, even this small plus implied a swing in budget results from one fiscal year to the next of $13 billion. As it turned out, the swing came to $13.6 billion.

Taken by itself, this transformation of budget results would impose a degree of restraint on the economy, but less than one would judge from the size of the swing. For one thing, a large U.S. contribution in the 1959 calendar year to the International Monetary Fund (counted as a budget expenditure in fiscal 1959) increased the size of the shift but had no immediate economic effect. And while the phasing out of certain antirecession programs helped hold expenditures down in fiscal 1960, and in that way helped enlarge the swing, any loss of stimulus from this adjustment was doubtless more than fully offset by the increases in employment and income that came with recovery.[117]

All the same, the administration was later subjected to much criticism for not having taken steps, either through tax reduction or spending increases, to prevent the swing from occurring. Some of the criticism was ultimately retracted, as the benefits of the administration's budget policies became more widely appreciated, but, entirely apart from the merits of the complaints, it is doubtful that the president could have aborted or significantly reduced the swing, even had he wished to do so.

In any case, there was no wish to do so. It was Eisenhower's view (with which I agreed) that closing the budget gap in 1959–60, which the swing did, would have important constructive effects.[118] It would ease the demand for capital and credit in financial markets and favor a trend to lower interest rates. It would help consolidate the trend to price stability that was already under way. It would strengthen the readiness of foreigners to hold balances in U.S. dollars and help check the outflow of gold. It would reduce the need to keep money tight. It would return the budget to where one could anticipate an early opportunity to carry out tax reduction on a fiscally responsible basis. And it would have political merit in what would be the last full fiscal year of the president's eight years in office. It was not a hard decision to make.[119]

Shaping a budget for fiscal 1961 presented much the same questions. There was reason to believe in January 1960 that the swing to surplus in fiscal 1960, which was occurring much as expected, would be followed in fiscal 1961 by a somewhat larger surplus (an expectation that failed), initially estimated to reach $4.2 billion. With this in mind, Eisenhower invited Congress in the January 1960 budget message to "join with me in a determined effort to achieve a substantial surplus . . . [which would] make possible a reduction in the national debt." Debt reduction would boost confidence in the U.S. dollar at a time when a boost was needed; in addition, it would "ease conditions in capital and credit markets and . . . increase the supply of savings for . . . productive investment."[120] Again, it was not a hard decision to make.

*   *   *

But there was all the same much criticism of the administration's conduct of policy in this period. Money policy did not escape criticism as unwarrantedly restrictive, but the main complaint, at the time and subsequently, was that the administration did not propose a tax cut.

Actually, however, there was no point in the entire three years, from 1958 through 1960, when a tax-cut proposal would have been either economically sound or politically practical. In 1958, with the economy in a brisk recovery, and with money policy (beginning in midyear) turning to restraint, it was to the latter, not to taxation, that one needed to look as the medium through which expansion could be encouraged. Indeed, it would have been grossly imprudent to have spent any part of the tax system's revenue-raising capability to give an expansionary thrust that could be given more adroitly and more promptly, to say nothing of more economically, by an easing of monetary restraint. To have proposed a tax cut in 1959 to revive activity that was being depressed by a paralyzing strike in the steel industry would surely have been a bizarre venture. And it would again have been an odd strategy, to say the least, to have proposed tax reduction to stimulate an economy that was being additionally restrained, as ours was at the time, by money policy. And to have put a tax-cut proposal before Congress in 1960, a presidential election year, with both houses controlled by the opposition party, would have invited a legislative contest that almost certainly would have ended with a greater loss of revenue than anyone could justify. Conversely, and given our confidence that there would be a Republican victory at the polls in November 1960, saving the opportunity to reduce the tax burden for another year and for another president would get the 1960s started in an economically favorable and politically auspicious fashion.

Reflecting these January 1960 expectations, the president's decision to recommend no change in taxes was put as follows in the Budget Message issued at that time:

> If expenditures are held to the levels I am proposing for [Fiscal] 1961 and reasonable restraint is exercised in the future, higher revenues in later years will give the next administration and the next Congress the choice they should rightly have in deciding between reductions in the public debt and lightening of

the tax burden, or both. Soundly conceived tax revision can then be approached on a comprehensive and orderly basis, rather than by haphazard piecemeal changes, and can be accomplished within a setting of economic and fiscal stability.[121]

*   *   *

Unhappily, these hopes were not realized. The surge of activity that followed the settlement of the steel strike in January 1960 continued for several months, but it became apparent early in the year that the economy's performance was beginning to fall below par and that steps were needed to improve it.[122] The principal reliance had to be on the easing of credit that was under way at the Federal Reserve, but with the gold outflow becoming steadily more troublesome there were limits to how far that expedient could be pressed. Accordingly, steps were taken once again to give the economy an upward thrust through the exercise of whatever Executive Branch discretionary authorities could be used to that end. A task force (which I chaired) was set up in the White House to design, activate, and monitor the program, with the accent on measures that would stimulate homebuilding, accelerate procurement, and ease the terms on which credit was available from federal lending agencies. A particular effort was made to speed up construction on federal and federally-assisted construction projects, including the Interstate Highway Program, which by that time had been authorized by Congress and was well under way.[123]

There were grounds as late as September 1960 for believing that these efforts, plus the Federal Reserve's credit easing, would prevent a downturn, but that expectation, and all that had been done to make it come true, was dashed by a sudden and unexpected shift in the fall of 1960 in the inventory-holding policies of business concerns.[124] A large buildup of stocks in the first quarter of 1960 (replenishing supplies that had been reduced during the steel strike) was followed first by two quarters of sharply reduced accumulation and then by six months of depletion. The effect was to turn a change in real GNP that had been positive in the first quarter of 1960 to changes that in the second, third and fourth quarters of the year were moderately negative. They were negative enough, however, to constitute the recession that is now dated as having started (though few would have said so at the time) in May 1960.

It is true that among the recessions since World War II the 1960 decline is one of the least severe: output and employment dropped less than half as much as in 1953–54 and 1957–58; disposable personal income did not decline at all; neither did aggregate consumer spending; and, in price-adjusted terms, final sales (GNP less inventory change) were up in the first and second quarters of the year, down only a shade in the third, and up in the fourth. And the decline didn't last long. Recovery is now dated as having started in March 1961, but there was sufficient evidence by December 1960 to justify the CEA asserting in the *January 1961 Economic Report* that the upturn "should not . . . be long delayed."[125]

But, shallow and brief though it was, recession in 1960 was a hugely disappointing close to Eisenhower's eight years of coping with the ups and downs of the economy. And it was a huge embarrassment to the Republican side in the November voting. As in all close elections, there were a number of negative factors in 1960 which, had they been absent, might have caused the outcome to be different. Recession was one of them. And the decline was all the more regrettable because it was in no sense necessary to pass through it in order to consolidate the price stability and achieve the structural balance in the budget that the policies pursued in 1958–60 helped bring about.

*   *   *

In this way the economy's performance in 1959–60 fell short of achieving the advance-pause-advance pattern we had hoped for, though it came close to doing so. Fortunately, however, the benefits inherent in having achieved price stability and a structurally balanced budget were not lost. All major elements of the economic environment needed to achieve growth at a good rate were in place when Eisenhower left the White House, his presidency ended. We spelled these out as follows in the *January 1961 Economic Report:*

As expansion is resumed, there is a good chance to realize more fully our economy's potential for growth. The basis for advance has been laid in recent years in the enlargement and improvement of our productive capacity and in policies that have brought the forces of inflation under control. Some temporary acceleration of growth might have been achieved if expectations of price increases had been allowed to persist and to become firmly rooted. But the unsustainable nature of such growth would now be confronting the economy with the need for far-reaching and painful correction. Because action to maintain stability and balance and to consolidate gains were taken in good time, the economy can now look forward, provided public and private policies are favorable, to a period of sound growth from a firm base.[126]

One does not expect the opposition party in politics to acknowledge its good fortune when its legacy on taking office is a good one, and there was no acknowledgment in January 1961. To a large degree, however, and not meaning to claim for the Eisenhower administration more than its rightful credit for this result, the benefits envisaged in the *January 1961 Economic Report* were realized, to everyone's advantage, in the first half of the 1960s.

Notes

1. At the March 6, 1953 cabinet meeting, Eisenhower assigned the function of countercyclical contingency planning to the CEA, to be started as soon as the council was reorganized, and the *January 1954 Economic Report* stated (p. 54) that "the Council of Economic Advisers was instructed early in the year [1953] to design plans for dealing with a business depression, although none was in sight." The president's June 6, 1953 letter to cabinet members requesting their participation in ABEGS indicated that "maintaining a stable prosperity" would be a major concern of the group (*Abilene Papers,* DDE Diary Series, Box 3, December 1953–July 1953).
2. Adams, *Firsthand Report,* p. 162.
3. From a speech to the Associated Press, April 20, 1953 (*Humphrey Papers,* p. 49).
4. *Economic Report,* January 1953, pp. 75–76.

5. *The Business Outlook, 1953,* National Industrial Conference Board, Studies in Business Economics, no. 37, p. 46.

6. *Public Papers, DDE,* 1954, pp. 231–31; *Economic Report,* January 1954, p. 72, and January 1956, p. 13.

7. *BCD,* December 1985, Series 525.

8. *BCD,* October 1985, Series 577 and May 1985, Series 578.

9. *Economic Report,* January 1961, Table C-52, p. 187.

10. *Economic Report,* 1954, Chart 12, p. 31, and Table G-14, p. 181.

11. Here I have relied on data in what I will refer to as the *Unpublished BCD,* precursor of *BCD.* Beginning in 1957, the unpublished compilation was prepared monthly under the CEA's direction by Dr. Julius Shiskin, at the time Chief Economic Statistician and Assistant Director of the Bureau of the Census and later Commissioner of Labor Statistics. The series included in it were compiled from a number of sources, public and private, including especially the privately-supported National Bureau of Economic Research. Preparation of the *Unpublished BCD* involved one of the earliest uses anywhere of electronic equipment for processing data in the analysis of the business cycle, on which Dr. Shiskin had been doing developmental work at the National Bureau.

The president took particular satisfaction every month in studying the charts and tables assembled in the early *BCD* document, speculating avidly on how the figures would move from one month to the next.

I use the last of the unpublished compilations (January 19, 1961), reflecting data largely as they were available to us between 1953 and 1960; there have, of course, been many revisions in the series since that time.

12. *Economic Report,* February 1986, p. 339, and *Flow of Funds Accounts, 1946–1975; Annual Total Flows & Year-end Assets and Liabilities* (Board of Governors of the Federal Reserve System, Washington, D.C., December 1976), p. 4. (The latter is hereafter cited as *Flow of Funds, 1946–75.*)

13. *Annual Report (1953) of the Federal Reserve Bank of New York,* pp. 6–11.

14. Policy discussions in the Open Market Committee throughout the 1950s tended to concentrate on the level and movement of net free reserves. Changes in money supply, interest rates and rates of inflation, and the prospects for production, employment and income, were by no means ignored, but if there was a primary target for money policy it was the net reserves of member banks, that is, excess reserves less borrowings by member banks at the Federal Reserve Banks. Data on reserves and member bank borrowings are from *Banking and Monetary Statistics, 1941–70* (a compilation published

by the Board of Governors of the Federal Reserve System, Washington, D.C.), pp. 596 and 667.

15. *Banking and Monetary Statistics, 1941–70*, pp. 17–18. Unless otherwise indicated, money supply will mean demand deposits plus currency in circulation. This was the most widely used measure of money supply at the time, corresponding to what is now called M1. It was of course necessary to take account also of changes in time deposits at commercial banks, but the narrower concept was generally adequate as an index of credit market conditions. Happily, the proliferation of money supply measures (M1, M2, M3, and so forth) was a later phenomenon.

16. Treasury bill yields are from the Federal Reserve's *Historical Chart Book* and the prime rate from *Banking and Monetary Statistics, 1941–70*, p. 707.

17. The committee was composed then, as it is now, of all members of the Federal Reserve Board and an alternating panel of five of the twelve Federal Reserve Bank presidents. Minutes of the meetings are available in microfilm (*Papers of the Federal Reserve System, Part 2*, University Publications of America, Inc., Frederick, Maryland) but were used here in offset form at the library of the Federal Reserve Bank of New York.

18. *Humphrey Papers*, pp. 99–100.

19. Composite indexes of indicators—leading, coincident, and lagging—were not calculated in the 1950s, but most of the series now combined in them were available in the *Unpublished BCD* and were of course scrutinized regularly. Of the sixteen separate indicators then available, there were early indications of a possible downturn in less than half. Had there been a composite index, the first warning would probably have been given in May 1953.

20. Said the January 1954, *Economic Report* (p. 50):

"The restrictive monetary and debt management policies pursued in the early months of [1953] had . . . a more potent effect than was generally expected. It was not that the policies were of themselves highly restrictive. . . . But the business and financial community, having become accustomed over many years to credit policies that facilitate the monetization of the Federal debt, no longer clearly remembered the discipline of monetary management aimed at preventing inflationary booms, with which an earlier generation had had experience. . . . The measures (taken) were new and startling to many bankers, mortgage lenders and businessmen who, while gravely fearing inflation and wishing to see it curbed, apparently underestimated the practical adjustments that its containment would require."

21. *Public Papers, DDE*, 1954, p. 715. The January 1955 *Economic Report* (p. 112) summarized the tax code changes as including

"more liberal depreciation allowances, a tax credit to reduce double taxation of dividends, a lengthening from one to two years of the period over which net business losses may be carried back, and more liberal treatment of research and development expenditures of business." Among revisions designed to correct inequities were "increased allowances for medical expenses and for certain dependents, a new allowance for child-care expenses, and more liberal rules governing the personal tax treatment of medical insurance and sick benefits received by employees."

22. *Public Papers, DDE*, 1953, p. 544.

23. *Eisenhower Diaries*, pp. 250–52.

24. Adams, *Firsthand Report*, p. 161.

25. *Economic Report*, January 1955, pp. 17–20.

26. In the dating of business cycles (done then as now by the National Bureau of Economic Research), it was first determined that a trough was not reached until August 1954 but a revision put it in May 1954.

27. *Public Papers, DDE*, 1954, p. 274.

28. *Public Papers, DDE*, 1954, pp. 340–41.

29. *Abilene Papers*, Cabinet Series, various dates.

30. Population data are from the February 1986 *Economic Report*, Tables B-30 and B-95, *Historical Statistics*, Part 1, Series A-335, B-1 and B-3, and *Current Population Studies, Special Studies, Population of the United States, May 1974*, p. 132.

31. *Economic Report*, February 1986, Table B-26, p. 283.

32. *Historical Statistics*, Part 2, p. 716.

33. *Study of Mortgage Credit, Report of the Subcommittee on Housing of the Committee on Banking and Currency*, U.S. Senate, 32861, pp. 12–15.

34. *Consumer Instalment Credit* (Board of Governors of the Federal Reserve System, Washington, D.C., 1957), Part I, Vol. I, p. 125, n. 4, and p. 128.

35. *Banking and Monetary Statistics, 1941–70*, p. 1081.

36. Calculated from data in various *Economic Reports* as the excess of longterm interest rates over the inflation rate.

37. *Economic Report*, February 1986, p. 358.

38. *Business Capital Formation—Putting it in Perspective, 1925–1979* (Machinery and Allied Products Institute, Washington, D.C., January 1980).

39. Comparisons with longterm trends utilize data from *Long Term Economic Growth, 1860–1970*, Series A2, A16, and A87. Data for real disposable personal income are available only from 1929.

40. *Economic Report*, January 1956, p. 29.

41. Minutes of the January 11, 1955 meeting of the Open Market Committee.

42. *Public Papers, DDE,* 1955, pp. 766–67.

43. Nominal GNP increased 5.6 percent a year, on the average, between the second quarters of 1955 and 1957; demand deposits and currency rose only 0.9 percent a year.

44. Alan Sproul, at the time president of the Federal Reserve Bank of New York and a greatly respected central banker, observed in the January 24, 1956 meeting of the Open Market Committee that the art of central banking in promoting growth without creating inflation was (paraphrasing his reported remarks) to approach the brink of activity without going over it. Unfortunately, it is almost never clear (until later) where the brink is.

45. *Abilene Papers,* Cabinet Series, Box 4.

46. Steps taken in 1955 to moderate the economy's expansion are described in the *January 1956 Economic Report,* pp. 28–43.

47. The circumstances under which the Federal Reserve Board was asked to study consumer installment credit control are described in the letter transmitting the finished report (*Consumer Instalment Credit,* 4 Parts, Board of Governors of the Federal Reserve System, Washington, D.C., 1957) to the CEA chairman. The report made no explicit recommendation on whether standby authority to control consumer credit should be requested, but its effect was to counsel against a request.

The inquiry into installment credit terms by bank examiners is described in the *January 1956 Economic Report,* p. 36.

48. Adams, *Firsthand Report,* pp. 168–70.

49. *Humphrey Papers,* p. 426, which reproduces testimony given to the Senate Finance Committee.

50. *Abilene Papers,* DDE Diary Series, Box 9, February 1955, Folder [1]. Press conference comments on the proposal are in *Public Papers, DDE,* 1955, pp. 282–84 and 309–10. See also *The White House Years,* Vol. I, p. 299.

51. Adams, *Firsthand Report,* p. 171.

52. *Abilene Papers,* Cabinet Series, Box 5, meeting of July 12, 1955. Budget data are from the *January 1956 Economic Report,* p. 214.

53. *Economic Report,* January 1956, p. 46.

54. *Abilene Papers,* Cabinet Series, meetings of April 30, 1954 and September 30, 1955.

55. *Abilene Papers,* DDE Diary Series, Box 15, April 12, 1956 telephone calls.

56. *Abilene Papers,* DDE Diary Series, Box 15, April 12, 1956 and Cabinet Series, Box 7, minutes of the April 20, 1956 meeting.

57. Humphrey's comment is in *Humphrey Papers,* pp. 539–40. Comments by Burns, Weeks and Mitchell were reported in *U.S. News and World Report,* June 1, 1956, pp. 130–32.

58. *Public Papers, DDE,* 1956, pp. 438–39. A similar comment

was made a few days later *(pp. 457–458)*.

59. *Abilene Papers,* Arthur F. Burns Papers, Box 10; DDE Diary Series, Box 15, April 1956 telephone calls.

60. *Abilene Papers,* Cabinet Series, Box 7.

61. *Abilene Papers,* DDE Diary Series, Box 17, September 1956 Folder, Misc, [1].

62. At the Joint Economic Committee's hearings on the *January 1957 Economic Report,* Federal Reserve Chairman Martin responded to a question on whether money policy had been "miscalculated in 1956" by saying:

> If we had the whole period to go through again, I think I would be inclined toward having a little bit more restriction in monetary policy from the latter part of 1954 to date. If we had been more restrictive, we would have had more influence, not that monetary and credit policy is the whole thing, but it would have been a more stabilizing influence on the economy (*JEC Hearings,* February 5, 1957).

63. *Public Papers, DDE,* 1956, p. 90.

64. *Public Papers, DDE,* 1956, p. 439.

65. *Abilene Papers,* Cabinet Series, Boxes 5 and 7.

66. *Economic Report,* February 1986, p. 303.

67. *Public Papers, DDE,* 1957, p. 40.

68. *Economic Report,* January 1957, p. 3.

69. Testifying before the Joint Economic Committee (January 31, 1957) a representative of the United Automobile Workers (UAW) rejected what he termed "general exhortation directed at all and sundry" and proposed an alternative, to be applied to "administered price industries" (where "a few corporations furnishing 'price leadership' . . . fix prices arbitrarily"). In the UAW plan, advance notice and public justification would be required when prices were to be increased by a company that accounted for more than a specified percentage of industry sales ("perhaps 20 or 25 percent"), and labor would be "bound by the policy that demands for wage increases and other economic gains in administered price industries . . . should be confined within the limits of the ability to pay, without price increases, of the efficient firm functioning under full employment conditions" (*Hearings,* p. 307).

70. On this, see the record of January 10, 1957 telephone calls (*Abilene Papers,* DDE Diary Series, Box 10) and the minutes of cabinet meetings on December 14, 1956 and January 9, 1957 (Cabinet Series, Box 8). Eisenhower agreed fully with the economic argument and had no concern whatever about adverse political effect, of which there proved to be little if any.

71. *Public Papers, DDE,* 1957, pp. 20–21.

72. *Report of the Joint Economic Committee on the 1957 Eco-*

nomic Report of the President, U.S. Government Printing Office, Washington, D.C., 1957, pp. 6–7.

73. *Historical Statistics,* Vol. 2, Series Q-148, p. 716.

74. Eisenhower's theory of why automobile sales collapsed in 1958 (a valid one, in my view) was that the industry's pushing of sales in 1955–57, aided by extensions of credit to buyers on much liberalized terms, made a subsequent drop inevitable. *Abilene Papers,* DDE Diary Series, Box 32, December 24, 1958 telephone calls.

75. John Maurice Clark, *Strategic Factors in Business Cycles,* National Bureau of Economic Research, New York, 1934, p. 33 and ff.

76. *Public Papers, DDE,* 1958, p. 434.

77. I put the case for credit easing before the cabinet at meetings on December 4, 1956 and February 27, 1957 (*Abilene Papers,* Cabinet Series, Box 8) and (as recorded in personal notes) before Federal Reserve officials at the same time.

78. *Economic Report,* 1957, pp. 44–46.

79. Shortly before the discount rate decision was made we were informed at the CEA that an increase was being considered, and one can safely assume that the Treasury was likewise alerted. I have no record of my reaction, but considering the cabinet statements I was making on the question, beginning in December 1956, it is hard to believe I could have given any encouragement to what was proposed.

80. The counteractive program was developed at the CEA with the help of ABEGS and was approved by the president on August 5, 1957 (*Abilene Papers,* Administrative Series, Box 20, and the *January 1957 Economic Report,* p. 7).

81. It is related in minutes of the November 12, 1957 Open Market Committee meeting that Dr. Winfield Riefler, the committee's senior policy adviser at the time, was surprised on returning to the Reserve Board after an absence of about a month at how greatly psychology had changed in credit markets and in the economy generally. As Hayes had done earlier, he noted that the System needed to maintain a correct public posture "if it hoped to retain the understanding and support of the people" and, to that end, advised a redirection of policy. His argument was that raising the discount rate in August had "made it clear to the world . . . that the Federal Reserve was not going to finance inflation" but that the System had now "done its job" and a reversal of the rate to its earlier level (3 percent) would show that it was acknowledging a "generally changed situation." He advised, however, against any change in reserve requirements and against any "flooding" of the banking system with reserves.

82. *Humphrey Papers,* pp. 236–54. When asked where depression might come from, Secretary Humphrey's response was: "A depression will come if, over a period of time, we keep on spending nearly $50 billion a year [the Defense Department budget at the time] in prepara-

tion for war, which contributes comparatively little to new capital and [to the] making [of] future jobs."

In one more attempt to explain his position, Secretary Humphrey stated in a February 8, 1957 interview with *U.S. News and World Report* (p. 57) that

> What I said was that if we did not begin a better control of our expenditures and reduce Government spending and taxes, then, over a sufficient period of time, the Government would be taking so much money that should be going into power, farms, factories and tools that we would not have enough jobs to keep our growing population well employed and that would make a depression.

83. *Public Papers, DDE*, 1957, p. 73. There were two papers: one, a proposed memorandum (or letter) from Humphrey to Eisenhower deploring the trend to higher spending and urging steps to reverse it; the other, the statement read to the press at the beginning of the Secretary's January 15 press conference. The first was discussed at the January 9, 1957 cabinet meeting (whether it should be from Humphrey to Eisenhower, or the reverse) and was questioned on the ground that it might (as it did) suggest a rift between the two. Eisenhower was not concerned about that possibility: he shared Humphrey's dismay at the trend of budget outlays but was less certain than the secretary that additional spending reductions of any size could be made, except at the expense of defense, which he would not endorse. Adams' account of the incident is the best (*Firsthand Report*, pp. 360–74). See also *Abilene Papers*, Cabinet Series, Box 8, minutes of the January 9, 1957 meeting, and *The White House Years*, Vol. II, pp. 127–31.

84. *CQ Almanac*, 1957, p. 724.

85. *Public Papers*, DDE, 1957, pp. 301–9.

86. The problem created when Congress, in its continual sparring with Eisenhower, balked at raising the debt limit even by the small amount needed at the time to meet a seasonal borrowing requirement. The scaling back of advance payments to defense contractors was the Treasury's reaction to this: it would conserve Treasury cash, obviate the need to borrow funds, and thus allow the Treasury to stay within the debt limit set by Congress. There are tracks of the incident in *Abilene Papers*, DDE Diary Series, Box 27.

87. Exports in the first quarter of 1957 were nearly 20 percent greater in real terms than in the comparable 1956 quarter, and continued so for another two quarters. Nonresidential investment outlays did not peak until the third quarter of 1957, and retail sales (price adjusted) were 3.4 percent higher than a year before. Housing starts appeared to be recovering in the late summer of 1957, but later revisions showed this to have been a misleading report.

88. By September 1957, efforts were under way at the CEA to

expand and systematize our capability for following cyclical developments. As a working assumption, I took July 1957 to be a cyclical peak
and, beginning with the data for August, compared subsequent
monthly changes in a sizable number of series with changes that had
followed the peak months of earlier cycles, especially 1953–54. It
would nowadays be called a study of "cyclical comparisons." Soon
after this project was started, Dr. Julius Shiskin was enlisted from the
Census Bureau to computerize the procedure and prepare a monthly
compilation and interpretation of results. The finished product had
circulation outside government only to the National Bureau of Economic Research, which was supplying much of the data and where
Shiskin had developed the data-processing techniques. One of the first
moves by the Kennedy administration's CEA was to have the Department of Commerce prepare the report for public release. It appeared
first as *Business Cycle Developments* and later (through April 1990) as
Business Conditions Digest. Since May 1990, a reduced form has been
merged into the Commerce Department's *Survey of Current Business*.

    89. Candor is much to be admired in the handling of economic
news by government but no White House wants to be the first to say
that the economy is in, or may soon be in, recession and, to my
knowledge, no White House ever has. Until it was clear in 1957 that a
downturn had started I kept the word recession out of my public
vocabulary, and was much chided for doing so. But unlike Federal
Reserve economists, for example, who discoursed on the subject only
within closed quarters, I spoke frequently in public and had to be
sensitive to a possible exploitation of my language by the administration's critics, as well as to the effect that premature comment on the
recession risk could have on public sentiment.

    90. Steps taken by the administration in 1957–58 to check reces-
sion, and requests made to Congress for additional discretionary
executive authority to act against a downturn, are described in the
Economics Reports for January 1959 and 1960.

    91. *Public Papers, DDE,* 1958, pp. 229–30.

    92. For all his reservations regarding public works spending as a
countercyclical measure it is doubtful that any president has made a
more systematic and sustained effort than Eisenhower to plan and
utilize public construction for countercyclical purposes. A February
2, 1954 memorandum from him to Dr. Burns (doubtless drafted at the
CEA) directed the Council to develop a program to that end. It listed
types of projects that might be activated, and said in part:

> Unless preparatory public works plans are carried to a relatively high
> degree of completion and (are) ready for instant use in the event of emer-
> gency, one of two things is bound to happen . . . Either there will be
> extravagant and wasteful use of public funds [or] there will be unconsciona-

bly long delay in getting such work started" [*Abilene Papers*, DDE Diary Series, Box 5].

Work under this assignment was started by a CEA unit, newly organized for that purpose; later it was done by a special Executive Branch Office under General John G. Bragdon (Retired), who served as Special Assistant to the President for Public Works Planning. General Bragdon's work was drawn on extensively in 1955–56 and in 1957–58.

93. *Public Papers, DDE*, 1958, p. 220.
94. *Public Papers, DDE*, 1958, p. 415.
95. *Public Papers, DDE*, 1958, pp. 307–10.
96. *CQ Almanac*, 1958, pp. 304–8.
97. *Public Papers, DDE*, 1958, pp. 234–35. Eisenhower was not alone in questioning the merits of an emergency tax reduction. In the Senate, a proposal by Paul A. Douglas (D Ill.) to have Congress enact one was defeated (March 13, 1958) by a vote of five to one. And while the April 1958 report by a panel organized by Nelson Rockefeller (*The Challenge to America*, Garden City, N.Y., Doubleday, 1958) is generally understood to have been clearly positive on tax reduction, Eisenhower read it, as I did, as reflecting uncertainty on that question. He wrote to Rockefeller:

> I can sense from the wording of the report the problem of composing the different views of the members of the panel on the timing and amount of a tax cut which your group apparently thought was desirable. I am faced hourly with the same division of opinion among people in the administration and [among] my good friends in the business world [*Abilene Papers*, DDE Diary Series, Box 32].

Economists testifying at Joint Economic Committee hearings on the *January 1958 Economic Report* were divided on tax cuts versus spending increases (which is the way the question was most frequently confronted), with most of them favoring spending increases.

98. *Economic Report*, January 1958, p. 50.
99. *Public Papers, DDE*, 1958, pp. 151–52.
100. *Public Papers, DDE*, 1958, p. 338.
101. An April 2, 1958 letter to Arthur F. Burns, *Abilene Papers*, DDE Diary Series, Box 32.
102. *Public Papers, DDE*, 1958, pp. 424–425.
103. *Public Papers, DDE*, p. 259. As the verse was cited in the transcript of Eisenhower's news conference it was "the voice of the turtle."
104. *The White House Years*, Vol. II, p. 310.
105. *Abilene Papers*, DDE Diary Series, Box 46, telephone calls of November 1959.
106. Summarizing the strike's chronology, negotiations that began

early in 1959 led to a proposal in which all major steel companies joined but which labor rejected. It offered a "modest" wage increase, some improvement in benefits, and certain contract changes affecting workrules. Negotiations broke off when the contract expired on June 10 but were later resumed at Eisenhower's request. When these failed, a strike was called, on July 15.

Eisenhower held meetings separately with both sides on September 30, but without success, and then appointed a Taft-Hartley Board of Inquiry to determine whether there were grounds on which the government could seek injunctive relief. When the board found (October 19) "no prospect for an early cessation of the strike [and no] issue of any consequence upon which the parties were in agreement," and when the CEA and other Executive Branch agencies had determined that continuation of the strike would imperil the nation's "health and safety," action was begun by the Department of Justice to obtain an injunction that would end the strike for the eighty days provided under Taft-Hartley. Relief was obtained on November 7 when the Supreme Court upheld an injunction granted earlier by a US District Court and affirmed by a Court of Appeals, allowing production to be resumed.

A settlement was reached in the "cooling off" period afforded by this injunction, largely through the intervention of Vice President Nixon and Secretary of Labor Mitchell, who were acting as the president's emissaries. Terms of the settlement were announced on January 4, 1960, less than a month before the injunction would have expired.

It was required by Taft-Hartley that if no settlement had been reached before the end of the "cooling off" period the dispute would go to Congress, which both the White House and the two opposing sides wished to avoid. Congress would almost certainly have put the dispute to compulsory arbitration.

There are accounts of the strike in William T. Hogan, S.J., *Economic History of the Iron and Steel Industry in the United States,* Vol. 4, Part 6, pp. 1637–1641 (D.C. Heath and Company, Lexington, Ma., 1971), and in *Collective Bargaining in the Steel Industry: Pattern Setter or Pattern Follower,* Harold M. Levinson (The University of Michigan/Wayne State University, Ann Arbor and Detroit, Michigan, 1962). The US Government's Supreme Court brief (the economic portion was written at the CEA) is included in *In The Supreme Court of the United States, October Term 1959, United Steel Workers of America, Petitioner v United States of America.* Related papers, including the Board of Inquiry Report, are in the *Transcript of Record, Supreme Court of the United States, October Term 1959, United States of America, Plaintiff, v. United Steelworkers of America.* All the president's published papers on the subject are in *Public Papers,*

DDE, 1959. See also *The White House Years*, Vol. II, pp. 453–59 and news conference comments on March 25 and May 5, 1959.

107. A January 21, 1960 letter from Vice President Nixon to Alexander F. Jones, Executive Editor of the *Syracuse Herald-Journal* of Syracuse, New York, gives a detailed account of the negotiations that brought the strike to an end (*Abilene Papers,* Official File, Box 636). Mr. Nixon's summary of the outcome on the workrules issue was that "the best that we were able to get the union to agree to was to set up a study commission with a neutral chairman."

108. *Public Papers, DDE,* 1959, p. 300.

109. *The White House Years,* Vol. II, p. 459. Eisenhower's agreement to the settlement was given on January 2, 1960 in a telephone conversation with his emissaries (*Abilene Papers,* DDE Diary Series, Box 47). He is reported to have stated in that conversation, as a final observation, that he "did not think that the Council of Economic Advisers would approve." He was right: I was gravely disappointed that the workrules question was left unsettled, troublesome as it might have been to pursue it further. And judging from what Eisenhower said in a January 31, 1962 address to the Los Angeles Chamber of Commerce ("we are not lacking in indications that we are drifting toward a featherbed economy"), he may well have felt the same. But the desire to reach a settlement, and thus to keep the issue from going to Congress, controlled the outcome.

110. Factors accounting for the reversal are discussed in the *January 1959, Economic Report,* pp. 122–27.

111. The *1967 Supplement to Economic Indicators,* p. 90 and the *International Economic Report to the President,* March 1975, p. 137.

112. *International Economic Report to the President,* March 1975, p. 137.

113. *Banking and Monetary Statistics,* pp. 899 and 932.

114. *Economic Report,* January 1961, pp. 39–40.

115. *Abilene Papers,* DDE Diary Series, Box 54, especially the memoranda dated November 11, 14, and 15 and December 1, 1960.

116. The administration's efforts to deal with the problem culminated in a trip to Bonn by Secretary Anderson and Under Secretary of State C. Douglas Dillon in November 1960 (after the presidential election) to persuade a reluctant West German government (Chancellor Konrad Adenauer, in particular) to make adjustments that would lower the foreign exchange costs to the United States of holding U.S. troops (and their dependents) in that country. It was of little avail.

117. Outlays that were made in fiscal 1959 but not repeated in fiscal 1960, thus contributing to the swing from deficit to surplus, included the following: $360 million from expiration of an authorization for Fanny Mae to make recession-oriented purchases of mortgages; $550 million from putting Fanny Mae and the Export-Import Bank on a

more nearly self-sustaining basis; $400 million from expiration of provision for temporary extension of unemployment compensation eligibility; $700 million from an already legislated termination of the Soil Bank Acreage Reserve program; and postal rate increases that were expected to reduce the postal deficit by $645 million (*Economic Report,* January 1959, p. 49).

118. Reflecting our view at the CEA that a budget balance would pave the way for significant tax reduction and reform, a December 23, 1958 letter of mine to the president included the following:

> Now that we have put forward a formula for bringing the budget into balance, I believe we should plan a constructive tax reform program and work hard at selling it to the American people. The danger . . . is that we will dissipate what budgetary surplus can be achieved in the years ahead in tax reductions that will be politically attractive but economically not very powerful [*Abilene Papers,* Administrative Series, Box 32].

119. In *The White House Years* (Vol. II, p. 460, no. 7), Eisenhower recalls a December 1958 warning from Gabriel Hauge (then chairman of a large New York City bank) that there could be unfavorable effects on the economy from a large swing in the budget from deficit to surplus, but wrote to Hauge that "an overwhelming consideration in my mind was the worsening situation in our balance of payments." It is evident from Hauge's first letter on the subject that his concern was not about a budget balance, per se, or about the possible effect on the economy of a swing from deficit to surplus, as some have thought it to be, but about achieving a balance through "some kind of broad tax increase" (which was not contemplated), by "stretching revenue estimates to an unrealistic point" (which we did not do), or by "proposals for expenditure reductions that informed people would know Congress would most likely ignore" (of which there were none). As he put it, the budget would have to be "credible," as of course it had to be.

Whether the budget was or was not credible depended, of course, on the perceptions of those who undertook to comment on it, but it was drawn up conscientiously by the Budget Bureau, under the close attention of the president, the Secretary of the Treasury, and the CEA, and there was never any doubt among us of its right to be believed. Moreover, our confidence was confirmed by events. Receipts in fiscal 1960 were $700 million more than the budget was counting on, which is a small error; and outlays were $500 million less than projected, also a small difference. The swing occurred principally because the economy moved from recession to recovery, which is what it was expected to do, and because there were a number of factors (see note 117, above) that ballooned expenditures in fiscal 1959 but were not repeated in fiscal 1960.

In the end, and despite the prospect of a swing in budget results from deficit to surplus, Dr. Hauge seems not to have been unhappy with the outcome, since a second letter to the president, written shortly after the Budget Message went to Congress, congratulated him on "turning the tide in the battle of the budget." (Hauge's letters are in *Abilene Papers*, Administrative Series, Box 18.)

120. *Public Papers, DDE,* 1960–61, pp. 37–38 and 40.

121. *Public Papers, DDE,* 1960–61, p. 40.

122. A March 7, 1960 aide-memoire of mine covering a conversation that day with Chairman Martin and Vice-Chairman Balderston confirms that I was not at the time urging the Federal Reserve to do more than what was already being done, which was to allow net reserves to move to smaller negative figures as market conditions brought this about. But things changed soon after that: a June 2, 1960 report of mine to the president noted that the discount rate reduction announced that day (at the Philadelphia and San Francisco Reserve Banks) "should have come three weeks ago" (*Abilene Papers*, White House Secretarial Records, Box 23). All the while, Eisenhower was following the movement of net reserves with some impatience; they were around minus $500 million when the year began and did not pass into plus territory until around midyear.

123. Actions taken by the task force are described in the *January 1961 Economic Report,* pp. 32–33.

124. There was less confidence at the CEA than at the Treasury that a downturn could be avoided, but I was persuaded until September 1960 that "the economy's next major move would be up," as I frequently put it. That, indeed, was the substance of a paper I read at a conference on the economic outlook at the University of Michigan in September 1960, and of cabinet presentations I made at several points in the earlier part of the year (*Abilene Papers*, Cabinet Series, Box 14, especially the May 12 meeting). May 1960 is now accepted as the first down month of the 1960 recession, but at the time few would have described what was occurring prior to October as more than a series of inconclusive ups and downs around a broadly flat trend.

125. *Economic Report,* January 1961, p. 43. There are important differences between the first and later datings of the 1960–61 recession, the effect of which is to show recession starting in the second quarter of 1960 rather than in the third, and ending in the fourth quarter of 1960 rather than in the first of 1961. On a monthly basis, the first decisively down month has been pushed back from June to May 1960, but the cyclical trough is still February 1961.

126. *Economic Report,* January 1961, p. 44.

V. Proposing a Legislative Program: Confrontations with Congress

Side by side with the intermittent problems Eisenhower faced in coping with the ups and downs of business was a set of structural problems that presented themselves more or less continuously. Finding a workable formula for getting the federal government out of farm price-support operations was one of them. Striving to give constructive direction to the nation's international economic relations was another. Government's involvement in housing and home finance was a third. And there were others.

In dealing with such problems, as in coping with the business cycle, the president operates with anything but a free hand; in the end, what he can do depends on the legislation he has to work with, and thus on what Congress is prepared to have him do. And, working as he did for six of his eight years in the presidency with both House and Senate controlled by the Democratic Party, there were not many aspects of this dependency with which Eisenhower was entirely happy. Indeed, his philosophical stance had him all too often colliding head-on with his political opposition.

We can begin the story of these struggles (they constitute a major part of what occupies the president in domestic affairs) with an account of what was perhaps the least rewarding of them all—trying to get a workable farm program from Congress.

Seeking a Workable Farm Program

When Eisenhower came to the White House, no part of the U.S. economy had government more deeply involved in it than agriculture. At the same time, no part of federal economic policy was more widely regarded, not least of all by farmers themselves, as wrongly designed and inadequate to its tasks. Moreover, although failing to achieve their goals, the programs were immensely expensive in budget outlays. And they were a complicated patchwork that few understood. As Eisenhower remarked in 1960, after nearly eight years of experience with them, "we talk about the farm problem [as if] there is just one [but] there are as many farm problems as there are commodities, as [many as] there are different localities . . . it is a real mishmash of problems."[1]

It was indeed a mishmash, but at its bottom were certain common elements. The prices of six "basic" commodities—wheat, corn, cotton, rice, tobacco and peanuts—were supported at 90 percent of "parity," with parity defined as the price for the commodity in question that would bear the same relation to operating costs currently as farm prices bore to operating costs between 1910 and 1914. In exchange for the government's support of this level of prices the farmer agreed to restrict the acreage he used to produce the crop in question; by adhering to this acreage-control requirement he was entitled to put his crop or part of it, if he chose not to sell it at market prices, in storage with the Commodity Credit Corporation (CCC) and to receive a loan (for which the commodity in storage served as security) for 90 percent of the commodity's parity price. Later, if market conditions made it to the farmer's advantage, an equivalent amount of the commodity could be reclaimed from storage, sold in the open market, and the loan repaid; if market conditions were unfavorable, the stored commodity could be signed over to the CCC as full payment for the loan. The effect was that the farmer was guaranteed a price that would produce something close to the cost-price relationship that existed prior to World War I, but could take advantage of a better price should that be available.

Being fairly arcane, the concept of parity caused the discussion of what government could do for agriculture to be subject to much misunderstanding. It did nothing to clarify things that the Republican Party's platform in 1952 called for "a farm program aimed at full parity for all farm products in the market place;" nor did it help when Eisenhower, in a 1952 campaign speech at the National Plowing Contest at Kasson, Minnesota, on September 6, stated (with Governor Stevenson, his Democratic rival, saying essentially the same thing) that agriculture was "entitled [to] a fair, full share of the national income," adding that this meant "not merely 90 percent of parity—it is full parity." Understandably, "full parity" was interpreted to mean price support at 100 percent of the 1910–14 parity, a commitment that was quickly dubbed a "golden promise."[2]

Clearly, the Kasson language went beyond what was intended. When Eisenhower restated his position, it was that the Republican Party would carry out the price-support laws then on the books (they were not due to expire until after December 1954) and in the meantime would devise better programs with the help of an advisory group on which agriculture would be appropriately represented.

As practically everyone acknowledged, what was on the books was full of faults. Acreage controls were rarely restrictive enough to offset the expansionary effects on supply of improvements in farming methods, leaving support prices chronically too high. In short, it was a race between controls and technology, with the latter typically the winner. With the large supplies traceable to high support prices tending to depress market prices, it was all too often to the farmer's advantage to repay his CCC loan by turning the pledged commodity over to the government. To make matters worse, the CCC's freedom to dispose of commodities so accumulated was subject to severe restrictions. As a result, commodities in storage rose sharply, creating an overhang that further depressed market prices and further encouraged farmers to turn their crops over to the CCC. Thus, the programs were more than merely self-perpetuating; they were self-aggravating.[3]

The formula for solving the problem was plain: enact a law

that would "modernize" parity by defining it in terms of cost-price relationships in a period more recent than 1910–14; set production controls at levels sufficiently restrictive to balance production with market demand at or around that modernized parity price; give the Secretary of Agriculture authority to "flex" price supports over a reasonable range, so they could be lowered if they were overly expansionary and raised if unduly restrictive; and give the Executive Branch greater authority to sell or donate CCC-held commodities at home and overseas. The formula for failure was equally plain: continue with overly attractive, inflexible price supports; put inadequately restrictive limits on production; and continue with overly severe limitations on the disposal of surpluses.

Eisenhower set about at once to persuade Congress to pass a better statute. Carrying out what was projected at Kasson, a bipartisan group—the National Agricultural Advisory Commission—was appointed on July 20, 1953 to study the problem, with full representation of farm interests. Six months later, proposals for a revision of existing programs were put before Congress.[4]

*   *   *

Passing over the detail in which all farm price-support programs abound, the proposals were built on three fundamentals. First, a modernized parity, based on cost-price relationships in the ten years preceding the most recent crop year, would be substituted for the 1910–14 concept and introduced gradually, in annual 5 percent reductions of the support mandated by the earlier formula. Second, flexibility would be introduced into the system by authorizing the Secretary of Agriculture to make adjustments in support prices within a range of 75 to 90 percent of the new parity, moving prices inversely with changes in supply. Third, government would be authorized to "set aside" commodities already held by the CCC for use in ways that would be as little disruptive as possible of commercial markets (e.g., in school lunch programs, disaster relief, foreign aid, and emergency reserves).

A vigorous effort was launched by Ezra Taft Benson,

Eisenhower's first and only Secretary of Agriculture, to have Congress enact these proposals. When the president was asked in his June 2, 1954 news conference whether he would be willing to compromise on them, he replied that he would "stand up and fight for the principles of [the] program right down the line," as he did.[5] The Agricultural Act of 1954, which was the congressional response, gave him part of what he had asked for, and he signed it into law on August 28, 1954.

*   *   *

It was clear within a year, however, that what had been asked for and what had been enacted was not enough. By June 30, 1956, commodity stocks in CCC storage had more than doubled, mounting to $5.4 billion. Nearly $6 billion in commodity loans were made by the CCC in the fiscal years 1954 and 1955 combined. Crop loans outstanding on June 30, 1955 came to over $2 billion.[6]

Addressing this unexpected and unwelcome outcome in his January 1956 State of the Union Message, and in a special message to Congress dealing exclusively with agriculture, Eisenhower called for a bolder attack on the problem. The program he asked for was simplicity itself: acreage under cultivation would be reduced by an amount sufficient to have a decisive effect on supply and thus on price. To accomplish this, there would be a "Soil Bank" made up of two parts: (1) an Acreage Reserve, under which farmers would volunteer to set aside a portion of their allotments for wheat, cotton, corn, or rice (possibly as much as 20 percent in wheat and cotton) and take cashable certificates in return equal to a percentage (high enough to make the exchange attractive) of the proceeds of what it was estimated the commodities would otherwise have produced; and (2) a Conservation Reserve, under which any farmer, regardless of crop or location of farm, would "shift into forage, trees and water storage [those] lands most needing conservation measures." In addition, there would be an enlarged and more flexible authority to dispose of surpluses. And to prevent the benefit of price-support operations from going in excess to the larger farms there would be a dollar limit on the size of the CCC loans available to individuals and single farming units.

It was hoped that these measures, jointly with certain other steps that had already been taken (the Farm Credit Administration reorganized to make it more nearly a farmer-owned operation; social security programs extended to farm families; gasoline used for farm purposes made exempt from federal taxation; and a Rural Development Program set up to help farm people obtain jobs outside agriculture, if they wished them), would help balance farm production with market demand, reduce CCC holdings of surplus commodities, and lessen the burden that price-support operations were putting on the budget.[7]

Because it was a set of mutually dependent parts the program would work only if it were taken as a whole. But what Congress did, as Don Paarlberg (at the time Assistant Secretary of Agriculture and later Special Assistant to the President for Economic Affairs) put it, was to "untie the package," leaving in it what the congressional majority (including a few dissident Republicans) wanted, taking out what it didn't want, and inserting features to its own liking.

It was not an unprecedented handling of a multisided legislative proposal, but the treatment was in this case particularly damaging. As delivered to the White House, the package contained the Soil Bank but coupled it with a return to 90 percent parity for basic commodities, called for a return to the old concept of parity when it required a higher price support than modernized parity, provided a high price support domestically for wheat and rice side by side with low, subsidized prices for sales abroad, and required mandatory supports for feed grains, the last of these provisions creating cost problems for livestock producers. As the bill was working its way through Congress, Eisenhower wrote in his diary, dismayed by what was happening:

> There seemed to be almost universal approval for the program the administration submitted. But the Senate Agricultural Committee promptly tacked on it a provision for the return to

90 percent rigid price supports. They are completely indifferent
to the fact that this feature . . . is in direct conflict with the rest
of the bill.

And citing three Republican Senators as having helped in the
deed, he continued:

> This is the kind of thing that makes politics a dreary and
> frustrating experience for anyone who has any regard for moral
> and ethical standards. . . . If we do not get a reasonable, coor-
> dinated program . . . we are soon going to have nothing but a
> completely political hodgepodge that will help push us ever
> closer and closer toward the brink of complete governmental
> control of our economy.[8]

The fate of what Congress sent him was thus settled. On
April 16, 1956 he turned the bill down, giving his reasons in a
veto message and, as follows, in a radio-TV speech:

> I could not sign this bill . . . because it was a bad bill . . . it
> would hurt more farmers than it would help. In the long run it
> would hurt all farmers. . . . It was confusing—in some aspects
> self-defeating, and so awkward and clusmy as to make its ad-
> ministration difficult or impractical. . . . [T]he Administration's
> Soil Bank was still in it [but] other provisions . . . would have
> rendered [it] almost useless. . . . [W]e got a hodgepodge in
> which the bad provisions more than canceled out the good.[9]

The veto was upheld and on May 24, 1956 a new bill was
enacted. It was again unsatisfactory. It included the Soil Bank,
but on terms that made it unlikely to have a significant effect in
1956. And it contained certain provisions especially objectionable to Eisenhower—a cotton export program that would have
adverse effects on foreign relations, and a freeze for two years
of acreage allotments for cotton and rice. But under pressure to
get legislation that would have an effect on 1956 plantings,
Eisenhower signed it, noting that he did so only because "its
advantages outweigh[ed] its harmful provisions.[10]

*   *   *

In 1958, following this disappointing result, another effort was made to deal with the technological revolution in agriculture that was at the bottom of the problem. The main thrust of the new proposal was to shift emphasis in the Soil Bank from the Acreage Reserve to the Conservation Reserve: the former frequently succeeded only in moving production from one crop to another; the latter aimed at taking land completely out of production. In addition, there would be a more workable parity, and greater discretionary authority for the Secretary of Agriculture in setting acreage allotments and price supports. In short, it was another try at getting basically the same formula as had been previously proposed.[11]

It was seven months before Eisenhower received a bill responding to these proposals that he was willing to sign. The first measure sent to the White House would have returned price supports to the 1957 levels (they had been reduced briefly under the immediately preceding legislation) and would hold them there for a year. Acreage allotments would be frozen for two years. Vetoing it, Eisenhower remarked: "What the farm economy needs is a thaw rather than a freeze."[12] A second effort was denounced by Secretary Benson as an "economic monstrosity" and it died in the House of Representatives.[13] Finally, a bill was received that was signed (August 28, 1958). It incorporated a number of the president's recommendations but again fell short of what was needed.

*   *   *

The next year produced still another special message (January 29, 1959) appealing for legislation attuned to the realities of agricultural technology and market conditions, and offering at least a modicum of administrative flexibility. Congress adjourned, however, without enacting anything that met those requirements. In the process, two bills were vetoed. One, a wheat bill, would have reduced acreage by 25 percent and raised price supports to 90 percent of parity. Eisenhower remarked in vetoing it that "this bill prescribes for a sick patient another dose of what caused his illness." The other, in his words, took "a long step backward by resurrecting 90 percent of 'old parity' as one basis for determining the support level for tobacco."[14] Both vetoes were sustained.

*   *   *

With time now running out for the Eisenhower presidency, the next proposal (1960) was a novel one, perhaps somewhat artful. Congress was invited to write whatever legislation it wished and it would be signed, provided it met certain tests: it should exclude price supports so high as to "stimulate still more excessive production, reduce domestic markets, and increase the subsidies required to hold world outlets"; it should exclude direct subsidies to farmers for crops already in surplus; and it should exclude subsidies for farm exports that would invite retaliation from friendly countries and (by tending to raise the prices of feed grains) hurt one set of American farmers by trying to benefit another.[15]

Unprepared or simply unwilling to fashion a law that would meet these tests, Congress ended its session with no legislation enacted except a price-support bill for dairy products, which the president signed (September 16, 1960) only reluctantly. Providing high price supports that required government to be deeply involved in the dairy business, it violated (as he told Congress) his "long-established and well known policies." But the 1960 presidential election campaign was already under way and he signed it because (as he explained) it would expire in a few months and do little harm in the interim and, if vetoed, would "engender intensely partisan political charges and countercharges in the dairy regions." In addition, he noted that it would be unfair to exercise his veto power when there was not enough time left for Congress to mount the effort necessary to override it.[16]

*   *   *

Coming in January 1961 to the end of this mainly fruitless effort, there was little for Eisenhower to do but record in his final State of the Union Message the pluses and minuses of farm developments during his eight years in office.[17] Despite many frustrations, there had been "notable advances": the efficiency of farm operations had improved enormously and the financial position and economic security of farmers and their families had strengthened greatly. But farming was still subject to the controls that Eisenhower had hoped to reduce and, if possible, to eliminate; and there was still a mismatch between the levels of price support mandated by Congress and prices that would clear markets, requiring huge amounts of supported commodities to be taken into government-held stocks and causing budget outlays for aid to agriculture to soar.

It was a disappointing outcome. Eisenhower had directed the legislative effort from the beginning and resented any implication that it was somehow the doing only of his Secretary of Agriculture. When asked in his August 10 1960 news conference, ". . . do you regret having kept Ezra Benson on as Secretary of Agriculture in view of the unresolved farm problem that is giving Mr. Nixon such a hard time in his campaign?" he replied:

> Ezra Benson has, to my mind, been very honest and forthright and courageous in trying to get enacted into legislation plans and programs that I think are correct. . . . For me to regret that he has been working for the administration would be almost a betrayal of my own views in the matter. I think we must find ways to give greater freedom to the farmer and make his whole business more responsive to market, rather than [to] just . . . political considerations."[18]

There is no mystery about what went wrong. A majority in Congress, including many Republican members, was simply unwilling to enact the legislation that market realities required, presumably out of fear of political "fallout." Actually, however, there was little evidence of negative political effect. As Governor Adams remarked, farmers voted Republican in 1960, when their impatience with Secretary Benson and the administration's farm policies was thought to be at a peak, just as, in a more amicable mood, they had voted Republican in 1956.[19]

*   *   *

Some years later, reviewing the history of this effort in his memoirs, Eisenhower wrote, despondently: "the whole farm situation remains a national disgrace."[20] Sad to say, presidents who have followed him have been no more successful than he was in obtaining rational, workable farm legisation. After more than twenty-five years, his statement still stands as a fair description of federal farm policy and the farm situation. If anything, both have worsened.

Remodeling the Housing and Home Financing Programs: Challenges to the Status Quo

In some respects, housing and home finance presented Eisenhower with problems much like those he confronted in agriculture—what to do about activities of great social and economic importance in which government was deeply involved at large and growing budget cost under congressionally-mandated rules that deepened the involvement and the expense when many people knowledgeable about housing, including several well and favorably known to him, believed that important parts of what government was doing could be done privately at less cost and with greater public benefit. There was also a belief that federal housing agencies should be pruned down and reorganized; indeed, there were those persuaded that the sprawling bureau that presided over most of what was being done—the Housing and Home Finance Agency (HHFA)—should be liquidated. Obviously, there was a formidable task here for the new president.

The Federal Housing Administration (FHA), one of HHFA's subsidiaries, was the centerpiece of the facilities coming under this scrutiny. Devised in 1934 to revive a home-financing industry devastated by economic depression and by its own mistaken strategies, it offered government insurance for home-purchase and home-improvement loans that had been made on acceptable terms by qualifying private lending institutions. It was designed to do this on an actuarially sound and self-supporting basis, and had succeeded in doing so. Operating with signal success (for much of the time alongside a basically similar activity of the Veterans Administration), it was widely acknowledged to be one of the soundest and most useful social inventions of the 1930s. From its inception through 1952 it had insured nearly $30 billion in home loans with remarkably little loss and at virtually no net cost to the federal government. It was a model of what Eisenhower wished to encourage as a partnership between government and business.[21]

Functioning in a totally different capacity, the Public Housing Administration (PHA), another principal HHFA component, was also a creature of the 1930s. But unlike FHA it was heavily dependent on federal subsidy. Public housing projects were assisted by planning advances, by low-rate interim financing, by subsidies to help meet the cost of servicing the long-term securities issued by local housing agencies to finance project construction, and by federal tax exemption. When the Eisenhower administration began, there were families living in 242,000 PHA-supported housing units, and construction was under way on another 50,000.

The third major HHFA division (uneasy under that agency's purview) was made up of the Federal Home Loan Bank Board (FHLBB) and its associated Federal Savings and Loan Insurance Corporation (FSLIC). Together, these agencies performed a unique set of functions: chartering, examining and supervising the federally-chartered savings and loan associations which, together with most state-chartered associations in that industry, constituted (along with a few mutual savings banks) the Home Loan Bank System's membership; insuring the share accounts (deposits) of member associations; and serving often as a lender to member associations.

Finally, several other agencies and activities were gathered under HHFA's Office of the Administrator (OA). Among them, the Federal National Mortgage Association (Fanny Mae) was the largest in point of business transacted and, next to FHA, the most important economically. It functioned in part as a "secondary market," in the correct sense of that term—buying FHA-insured and VA-guaranteed home mortgage loans when private funds were temporarily inadequate and selling them back into the market when funds were plentiful. Increasingly, however, Fanny Mae was used as a "primary market" agency (though still called a secondary facility), buying and holding "special-assistance" (low-interest rate) mortgages made to finance projects (cooperative housing, housing for the elderly, housing in disaster areas, and military and defense-related housing) for which Congress had mandated subsidy aid. Because special assistance loans were made at below-market interest rates, selling them back to private investors normally required that they be sold at prices below par; but since Congress typically insisted that sales be made at par, it was more often than not impossible to complete them. When funds spent to acquire mortgages exceeded funds received (proceeds of mortgage sales plus principal and interest paid to the agency on its holdings of mortages), there was a charge on the federal budget. In fiscal 1953 this amounted to $379 million.[22]

The Office of the Administrator was also responsible for low-interest loans to finance the construction of college housing (a program for which the demand was high and rising even in the 1950s, when college enrollments were low) and to carry out urban renewal projects (next to public housing the most visible of all federal housing programs).

Through 1952, 115 urban renewal projects had been assisted through planning advances and development loans. In these programs, as in all other federal programs in which there was assistance to local governments for projects of a purely local character, the major sticking point between Eisenhower and Congress was the extent to which the local community would be required to participate in meeting project costs. Eisenhower believed these should be divided about equally, because that seemed equitable and because it would help assure that the projects were built and operated economically. Congress, on the other hand, typically preferred a more liberal sharing of costs by the federal government. In this it had, of course, the full support of most local officials.

*   *   *

Eisenhower's first guidance on how to approach this melange of problems came in a memorandum prepared for him by Aksel Nielsen, a longtime family friend and confidant from Denver, Colorado, and a greatly respected figure in the mortgage banking industry. There were recommendations later from an Advisory Committee on Governmental Housing Policies and Programs set up early in 1953 at Nielsen's suggestion.[23] In 1954, a reform measure based in good part on the recommendations of these outside persons was put before Congress. Some thought it did not go far enough; some thought it pointed in the wrong direction; by any test it was bold and far-reaching—a direct challenge to the status quo.[24]

First, there would be a new approach to public housing. Congress was asked to continue PHA's construction authorization at 35,000 units a year, which would extend current practice, but to make this commitment for four years rather than for the one year which was its regular practice. It was hoped (and expected) that within the span of this longer extension, and with the help of certain new programs which the administration planned to propose (and to which we will shortly turn), families that would otherwise be seeking accommodation in public housing would make provision for themselves by buying a home outside the public housing system.[25] Thus, although the four-year authorization would leave the federal government with a large stake in public housing already constructed and in use it would enable PHA to phase out construction of new units.

Second, the practice of total clearance in urban renewal projects would be abandoned. The "federal bulldozer," as Martin Anderson had dubbed the urban renewal program, would henceforth operate selectively, allowing still-usable structures to be saved.[26] And the program's authorization would be broadened to encompass the rehabilitation or construction of nonresidential facilities essential to neighborhood life.

Third, it was proposed that communities seeking federal assistance, such as in urban renewal, be required to show that they had a "workable program" into which it would fit.

Fourth, with slum "prevention" rather than "clearance" in mind, a new FHA program would offer insurance on a preferentially-liberal basis for loans to homeowners wishing to rehabilitate dwellings located in declining areas. It was a type of credit previously not eligible for federal insurance. Again, a community wishing to avail itself of this assistance would have to show that it had a "workable program" for using it.

Fifth, Fanny Mae would be rechartered, reorganized, and given authority to issue its own debentures, without federal guarantee. Anyone using Fanny Mae's facilities would be required to purchase stock in the corporation in amounts that ultimately would permit total withdrawal of federal funds. In short, it would be privatized. Special assistance operations would continue, but in limited amount, and would be plainly identified as involving federal subsidy.

Finally, to help stabilize homebuilding, and thus to help smooth the business cycle, Congress was asked to increase the president's authority to adjust the terms of downpayment and maturity on which FHA and VA would insure or guarantee home loans.

*   *   *

Not to this day has Congress been presented with a more comprehensive and innovative program for reform of federal housing and home financing activities, but Congress dealt with it as it dealt with Eisenhower's program for rationalizing farm price-support programs: it picked it apart and turned aside almost entirely its challenge to current arrangements. The public housing construction authorization was held again to one year, assuring that Congress would have a housing bill up for debate in another year, which left the administration's housing and home financing programs locked as before in a hostagelike condition; Fanny Mae was restructured and moved toward privatization, but those provisions of the underlying law that set ceiling interest rates at below-market levels on special-assistance loans, and required that the loans be bought (and sold) at par, were left as they were, assuring a continued heavy drain on the budget; and the president's request for greater authority to adjust the terms on which federal agencies would be permitted to insure or guarantee home loans (much wanted at the CEA) was turned down. To boot, and on its own initiative, Congress liberalized the terms on which the FHA and

VA could insure or guarantee home loans, raising questions about the quality of loans for which the federal government was accepting a significant financial responsibility.

Although disappointed in a number of the bill's features, Eisenhower signed it with an expression of thanks that (in my judgment) was more generous than was warranted.[27] Shortly thereafter, however, perhaps after second thoughts on what Congress had done, a press conference remark by the president made it clear that in another year there would be another try for what had not been achieved in 1954.

The next (1955) legislative session was again a disappointment. The bill that was passed had many constituency-pleasing features (its treatment of public housing, especially), but the session was notable mainly for its relatively quiet resolution of an intramural struggle between the Federal Home Loan Bank Board (backed by the savings and loan industry) and HHFA (backed by the White House).[28] The Bank Board wanted independence from the HHFA; HHFA wanted to retain dominion over the Bank Board, arguing (wrongly, I thought) that only under its (HHFA's) surveillance would the Bank Board's activities be adequately coordinated with the administration's economic and financial policies.

In the end, the Bank Board gained the independence it sought. Eisenhower signed the bill, expressing "serious objections" to the result and calling it "a backward step which will seriously impair [policy] coordination and thrust an unnecessary supervisory burden on the President."[29] But it was a mistaken view of the outcome. As an independent agency the Bank Board worked to coordinate its policies with those of the White House and the Federal Reserve if anything more closely than it had when under HHFA's thumb, doing so entirely to the president's satisfaction. In short, dust had been raised within the bureaucracy over a jurisdictional question, fortunately without significant effect on economic policy.

*   *   *

But Congress returned soon to headier stuff. Legislation was enacted in 1956, 1957, and 1958 largely in the image of the 1954 act and increasingly less agreeable to Eisenhower. As usual, the bills were of the "omnibus" type, making it necessary for the president (not having the item veto he repeatedly asked for) to accept features not to his liking in order to obtain others that were vitally necessary. By 1959, however, this legislative struggle had reached the point where Eisenhower's willingness to make concessions to release FHA from its perennially hostagelike status (i.e., needful of additional loan-insuring authority) was exhausted. Relying on estimates made jointly by the Budget Bureau, HHFA, and the CEA that said FHA could operate for a few months (perhaps even for a year) with the insurance authorization carried over from the preceding year (plus a precarious arrangement involving "commitments to insure" that actually exceeded current insurance authorization), a battle of wills began between Eisenhower and opposing elements in Congress in which two housing bills were vetoed (with vetoes sustained) before one was on his desk that he was prepared to sign.

What Eisenhower wanted had been put before Congress in the January 1959 Budget Message: public housing construction held to a roughly constant annual volume, with available units allotted to families displaced by public action (most often by urban renewal); longterm authorization for the urban renewal program, with local communities required to bear a share of project costs graduated up to 50 percent, and to have a "workable program" for using federal funds; interest rates on special-assistance loans set at levels sufficient at least to cover Treasury borrowing costs; ceiling interest rates on FHA-insured and VA-guaranteed loans set at levels high enough to assure a supply of private financing; greater authority for the president to "flex" loan insurance and guarantee terms in keeping with market conditions and the economy's stabilization needs; and (the major sticking point in the bill) an open-ended loan-insurance authorization for FHA, which would eliminate the recurrent paralysis of the building industry that occurred when authorizations adequate for not much more than a year were close to being exhausted.

The first bill enacted by Congress was turned down for

reasons that illustrate well the differences between what Eisenhower wanted and what the congressional majority was disposed to give him. They were spelled out in the veto message:

- the bill was "extravagant," proposing to spend $2.2 billion where $810 million had been requested;

- it would be an obstacle in the fight against inflation: "We have made good progress . . . but we cannot win that fight if we add one spending program to another without thought of how they are going to be paid for, and invite deficits in times of general prosperity. No one can gain from a fiscal policy of this inflationary type—least of all, the housing industry;"

- the requirement that Fanny Mae buy mortgages at par under its special assistance program, regardless of the price that these mortgages command in the open market" would tend to "substitute Federal spending for private investment [and] drive private credit from areas where it is urgently needed;"

- "instead of removing the wholly unnecessary limit on the amount of the mortgage insurance authority of [FHA], the bill would continue these important programs on an uncertain, hand-to-mouth basis;"

- through lower downpayments and longer maturities [the bill] would introduce underwriting provisions of questionable soundness into a number of FHA's loan insurance programs;" and

- it would put the urban renewal program on a basis that would discriminate in favor of large as against small cities and reduce the share of project costs borne by local communities, already thought to be too low.[30]

The second bill came to the White House not sufficiently changed from the first to warrant being signed and, amid renewed warnings from the building industry that it would collapse in ruins unless the legislation was signed forthwith, it too was vetoed.[31] This second veto was also sustained, again without collapse of the building industry.

The third bill sent to the White House gave enough loan-insurance authorization to FHA to last only about one year and fell short in several other respects of what Eisenhower was seeking, but it made adjustments in some features of the preceding bills sufficient to overcome his major objections to them, and he signed it on September 23, 1959, without comment.

*   *   *

Relatively little was done by Congress on housing in 1960, leaving the law as Eisenhower left the presidency much as it was when he entered into it. It was an outcome with which no one was satisfied. It was a defeat for the administration that arrangements were continued that guaranteed a deepening federal involvement in public housing and home financing at increasing budgetary cost, with no believable prospect of improvement in either the volume or stability of homebuilding. It was also a defeat that the president was not given enough authority to adjust the terms on which home loans could be insured and guaranteed to make these programs as effective as they could be for helping stabilize the construction industry and the economy.

The sum of it is that Eisenhower's challenge to the status quo in federal housing and home financing programs was rejected by Congress in what was, at bottom, a conflict of philosophies. Whether his programs would have produced all that was expected of them by their architects no one can say, but there is nothing in the continued instability of homebuilding, or in the mounting costs of federal programs that have yet to deal adequately with the housing problems of low-income families, that denies the possibility that they might have done so.

Extending Social Security

Writing in 1980 on welfare reform, two students of the subject observed that, "[c]ontrary to the impression left by historians, neither welfare expansion nor welfare reform died in the 1950s."[32] They were right: then as now, liberals and conservatives divided sharply on what needed to be done to maintain a reasonable level of personal income against circumstances that could interrupt it—old age, unemployment, disability, illness—but the 1950s was all the same a period not of inaction but of significant extension in what we nowadays call "safety net" or "social guarantee" programs. In the controversies of the period, Eisenhower was in a position intermediate between two extremes. His accent on individual responsibility, limited government, and actuarial and financial soundness made him a target of welfare activists; at the same time, being sensitive to the hazards to personal economic security in an industrialized, market-oriented society and the responsibility of government to assist individuals in coping with them, he was often equally under attack from the right.

Essentially, his problem was that too few people understood that to make democratic government work it was necessary to combine liberality in dealing with human concerns with conservatism in fiscal affairs. In any case, achieving a combination of fiscal soundness and social liberalism is what engaged his efforts in the social security area—that, plus seeking ways to deliver assistance without creating, as he put it, "permanent dependency" in the beneficiaries, and "going so far in the direction of socialism that a centralized bureaucracy [gained] excessive control over the lives of all of us."[33]

As he saw it, there were political as well as economic realities that made the extension and strengthening of programs to protect personal security a "practical necessity." He put the political realities bluntly in a 1954 letter to his conservatively inclined and outspoken brother Edgar, who had written to him apparently to protest that there was not enough difference between what the new administration was doing and what its immediate predecessors had done. The president replied, somewhat heatedly:

". . . [I]t is true that I believe this country is following a dangerous trend when it permits too great a centralization of government functions. I oppose this [and] in some instances the fight is a rather desperate one. But to attain any success it is quite clear that the Federal Government cannot avoid or escape responsibilities that the mass of the people *believe* should be undertaken by it. The political processes of this country are such that if a *rule of reason* is not applied in this effort we will lose everything—even to a possible and drastic change in the Constitution. This is what I mean by my constant insistence on "moderation" in government. Should any party attempt to abolish social security, unemployment insurance, and eliminate labor laws and farm programs you would not hear of that party again in our political history. There is a tiny splinter group . . . that believes you can do these things. . . . Their number is negligible and they are stupid [Eisenhower's italics].34

The economic realities were alluded to again in the 1954 letter (already referred to) to General Bradford G. Chynoweth (Retired), an old friend, also outspoken and also impatient with what he judged to be the president's liberalism. Eisenhower responded to him, in part:

It seems to me that no great intelligence is required . . . to discern the practical necessity of establishing some kind of security for individuals in a specialized and highly industrialized age.

When this observation elicited only more protests from Chynoweth, along with certain proposals that Eisenhower called "alarming," he responded with a second letter:

Mass production has wrought great things in the world, but it has created social problems that cannot be possibly met under ideas that were probably logical and sufficient in 1800.

What I mean by the "Middle of the Road" [Chynoweth had questioned the concept] is that course that preserves the greatest possible initiative, freedom and independence of soul and body to the individual, but that does not hesitate to use government to combat cataclysmic economic disasters which can, in some instances, be even more terrible than convulsions of nature.35

But the uncomfortable reality was that a middle-of-the-road position left Eisenhower widely separated on a host of specific issues not only from many of the conservative wing of his party but also from the main body of welfare expansionists. Among these issues were: How much provision should the individual be expected to make for his own and his family's economic security, and how could government assist most constructively to that end; to what extent should income-support programs be federalized, and to what extent should they require participation by local government in their management and in the bearing of costs; should Social Security arrangements be actuarially sound and self-supporting or should they be unfettered by such restraints and financed if necessary out of the federal government's general revenues; how important was it that the provision of health insurance and medical services remain private? And so on.

*   *   *

Eisenhower encountered all these complicated and vexing questions during his presidency, but the one he faced first was, on the surface at least, relatively simple and straightforward: Should his initial social security proposals be limited to extending the coverage and improving the benefits of existing programs—Old Age and Survivors Insurance (OASI)—or should they extend protection into new fields, such as disability and health insurance?

The question was a crucial one for welfare expansionists. Their goal was to establish an all-encompassing income-maintenance system, and their view of how best to reach it was to concentrate on getting activity started in still-uncovered areas. Disability insurance was such an area. If even a modest start could be made there, a natural process of program expansion would take over. Berkowitz and McQuaid, already cited, described what was expected (without necessarily endorsing it):

> [T]he existence of a law was an invitation to its liberalization. The trick was to get a law passed creating a new federal welfare program. The expansion of that program would follow."

By this test, the administration's initial proposal was clearly less than what welfare expansionists wanted. As described in the White House message presenting it to Congress (August 1, 1953), it was "a specific plan for a specific purpose—the extension of coverage." To be sure, it would do this on an immense scale, extending protection to an additional 10.5 million persons, but there was no extension of programs into new areas.[36]

It was stated by the administration when its first proposals were made that others would follow, and there was no delay in keeping that promise. It is hard to believe, however, that what was recommended in the second round did not go significantly beyond what the White House had originally intended. In these second proposals, benefits under OASI would be liberalized by a more generous method of calculating them and by an increase in the amount of income retirees could earn without loss of benefits; in addition, a step would be taken into the hitherto uncovered area of disability insurance. Doubtless responding to pressure from welfare activists, it was proposed that benefits owed to a qualifying person who suffered total or extended disability prior to retirement would be preserved, under a "disability freeze," until retirement at 65.

Delayed by drawn-out hearings, Congress did not respond to these proposals until late in 1954. In the end it did so largely as the White House had requested, but because the "disability freeze" had now to be included in the calculation of the program's likely cost, the payroll tax, which in the first round of proposals was to be left unchanged at 3 percent, would be increased to 4 percent. With these changes, what had been Old Age and Survivors Insurance would become Old Age, Survivors and Disability Insurance (OASDI).[37]

*   *   *

Efforts continued in 1955 to strengthen what the *Economic Report* called the "floor of security for the individual" (a more felicitous expression than the earlier "floor over the pit of personal disaster"), producing amendments in 1956 which, with two exceptions, were in line with the administration's recommendations.[38] But the exceptions gave Eisenhower some pause, and illustrate again how his more cautious thinking separated him from welfare expansionists.

First, there were reservations about a provision (modified from an earlier and more liberal proposal) that would permit women in covered employment to retire at 65 with full benefits, or to accept reduced benefits at an earlier age. The fear was that the change would encourage employers to lower the maximum age at which they would offer employment to women.

Second, exception was taken to an amendment of the underlying law which, in the familiar manner of step-by-step program liberalization, would lower from 65 to 50 the age at which a covered employee could become eligible to receive disability payments. What troubled Eisenhower was not the merits of disability insurance per se, but the actuarial implications of the terms on which it was being made available. He stated his reservations about it during a news conference on the day (August 1, 1956) the bill was signed: "we are loading on the [social] security system something I don't think should be there, and if it is going to be handled, should be handled another way."[39]

Later developments justified that concern, but in 1956 it was a purely speculative worry. Noting that the bill had been passed overwhelmingly by Congress, Eisenhower put his doubts aside and signed it.

*   *   *

It was not long, however, before it became evident that the cost of meeting the commitments undertaken in successive program liberalizations would outrun the system's resources. Trustees of the OASDI Trust Fund reported in mid-1958 that, for the first time in the system's history, what was being paid in benefits was exceeding what was being collected in payroll taxes and earned in interest on reserves.[40] At the same time, there was pressure to increase benefits to compensate for the cost-of-living increases that had accelerated in the mid-1950s. Facing these problems, Congress proposed that the payroll tax be raised from 4.5 to 5 percent and that the wage base on which the tax was calculated be lifted from $4,000 to $4,800.

Eisenhower signed the 1958 bill without raising questions about the tax increases. But he had strong reservations about portions of the bill that dealt with federal-state sharing of the costs of welfare programs of the "public assistance" type (arrangements outside the OASDI system, under which assistance was given to needy individuals on a grant basis). His signing message noted that the bill would raise to 58.5 percent a federal share that had moved up from 45 percent in 1946 and stated:

> I believe deeply in the concept that the States and communities can best determine the actual needs of individuals and best administer programs of assistance to them—and that State and local financial responsibility in these programs should be strengthened, not weakened.[41]

Again, however, the trend he deplored had not gone so far as to cause him to veto the bill. As with his concern about the actuarial basis and likely cost of the disability program, it was too early for his worries to be more than vaguely disquieting doubts, and too early for many to share them.

*   *   *

The approaches Eisenhower preferred to have government take in helping protect individuals against interruptions of income had him at loggerheads with Congress on two additional programs which commanded major attention during his presidency—unemployment compensation and health insurance. Of the two, the need to strengthen unemployment compensation presented the simpler problem. The system had been set up in 1937 as a federal-state partnership, in which the federal government's role was to specify coverage, levy and collect a payroll tax on covered businesses to meet costs, and credit the receipts to reserves held in trust separately for each of the states. Benefits were paid from these reserves on terms (amount and duration) set by the states themselves, and they varied from state to state.

Virtually everyone shared the view that benefits should be more nearly uniform among the states, but there was disagreement on how this should be accomplished. Welfare activists would do it by federalizing the system; Eisenhower, in keeping with his distaste for the centralization of governmental functions, would preserve the federal-state partnership basis and, to obtain greater uniformity among state programs, would rely on White House appeals to laggard states to upgrade their benefits.

The administration's plan called for action at both the federal and state levels. On the federal level, Congress was asked to extend the system's coverage to federal employees vulnerable to layoff or dismissal, to persons employed in establishments that processed farm products "as an incident to farming," and to the employees of all businesses, regardless of size (at the time, firms employing fewer than eight were not covered). Congress was also asked to shorten from three years to one the period required for a firm to qualify for a reduced payroll tax (which a business could do when it could report a favorable employment experience) and to provide assistance through non-interest-bearing loans to states whose reserves were nearing exhaustion. At the same time, there was an appeal to the states to bring benefits up to certain minimum levels of amount and duration (one-half of an individual's recent earnings, for at least twenty-six weeks).[42]

There was a mixed response to these proposals, but the outcome was in the main a victory for Eisenhower. The federal-state partnership was continued, and appeals to the states to improve benefits where they were below recommended minimum levels were in most cases acted on favorably. The principal disappointment was that Congress, deferring to representatives of small businesses who claimed that applying the system to small concerns would be administratively impractical and unduly burdensome, left businesses employing fewer than four persons still in the "uncovered" category.

As already noted in connection with what was done to stem recession in 1957–58, Congress was asked in 1958 to provide for a temporary extension of eligibility for benefits beyond whatever limit was in force in a particular state. Ultimately it did so.

*   *   *

Health insurance was an infinitely more difficult issue. By 1953 it had been debated in the United States for twenty years (much longer abroad), with proposals ranging all the way from those under which a nationalized system would provide virtually all health services (on the British model) to those in which reliance would be mainly on private insurance and private health care, with government assistance limited to needy persons. An intermediate and widely-favored approach would leave medical and health services private, but fold health insurance into the social security system. A plan of the last type had been proposed in the 1940s in the Wagner-Murray-Dingell bill but failed to be accepted on three occasions. And in 1952 a National Health Act, sponsored by President Truman (also designed to establish a national health insurance plan within the social security system), failed of enactment.

Given this history, it was inevitable that health insurance would be an issue in the 1952 presidential campaign, and Eisenhower was drawn deeply into it. Not much would violate his convictions more gravely than to have government intrude itself between physician and patient.[43] At the same time, he recognized an urgent need to make health services more readily available, especially to persons in rural areas and to those who were both elderly and needy. The problem was to devise a system that would meet these needs while preserving the traditional arrangements of private medicine, and to do it to the extent possible through private insuring institutions. When he put a plan before Congress that would meet these tests, he cautioned the lawmakers:

> [W]e must be careful and farsighted in the action we take. Freedom, consent, and individual responsibility are fundamental to our system. In the field of medical care, this means that the traditional relationship of the physician and his patient, and the right of the individual to elect freely the manner of his care in illness, must be preserved.
>
> In adhering to this principle, and rejecting the socialization of medicine, we can still confidently commit ourselves to certain national health goals.[44]

The program he proposed called first for a strengthening of

existing programs. There would be increased support for the Public Health Service, significantly increased federal aid for the construction of medical facilities, and an increase in the resources directed to the rehabilitation of disabled persons. But to this would be added a totally novel arrangement: the federal government would "encourage the development of more and better voluntary health insurance" by offering to reinsure policies issued by private companies. Out of a $25 million fund, the federal government would absorb three-quarters of the abnormal losses incurred by companies that offered health insurance in areas (predominantly rural) where protection would normally not be available without federal aid. It was expected that this would lead to an expansion of private health insurance, and that, as that happened, the portion of the cost borne by the federal government would be reduced. Private voluntary health insurance would take over.

The plan was supported vigorously by Eisenhower against much opposition. The American Medical Association thought it went too far; others thought it did not go far enough. Welfare expansionists wanted health insurance folded into the social security system; Eisenhower argued that to do so would in effect make it compulsory, and that compulsory health insurance would be a step toward socialized medicine. For him, the last point was the crucial one: as he put it in a 1960 news conference:

> The only thing to which I am utterly opposed is compulsory insurance in this field; and to put the matter in the OASI . . . does not seem to me suitable because I regard that as a compulsory affair.[45]

The 1954 congressional session was a standoff on the issue. A Senate version giving effect to Eisenhower's reinsurance proposal was not voted on, and a House version was held over for further study. Eisenhower made no secret of his disappointment. Responding to a July 14, 1954 news conference request for his comment on Congress's sidetracking of his proposal he stated that:

In the campaign I made two promises that have to do with the health of the American people. I said, first, that I was opposed to socialized medicine and would use every single attribute and influence of the Presidential office to defeat any move toward socialized medicine; also, in talking about the great deficiencies in medical care in this country and, particularly, for people who can't afford the expensive type of service that is now available to us in our best hospitals, that something must be done. We were going to study ways and means to bring together better medical care to the rural areas, and bring good and fine medical care within reach of the average household budget. That is what we have been trying to do.

I am sure that the people who voted against this bill just don't understand what are the facts of American life.

I don't consider that anyone lost yesterday, except the American people. There is nothing to be gained, as I see it, by shutting our eyes to the fact that all of our people are not getting the kind of medical care to which they are entitled. I do not believe there is any use in shutting our eyes to the fact that the American people are going to get that medical care in some form or other.

As I say, I am the last to believe that the answer lies in socialized medicine, and I am trying to provide [an alternative] plan. . . . This is only a temporary defeat; this thing will be carried forward as long as I am in this office.[46]

Returning to the subject three months later in a notable public address (at the Alfred E. Smith Memorial Dinner in New York City), he vowed to resubmit the voluntary health insurance plan to the next session of Congress. It was, he said, "the logical alternative to socialized medicine."[47] But things went otherwise. It was evident by 1956 that private, voluntary health insurance had increased as much as could be expected, even with federal aid, and Eisenhower's proposal to promote its growth was not resubmitted. Instead, the administration shifted its emphasis to a broadening and improving of federal health programs already in place, including an increase in funds for the Institutes of Health, and a shifting of the Hill-Burton hospital construction program away from expansion of medical care facilities, which were in many cases in surplus, to the construction of facilities for the training and support of medical personnel and research, where serious shortages existed.

But pressure continued for health insurance that would be built into the social security system, though it was not until 1965, five years after Eisenhower's presidency was over, that this was authorized in legislation that established the Medicaid and Medicare programs. What Congress created in that action was a vast entitlement system, in part voluntary but principally compulsory, and not fully self-supporting. Financing was in part by payroll taxation, in part by voluntary payment of insurance premiums, and in part by drains on the Federal Treasury, a system that departed in basic respects from what Eisenhower had sought to have legislated.

As they developed, the Medicare and Medicaid plans inevitably involved, among other things, a certain bureaucratizing of the accounting and payment aspects of health services, with considerable uhappiness in the medical professions over that consequence. But what happened as a result of folding the arrangements into the social security system was clearly not the socialization of medicine that Eisenhower had feared. The problems that did develop were principally financial and administrative. By 1984, federal budget outlays for the two programs combined had reached $80 billion. And in June 1983 the Medicare Board of Trustees reported that, even on optimistic actuarial and financial assumptions, the resources of the Hospital Insurance Trust Fund would be exhausted by 1996; on less optimistic but still not unreasonable assumptions they might be exhausted by 1988.[48]

It was the kind of problem that Eisenhower would have been quick to recognize and quick to act against, but it was not the problem he had anticipated. For that matter, it is doubtful that anyone involved significantly in the debates over health insurance in the 1950s anticipated the magnitude of the financing and administrative problems that lay ahead. If they did, they left no track of their foresight in the legislative history of the time.

*   *   *

Thus, the notion alluded to at the beginning of this account— that welfare reform and expansion died in the 1950s—was clearly mistaken. Actually, there was an immense expansion of the income-maintenance safety net, though not in all respects as welfare expansionists desired, or as Eisenhower thought entirely sound. Granted, the years of greatest program expansion were yet to come, notably in health and disability insurance; but so also were the problems of actuarial unsoundness, financial overcommitment, and economic burden that the more cautious approaches favored by Eisenhower were designed to avoid.

Aiding Education

No question tested Eisenhower's convictions on intergovernmental relations more severely than how responsibility for the support of education should be divided among federal, state and local governments. At the same time it would be hard to identify a task, other than finding a path to world peace, about which he felt more deeply and on which his views were more fully developed.

He confronted the higher-education aspect of the problem at once when, in 1948, he assumed the presidency of Columbia University. venting his feelings on it in a diary note shortly after entering into that position. It made a point that was central in his thinking on the subject:

> The private institution has a most important function. . . . Its thinking, its research, its processes are free—not dominated by politicians seeking reelection. Therefore it sets up and maintains standards that have a direct and beneficial effect on the many state universities. Without these standards of quality, without this example, instruction in state universities would gradually fall under the domination of politicians. The state university, today, is a valuable, necessary and very wonderful institution. But let private institutions fall under federal domination and the next step is for all institutions to demand federal help. This means federal control, eventually. And the best way to establish dictatorship is to get control of the educational processes"[49]

Expressed by the president of a leading university, and not

at all in the mainstream of thinking on the role of government in higher education, these views put Eisenhower at once into the center of debates on the subject. A prominent New Yorker with close and longstanding affiliations with Columbia, concerned about the financial needs of privately-supported institutions, wrote at once to the university's new president to warn him against taking too severe a stand against federal aid. Respectful but undeterred, Eisenhower replied, again making his point regarding the joint interest of private and tax-supported institutions of higher learning:

> I well realize that in taking a stand against direct governmental support of higher education I am among those who place in front of all our privately endowed institutions a critical problem, indeed one that can actually become calamitous unless promptly solved.
> [B]asicly . . . I believe that the perpetuation and health of our form of democracy require that education be forever free of political domination. One great function of the privately endowed institution is to establish such standards in free education and research that any attempt to stultify education in tax supported institutions will always be doomed to defeat. It is my belief that democracy can never afford to dispense, therefore, with the privately endowed institution and I believe further that realization of this truth can be brought home to the American public.[50]

There was obviously a challenge here for the fund-raising responsibilities of private institutions. The letter continued:

> This means that a vast army of individuals will have constantly to be spreading this gospel and working to secure the necessary material support. This is what Columbia is trying to do.

But efforts to increase federal aid for education at all levels of the educational process continued, causing Eisenhower to turn attention increasingly to how it could be provided with the least intrusive effect. A long letter to Congressman Ralph W. Gwinn (R N.Y.) dealt with ways of doing this.[51] There were several possibilities: for institutions of higher education, there

could be "contractual arrangements . . . for scientific research
. . . essential to the public interest (and) certain types of fel-
lowships and scholarships to meet unusual Federal requirements . . . ;" for primary and secondary school systems, there
could be help in financing the construction of facilities, where
the involvement of government would entail no intrusion into
the classroom and would end automatically when construction
was complete.

Taking an opposite view, advocates of federal aid to education typically wanted assistance for the full gamut of school
activities—for teaching and school administration as well as for
the construction of facilities. Eisenhower recognized the need
in some circumstances for going that far, but only where there
was a "proved need and proved lack of income." His letter to
Gwinn dealt with this:

> I am well aware that there are certain sections of this country
> where the tax revenue potential of each will not provide for all
> of the children in that area that level of education deemed
> generally required in discharging the duties of [an] enlightened
> electorate.
>
> In such areas I would heartily support Federal aid, under
> formulas that would permit no abuse, no direct interference of
> the Federal authority in educational processes and no opportu-
> nity to expand the flow of Federal money into areas where need
> could not be clearly demonstrated. I would flatly oppose any
> grant by the Federal government to all states in the union for
> educational purposes. Such policy would create an ambition—
> almost a requirement—to spend money freely under the im-
> pulse of competition with other localities in the country. It
> would completely decry and defeat the watchful economy that
> comes about through local supervision over local expenditures
> of local revenues.
>
> In short, unless we are careful, even the great and necessary
> educational processes in our country will become yet another
> vehicle by which the believers in paternalism, if not outright
> socialism, will gain still additional power for the central govern-
> ment. . . .
>
> I firmly believe that the army of persons who urge greater
> and greater centralization of authority and greater and greater

dependence on the Federal Treasury are really more dangerous to our form of government than any external threat that can possibly be arrayed against us.

*   *   *

There were tests at once of these convictions. The history of federal involvement in helping local governments meet school costs, including instructional costs, was a long one, and Eisenhower, in the White House, was drawn early into debates concerning two versions of it.

The first was a relatively minor but thorny question. It involved federal aid to local governments in what were called "impacted areas," meaning areas where instruction was supplied to children of families housed on federal property (e.g., a military base) and where, because the local government was not being compensated through the receipt of property taxes, there was a legitimate claim for federal reimbursement. The problem was that aid once received on this basis was not readily relinquished, even if the federal impact had receded, perhaps vanished altogether. Also, because legislation to relieve these situations typically reached the president's desk as an "emergency measure," needing to be signed at once, it was hard to veto what Congress, tending to be generous in such matters, chose to pass. Thus, when Eisenhower signed the 1957 bill, he noted, obviously with some annoyance, that he was doing so "only because I have been assured that, without this extension, school facilities which will be needed for children by September 1959 would not be available."[52] And a 1958 bill that in his view was "so drawn as to constitute a threat to our traditional definition of responsibility for American education" had to be signed "despite serious reservations regarding (its) wisdom . . . in order to avoid depriving 3,300 school districts of many millions of dollars for their operating expenditures during the coming school year."[53]

A succession of presidents has continued the effort to bring "impacted area" school assistance under control, some with more success than Eisenhower and some with less. Although budget outlays under the program remained roughly unchanged at about $200 million between the fiscal years 1953 and 1961, the number of school districts receiving assistance increased to 4,275. In the January 1984 budget the number of areas proposed to be assisted had been reduced to 1,300 (perhaps in part by the consolidation of school districts), but estimated expenditures had increased to $572 million.

The second of Eisenhower's tests on aid to education, many times more important than the "impacted areas" question, was a problem unique to the 1950s, created by the wave of students that swept into the schools in those years. It was the post-World War II "baby-boom" generation. Nothing before had equalled it: between 1950 and 1959 the 4 to 14-year-old age group increased by nearly half, five times as fast as in the comparable period following World War I, and public school enrollments (kindergarten, primary, and high school) increased 40 percent.[54] Eisenhower was fully aware of this but saw no reason for altering his basic position on federal aid, stating in the January 1954 Budget Message that

> I do not underestimate the difficulties facing the States and communities in attempting to solve the problems created by the great increase in the number of children of school age, the shortage of qualified teachers, and the overcrowding of classrooms. The effort to overcome these difficulties strains the taxable resources of many communities. At the same time I do not accept the simple remedy of Federal intervention.[55]

Unlike the stringencies felt by local governments in what was a relatively limited number of "impacted areas," the classroom shortage was felt by virtually every community in the country and obviously needed to be addressed by a federal program of national scope. White House-sponsored conferences on education held regionally in 1953, and a summit-type meeting in 1955, were helpful toward developing an official position, but what was presented to Congress in February 1955 was primarily a product of planning done at the newly-established Department of Health, Education and Welfare (HEW). It reflected Eisenhower's view that aid could be appropriately supplied by the federal government to help communities finance the onetime cost of constructing physical facilities, but that responsibility for continuing costs—teachers' salaries, in particular—should remain with local government.[56] What the plan proposed was aid styled separately for each of three groups of communities.

- Those unable to sell school construction bonds at "reasonable" rates would be able to borrow from a federal fund set initially at $750 million.

- Those able to service debt but unable to issue it because of debt ceiling limits (even though selfimposed) would be able to lease facilities constructed by state agencies with funds obtained from the federal government; ultimately, lease payments would retire the debt and enable ownership of the facilities to be transferred to the local government.

- Those unable to meet either the debt-service or lease-payment requirements would be assisted under a grant program, funded equally by state and federal governments.

The plan was attacked principally on the ground that it was overly complex, though it is hard to see how this could have been a legitimate complaint from a Congress with a fair amount of sophistication in the design of aid programs. In any case, the alternative that emerged in Congress was simplicity itself: it provided that the federal government would buy school construction bonds issued by state agencies which, in turn, would make funds available to local governments on a loan basis, without regard to differences in need or in ability to raise revenues. It was, in short, a something-for-everybody piece of legislation, at the opposite pole from the help-for-those-who-need-it plan proposed by Eisenhower.

Under normal circumstances, a bill such as that favored by the majority in Congress would have come fairly promptly to the president's desk, but the attachment to it of an antisegregation amendment prevented that from happening, and Congress ended its 1955 session with no action on what was by that time described widely, if exaggeratedly, as a "standing room only" condition in the nation's classrooms.

*   *   *

Eisenhower returned to the legislative fray in 1956 sensitive to the need to present a plan that would be viewed as less complicated and (doubtless more important) would be subject to less restrictive eligibility requirements. Three elements of the 1955 proposal were retained—federal purchases of construction bonds that local governments could not sell at "reasonable" rates of interest; grants to help states finance the construction of facilities that would be leased to communities that were blocked from doing their own financing by (often selfimposed) debt-ceiling limitations; and a separate grant program to assist school planning at the state level. But to these elements was added a $1.25 billion program of matching grants to help states construct facilities for communities unable to meet either debt service or lease-payment requirements. Access to this assistance was made subject, however, to states being able to demonstrate not only that they had a need but that an effort had been made locally to meet it.[57]

In the mood of Congress at the time, even this liberalized plan would almost certainly have been judged inadequate, especially in view of the "need and effort" requirement, but action on it was again precluded by the racial segregation issue, and once more Congress adjourned without sending a bill to the White House.

Still anxious to have a program to meet what was regarded widely among school administrators as an emergency that only federal funds could solve, the administration repeated in 1957 the proposal it had made in 1956 but, as a concession to Congress, softened the "need and effort" feature. There was also a request that the program be completed in four years rather than five ("since one year has already been lost") and that it be judged "on its merits," uncomplicated by the racial segregation issue.[58]

As before, Eisenhower's formula lacked enough friends in

Congress to secure its enactment. The preference was for alternatives that involved no test of "need and effort" and included a provision (to which he took particular exception) authorizing federal aid to help meet teachers' salaries. But Congress was again unable to resolve the racial segregation issue. With no bill sent to the president, the administration ended with nothing done at the federal level to ease the classroom shortage.

Fortunately, however, and to the surprise of many, this last setback did not prevent the problem from being met. Between 1952 and 1958, while Congress was debating the civil rights question as it applied to federal aid to education, and advocates of large and generous aid programs were forecasting disaster unless action on the lines they proposed was taken forthwith, capital spending by local school systems nearly doubled, while school enrollments were rising by about 30 percent.[59] Thus, the problem that had been deemed by many as impossible of solution without a large-scale infusion of federal funds was met, in most cases adequately, by local effort, confirming Eisenhower's belief that local governments had more capability to meet local needs than they were commonly credited with.

*   *   *

One additional aid-to-education problem remains to be noted. As measures to correct the shortage of classroom space were being debated the Soviets, on October 5, 1957, launched *Sputnik,* the first of the space vehicles, putting Eisenhower's aid-to-education philosophy to a test by focusing attention on deficiencies in teaching (especially on the teaching of science and mathematics), the aspect of education in which he was most reluctant to see the federal government become involved. All the same, proposals were sent quickly from the administration to Congress which, while directed to the teaching function, were consistent with his views on how aid should be made available to local communities. They called for help that would not involve the federal government in an open-ended commitment ("This is a temporary program and should not be considered as a permanent Federal responsibility") and that would not diminish the responsibility of local governments to support their own school systems ("The keystone is State, local and private effort; the Federal role is to assist—not to control or supplant—those efforts").[60] There would be a fivefold increase in appropriations for the education activities of the National Science Foundation (which operated mainly through scientific societies and the science departments of college and universities) as well as a four-year program (to be administered by HEW) aimed at strengthening general education (including language education) and science education. And there would be federal funding annually of 10,000 merit scholarships (to rise in four years to 40,000), to be awarded with "reasonable preference . . . to students with good preparation and high aptitude in science or mathematics."

Congress's response was in the main a success for Eisenhower's proposals, though in an omission that must be judged to have been ultimately deeply damaging to the nation it made no provision for the merit scholarships he had requested. After expressing his regret at that omission, the final sentences of his signing message for the bill were a restatement of his commitment to maintaining a proper balance in aid to education between what the federal government should do and what should remain the responsibility of state and local governments:

> Much remains to be done to bring American education to levels consistent with the needs of our society. The Federal government having done its share, the people of the country, working through their local and State governments and through private agencies, must now redouble their efforts towards this end.[61]

Assisting "Distressed Areas"

Attention was drawn increasingly during the 1950s to what was known as the "distressed areas" problem—unemployment in certain sections of the country that, over extended periods, was consistently higher than in the economy generally. Unlike today's "structural unemployment," which mainly affects specific industries and occupations and certain population groups, it was largely a geographical or locational condition.[62] Unemployment in West Virginia was the most dwelt-upon example of it.

The problem had all the attributes necessary to make it a sensitive political issue. There was agreement on all sides that something needed urgently to be done, but wide differences on what to do, pitting Eisenhower's insistence on a prudent financial design in whatever was done and his stress on the responsibilities of local government against approaches that were less limited, if limited at all, by these constraints.[63]

Debates on distressed areas often sounded as if nothing was being done about the problem they presented. Actually, everything done to promote the economy's growth and stability was helpful at least indirectly, and there were numerous selectively-designed programs through which assistance was made directly available. The Small Business Administration shaped its lending policies to favor companies that would provide jobs in areas where unemployment was chronically high, and (whenever possible under existing law) companies operating in what had been designated as distressed areas were given preference in government procurement and in the placement of contracts for government construction. An Office of Area Development had been established in the Department of Commerce to advise communities on the design and administration of economic development programs. Still, legislation was needed to authorize and fund a more far-reaching effort.

*   *   *

The first of Eisenhower's requests designed to meet this need was sent to Congress in 1956.[64] Under its terms there would be an Area Assistance Administration in the Department of Commerce, empowered to "provide technical assistance to communities or larger areas, either directly or through grants, for studying their resources and preparing practical plans for industrial development." It would have the power also to make "capital improvement loans for projects that promise to improve a community's longrun economic outlook . . . for which financing [could not] be obtained on reasonable terms from private sources." For the loan programs there would be a $50 million revolving fund, with the Area Assistance Administration advancing 25 percent, state or local governments 15 percent, and private sources the remainder. Advances would be available only to communities where unemployment had been 8 percent or higher for the greater part of the preceding two years, and for projects having a reasonable chance of providing jobs that would be both lasting and additive, the latter in the sense of not being shifted ("pirated") from other areas. In addition, HHFA would be authorized to give priority under its community facilities program to projects in areas of chronically high unemployment; and urban renewal assistance (normally available only for housing and closely related projects) would be available for industrial development in qualifying areas. There was provision also for "skill improvement" programs.

Alternatives appeared quickly, with the leading one a bill sponsored by Senator Paul H Douglas (D Ill.) that differed in virtually all basic respects from what Eisenhower proposed.[65] It would distribute aid to rural as well as urban areas (the administration believed it could assist the former more constructively under a Rural Development Program which it had already established). It would make aid available to communities in which unemployment was lower and had persisted over a lesser time than was required to qualify for assistance under the administration's bill, would set a lower requirement on the sharing of costs by state and local governments, and would be administered not by the Department of Commerce but by a new, independent agency. Finally, it was stripped during debate of an "anti-pirating" provision that would have required borrowers to show that their projects would not simply move jobs from one area to another.

Against this competition the administration's formula won relatively little support. It did not propose to spend enough money, its critics thought, and its spending controls were too tight. But the Douglas bill fared not much better. It passed the Senate with the help of sixteen Republicans but was not cleared by the House Rules Committee. The 1956 congressional session ended, accordingly, with no legislation passed on area assistance.

*   *   *

It was two years before the subject again became an issue in Congress (largely because economic growth in 1956–57 greatly reduced the number of areas that would qualify as "distressed") and in the interim the Douglas bill, sponsored now also by Senator Frederick G. Payne (R Maine), making it the Douglas-Payne bill, had been revised to reduce its differences from the administration's plan. In its revised form it passed both chambers of Congress but still differed so sharply from what Eisenhower thought was appropriate that he vetoed it, pointing out that it would have the federal government supplying too large a proportion (65 percent) of the funds for local development projects ("This is a field in which, if the Federal government participates at all, it should be able to rely on local judgments backed up by significant local contributions"), that the repayment period for loans was too long (forty years, as against the administration's twenty-five), that there was a "serious question . . . whether Federal loans for the construction of industrial buildings in rural areas (which the Douglas-Payne bill would authorize) would be a proper or effective approach . . . to the problem of surplus labor in essentially agricultural communities," that interest rates to be charged on development loans were too low relative to Treasury borrowing costs, that grants could be made under the bill with "no local participation whatever," and that responsibility for administering the program would go to HHFA, not to the Department of Commerce, where he still thought it belonged.[66]

Congress adjourned in 1958 before the Douglas-Payne bill had been on the president's desk for ten days, which qualified his failure to sign it as a "pocket veto." But since Congress had failed to appropriate funds to carry out what it had authorized, this did not delay the availability of assistance, provided Congress would act promptly on a substitute measure when it reconvened. With that in mind, Eisenhower promised in his "memorandum of disapproval" to submit another plan in January 1959 and urged Congress to act on it promptly.

The administration's plan was delivered as promised, competing with a Douglas-Payne bill sponsored now by an increased number of Republicans. Again, the two approaches had moved closer in some respects, but they were still apart on the definition of eligible areas, on the extent to which local governments and groups would be required to participate in financing development projects, on the limitation of aid to areas that were essentially nonagricultural, and on where responsibility for administering the program would be located.

The White House bill got little notice. The Douglas-Payne bill passed the Senate, but a House measure broadly similar to it stalled in the Rules Committee. Once more, Congress adjourned with no area assistance legislation enacted.

*   *   *

By this time, with the 1960 presidential election campaign to begin soon, the debate had become patently political. A January 1960 letter from Eisenhower to Senator John Sherman Cooper (R Ky.) helped give visibility to what was already being done from the White House to assist affected areas, and efforts to obtain legislation consistent with the president's views were intensified.[67] To this end a May 3, 1960 message from Eisenhower to Congress, chiding it on what remained for it to do on his legislative program, had area assistance high on the list. There was, however, no disposition to accept anything Congress chose to enact. He said in his message:

> [I]t is basic that we reject the various schemes that would perpetuate insecurity by making distressed areas dependent upon the uncertainties of continued Federal subsidies, or that would pour Federal dollars into areas where distress has been temporary and which are competent to meet their problems themselves. Moreover, it will injure, not help the chronically affected areas if funds and loan advantages are indiscriminately broadcast to other areas that do not urgently require such assistance.
> The only way this difficult problem can be sensibly solved is

through healthy government-community cooperation that creates self-sustaining local economies. It cannot be solved by a dispiriting and misplaced benevolence on the part of the distant central government.[68]

What followed in Congress was again inconclusive. It began when a version of the Douglass-Payne bill was called up for debate by the Speaker of the House under the rarely-used "Calendar Wednesday" procedure, which permits a measure to be debated for two hours despite not having been cleared by the Rules Committee. Debate produced only one change in what the Senate had approved (an amendment, introduced by members from certain eastern states, which tightened the bill's provision against "pirating" jobs from one area to another) but it inspired the invention of what must be a textbook case on the variety of tactics available under House rules to delay substantive debate on a measure if there is a will (and the votes) to do so. In the end, however, a bill was accepted by House and Senate (in neither case by very wide margins) and sent to the president.

It had again the defects that caused earlier bills to be vetoed and had a cool reception at the White House. It was not Eisenhower's practice to comment publicly on bills in advance of making a statement to Congress on them, but in this case he said during a news conference, two days before the measure was vetoed, that its definition of eligibility for assistance was so broad that, even though it called for significantly more money than the administration's bill, it would supply less aid to areas of persistently high unemployment than would the measure he favored. He summed it up with the observation that "it's getting to be a pork barrel bill, as I see it."[69]

The president's judgment was sustained when the Senate failed by eleven votes to override his veto, and shortly thereafter Congress adjourned to attend the presidential nominating conventions. When it returned, there was another message from the White House reminding it of its unfinished business, including its failure to write an acceptable area assistance bill. In it the president recalled:

For five years in a row I have recommended area assistance legislation. Regrettably I had no choice but to veto the legislation the Congress did pass this session. It would have frittered the taxpayers' money away in areas where it was not needed and on programs that would not have benefited those truly in need of help.

A new area assistance bill, with Administration backing, was introduced immediately after my veto. It would channel more help directly into stricken areas than any previous measure proposed. Failure to act will deny this help for months to come. Human distress demands action now. If later we find there should be changes either in the dollar amounts or the methods used, experience will dictate the kind of adjustments to be made.[70]

Some reconciling of differences between Congress and the White House on what would be done to aid distressed areas might have been possible in a less partisan year, but not in 1960. When Congress reconvened, attention to the question was limited to an inconclusive, one-day hearing before a Senate subcommittee, leaving the issue to be carried over into the fall election campaign.

*   *   *

Thus, the Eisenhower period ended with no area assistance program agreed on, due partly to political considerations germane entirely to the times, but more fundamentally due to deeply dividing differences between what Eisenhower thought best and what was proposed in the various versions of the Douglas and Douglas-Payne bills. In short, it was a contest between two philosophies of government, ending in this case in "no decision."

For the most part, that inconclusive result still prevails. Following the Eisenhower period, interest centered for some years on the expansion of aggregate demand as a way of correcting even the hard-core unemployment that characterized "distressed areas." But that approach failed and the distressed areas problem has remained, transformed from what it was in the 1950s to joblessness that is more widespread geographically, that has more to do than formerly with skills and the lack of them, and that is more needful of being attacked in a broad-based but still selective manner.

To date, it has not been attacked in that way, but when it is, as ultimately it will have to be, there will be much to learn from the Eisenhower experience, and from his views on how the problem should be approached.

Helping Small Business

Small business has never lacked advocates in Washington, some of them true believers in its causes and all of them alert to the political benefit of being helpful to its interests. Eisenhower was not unaware of these benefits, nor backward about claiming his rightful share of them, but his ingrained individualism, the roots of which were set firmly in place during his Kansas boyhood, made him a natural ally of the small enterprise and the individual entrepreneur, and he worked with genuine conviction throughout his presidency in their behalf. When it became evident that a cabinet-level group was needed to develop new programs helpful to small business and to strengthen programs already available he agreed eagerly to its establishment. The result was the Cabinet Committee on Small Business, which operated without interruption to the end of his presidency under the chairmanship of the CEA chairman and with the president's close attention.[71]

An opportunity came early for Eisenhower to put his convictions on small-scale entrepreneurship to work. As we have seen, when the Reconstruction Finance Corporation was liquidated in 1953, disposition had to be made of its function of lending to small companies. There were questions then, as there had been even in the 1930s and as there still are, whether a lending agency with this purpose was needed. Not everyone in the cabinet thought so, but Eisenhower was not among the skeptics. He gave full support to the legislation that established a Small Business Administration (SBA) and authorized it to serve small companies as the RFC had done.

At the start, SBA was given only a two-year lease on life, but it quickly established itself as a well-managed and useful agency, with none of the taint of political favoritism that had been RFC's undoing, and after extensions of two years in 1955 and one year in 1957 it was given permanent status in 1958. It began its operations with a relatively modest lending authority—a revolving fund of $275 million, of which $150 million was earmarked for secured, intermediate-term business loans, with the remainder reserved for disaster loans and the "commitments to lend" that small companies sometimes needed when, as bidders for government contracts, they had to have an assured source of credit. Loans to a single borrower were at first limited to $150,000, later to $350,000. The interest rate was 5.5 percent, which involved a small subsidy, and loan repayment periods were normally set at not more than three years, though longer periods were possible.

Operating with these powers and within these limits, SBA quickly became a vigorously active agency. From 1953 through fiscal 1960, it made nearly $1 billion available to small companies, either from its own resources or jointly with private lenders under "participation" or "take-out" arrangements. Under the former, it advanced only part of a loan and a private lender put up the rest; under the latter, it agreed to assume all or part of a loan originally made by a private lender, if called on to do so. Both arrangements were designed to draw private banks into the activity.[72]

*   *   *

It was helpful to small business to have access to short- or intermediate-term credit, but a small company's most urgent financial need is often for longterm credit or for equity capital, and finding ways to supply these, especially equity, became a major task of the Cabinet Committee. Needless to say it had an equally high priority with the small business committees of Congress.

It was not easy, however, to devise a constructive and financially prudent formula for meeting this need. Nothing facilitates the raising of equity capital more effectively than a rising stock market, and it was enormously helpful that stock prices were on a rising trend through the Eisenhower years (Standard & Poor's index of prices of 500 common stocks was 2.3 times higher in 1960 than in 1952, an average annual increase of nearly 11 percent). Still, many small companies were unable to raise longterm funds on terms they could afford.[73]

Plans were debated at length between the White House (represented by the Treasury) and congressional committees on how best to meet this need, but there was a considerable gulf between the two sides. The White House was striving for an arrangement that, while adequate to the need and sound on grounds of credit standards, would not be overly dependent on federal support; the controlling forces in Congress were less constrained by budgetary cost or by the possibility that what was done might invite the taking of undue business risks.

The problem was discussed through several sessions of Congress with no resolution of the differences but was settled in 1959 when Congress passed, and the president signed, the Small Business Investment Company Act. The small business investment companies (SBICs) which that legislation authorized were empowered to raise funds by borrowing from the SBA or from state and local development agencies and by selling their own securities in the open market (originally only in debt form, but later also as equity). The proceeds would be invested in small companies.

Though the SBA was happy with the results, as were the bill's supporters in Congress and the Washington representatives of small business, the White House, the Treasury, and we at the CEA were chary of it, fearing that it would invite the taking of unduly high business risks. But there are limits to how free a president is to reject a bill on essentially speculative grounds that comes to his desk with backing as broad as had been won by the Small Business Investment Company Act, and it was signed.

The result was a surge of applications to form SBICs, exceeding even the large response that the SBA had anticipated, and many more of the new entities were licensed than in the end survived. As many as 700 were reported to have been in existence in the 1960s, but by 1979, twenty years after the authorizing legislation had been passed, the number had been reduced to around 300. There is no estimate of the losses that must have been involved in this shrinkage, but, on the positive side, an estimated $3.1 billion had by that time been invested in some 50,000 small companies.[74]

* * *

As the debates that culminated in passage of the Small Business Investment Company Act went forward, the Cabinet Committee on Small Business searched for additional ways to help small companies meet their problems, financial and otherwise. Several were identified.

First, to help them raise equity funds, it was proposed that the upper limit on issues of securities that could be cleared by the Securities and Exchange Commission (SEC) on a simplified (Regulation A) basis be raised from $300,000 to $500,000. It was obviously not a revolutionary proposal, but it was expected to be useful to small and medium-sized companies seeking to raise equity capital without significantly increasing the risk to investors. However, neither Congress nor the SEC could be persuaded to that view, and legislation that would have allowed it to be tried was not enacted.

Second, small companies needed tax relief. The expiration of the excess profits tax and the reduction of rates on personal income that went into effect in 1954 were helpful, as were several of the changes made in the tax code by the Revenue Act of 1954; but the Cabinet Committee worked assiduously for more. Because the federal budget at the time permitted no more than a small loss of revenue, not much could be done, but it was possible to make a number of useful adjustments. One of these accorded corporations of small size the right to be taxed in the same manner as partnerships; another allowed small companies to accumulate surplus in larger amounts than had previously been permitted without running afoul of the "incorporated pocketbook" rule; and a third (of major importance to small, closely-held companies) permitted the payment of estate taxes in installments rather than in the one lump sum that had previously been necessary and that often could not be raised without liquidating the company.

Third, an enormous effort went into devising ways to help small companies compete for federal procurement or construction contracts.[75] The methods used took several forms: "set asides" gave small businesses priority in the bidding process; procurement agencies were authorized to require prime contractors to make greater use of small companies as subcontractors; the SBA was authorized to issue "certificates of competency" to qualifying small businesses when such a document was required; procurement rules (famed for their complexity) were simplified and codified to make it easier for a small company to find its way through what might otherwise be an impenetrable barrier between it and a government contract; and manuals were prepared and circulated widely that described the numerous forms of assistance available to small companies and the conditions on which it could be obtained.

Partly because of the difficulty of defining "small business," but for other reasons as well, it was difficult to determine the effectiveness of these efforts. But it was estimated that they contributed to keeping the share of defense contracts going to small companies about constant, at 16 to 17 percent. This was no small success, considering the changes that were occurring in the nature of "weapons systems" and how these tended to shift competitive advantage to large companies with large research and manufacturing capabilities.

Fourth and finally, an effort was made to increase the accessability to small businesses of the results of research done under government contract. Typically, the research was done by a large company, leaving most small companies unaware of the work's existence, or what was in many cases their rightful access to it. The first need, obviously, was to have contracts so written as to withhold research results from public access only where there remained compelling reasons of national security. What remained was mainly an educational task: preparing and distributing manuals on how to obtain access to such research results as were in fact available. In the end, however, it was essential to spark the interest of small companies in helping themselves.

With that purpose in mind, a two-day Conference on Technical and Distribution Research for the Benefit of Small Business was held in Washington in September 1957, addressed in separate working sessions by representatives of the major procurement and contracting agencies and in a plenary meeting by the president. Over a thousand owners and operators of small businesses and representatives of associations and groups serving the small business community attended, with many more at meetings that followed in other cities. Responsibility for the project and for the preparation of a brochure that it inspired (*Federal Policies and Programs That Benefit Small Business*) was borne by the Cabinet Committee on Small Business.[76]

* * *

The importance to small businesses of what can be accomplished by such efforts as were made by the Cabinet Committee is small compared with what hangs on keeping the economy prosperous, competitive, and open to the establishment and expansion of new companies, but it would be a mistake to underestimate them. When the Cabinet Committee made its final report to the president it felt justified in asserting that what it had done amounted to "a major advance in federal economic policy," though there were no illusions about its permanence. Much of what was accomplished would be lost if the effort was not continued. As the report put it,

> [T]he task of preserving an economic environment favorable to the establishment and successful operation of small businesses can never be fully accomplished . . . [T]here will always be a need for Government to follow the economic fortunes of small enterprises with the closest care, and regularly to evaluate its existing and proposed programs for promoting the welfare of small concerns.[77]

The Cabinet Committee was disbanded after 1960. Efforts of the sort it made were subsequently continued under various auspices, but I believe it is fair to say they have at no time been pressed with the same zeal or as systematically as under Eisenhower. And it is doubtful that there has been at any time the same breadth of participation within government in them.

Amending the Taft-Hartley Act

One of the most sensitive legislative questions facing Eisenhower as his presidency began was what to do about Taft-Hartley, a major statute among the federal laws governing labor-management relations. It had been passed in 1947 over a veto by President Truman and opinions regarding it were still deeply divided. To its most severe critics it was a "slave labor law" that should be wiped from the books; to its friends its enactment was a step, which they hoped to extend, toward redressing an imbalance between labor and management that was created in 1934 by passage of the Wagner Act. There was agreement on both sides that extensive amendment was called for.

Eisenhower made no secret of his lack of familiarity with certain of the questions that amendment of the law would raise, notably what to do about "right to work" laws (state laws mandating that union membership could not be made a requirement of employment).[78] His general position was that there was merit on both sides of the debate about what needed to be done: some features of the law were unfair to labor; others were unfair to management. The task was to correct both.

Not everyone in Eisenhower's official family shared the confidence he had that these differences could be satisfactorily resolved. As Sherman Adams later wrote,

> Now and then, in his determination to reach a difficult but desirable objective, the idealistic and optimistic Eisenhower would reveal a faith in the higher motives of mankind that astonished the more cynical members of the cabinet.[79]

As it turned out, the cynics were right. Preliminary meetings in 1953 revealed strong support by some members of the cabinet (Weeks, Summerfield, Wilson and Humphrey) for changes which, from their nature, would be adamantly opposed by

Labor; on the other side, Martin Durkin, Eisenhower's first Secretary of Labor, was pressing for changes that management would oppose with equal vigor. Finally, there were some at cabinet level who counseled against doing anything at all until 1955, for fear of adverse effects during the 1954 congressional election campaign.[80]

Eisenhower rejected the counsel to do nothing and chose to move the debate along by establishing a cabinet-level task force to prepare a list of proposals that could be considered for presentation to Congress. It was reported early in the deliberations, however, that Weeks and Durkin were "poles apart," and it was not until Durkin had resigned and been replaced by James Mitchell that the group was able to agree on even a preliminary package of proposals.[81]

What was finally put before Congress was a mixture. In it were items that labor would welcome and management would oppose: limitations on the use of injunctions in labor disputes; less restrictive rules on secondary boycotts; greater protection of the representational rights of unions; and (until legislation could be prepared and enacted that would make this unnecessary) the application to management of a requirement already applying to trade union officers that called for an affidavit disclaiming membership in Communist organizations. Management, on the other hand, would approve and labor would resist proposals to retain that section of the act (14b) protective of "right to work" laws, to authorize government-sponsored, secret-ballot strike votes, and to give union members the right to revoke a dues-checkoff agreement at any time, not just when a contract was being terminated. Certain issues would be held over for further study: the "no-man's land" question (what to do about jurisdictional conflicts among federal and state authorities that left some labor disputes in a kind of limbo) and rules governing the handling of union welfare and pension funds.[82]

Although the White House proposals seemed at the time to be both far-reaching and balanced, reactions to them in some quarters of Congress made it quickly clear that there was more to be done than they touched on. Evidence of sentiment to that effect had surfaced in congressional hearings that revealed highly objectionable practices in picketing, in the use of boycotts against third parties to achieve union purposes (including so-called "hot cargo" cases), in the management of union welfare and pension funds, and in collusive ("sweetheart") arrangements between labor and management. In the light of these revelations, White House proposals began to look somehow inadequate. The effect was to stall legislative activity, and it was announced by the White House that for the time being it would make no further moves relating to Taft-Hartley. The 1954 congressional session ended, accordingly, with no labor legislation of importance enacted.

*   *   *

The next two years were similarly unproductive. Eisenhower's 1954 recommendations were resubmitted in 1955 and 1956, but Congress passed no labor legislation. In January 1956, however, a step was taken destined ultimately to change the climate of opinion on what needed to be done. Building on what had been revealed in earlier investigations, the Senate established a Select Committee on Investigations of Improper Activities in Labor-Management Relations, chaired by the greatly respected Senator John McClellan (D Ark.), to study abuses of power in the conduct of union affairs and in labor-management relations generally.

But even in this more reform-minded congressional context, White House initiatives continued to be relatively timorous, undoubtedly due to differences within Eisenhower's official family on what should be done.[83] Reflecting this condition, the 1957 State of the Union Message promised a special communication on labor-management legislation, but it was a year before it was readied and delivered. In the meantime the McClellan Committee was giving exposure to dealings between labor and management, and practices in the conduct of union affairs, so flagrantly corrupt that a need for rigorously corrective legislation became increasingly apparent.

To some extent, Eisenhower's January 1958 proposals took account of this change in mood, but still not fully. For the most part, the new program merely carried over what had been asked for in 1954—an easing of the Taft-Hartley secondary boycott prohibition as it applied to "farmed out" work and to "on site" construction, and a closing of the "no-man's land" gap—but proposals were added to prohibit picketing in certain representational and organization disputes, to outlaw corrupt dealings between labor and management, or between their agents, and to require financial reports by unions.[84]

Congress also was acting timorously. It passed a Welfare and Pension Plan Disclosure Act that touched only tentatively on some of the most important issues under investigation and was silent on others. Eisenhower signed it with a statement critical of its deficiencies, saying that while it established a precedent of federal responsibility concerning the management by unions of welfare and pension funds it did "little else." Listing what he called "just some of the bill's shortcomings," he noted that the reports it required would be so summary as to permit concealing many of the abuses they were intended to reveal, that there was no assurance of uniform interpretation of the bill's many technical terms, that it was unrealistic to rely (as the bill did) on legal action by individual employees to compel compliance, that it gave the Secretary of Labor no "investigatory or enforcement powers," made no provision for "dealing directly with the most flagrant abuses [such as embezzlement and kickbacks] once they were uncovered," and appropriated no money to administer the custodial and other functions placed on the Secretary of Labor. In short, it would require "extensive amendment at the next session of Congress."[85]

As this rebuke reflected, Eisenhower's involvement in the effort to reform labor law, which at the outset had been not strongly assertive, had become sharply focused and determined. Giving expression to the reformist sentiment inspired by the McClellan Committee's findings, the White House served notice in the January 9, 1959 State of the Union Message that legislation would be proposed to "safeguard workers' funds in union treasuries," assure "free and secret elections of [union] officers," advance "true and responsible collective bargaining," and "protect the public and innocent third parties from unfair and coercive practices such as boycotting and blackmail picketing." Shortly thereafter (January 28, 1959), a 20-point legislative program to accomplish these purposes was put before Congress in a Special Message on Labor-Management Relations.[86] And in news conference remarks on April 29, July 22, and July 29, 1959, as well as in a radio-TV address on August 6 on "The Need For An Effective Labor Bill," the president stated that what the administration wanted was "a law to meet the kind of racketeering, corruption and abuses of power disclosed . . . by the Senate Investigating Committee headed by Senator McClellan."[87]

As Eisenhower's views were hardening, steps were being taken also on the Democratic side in Congress (inadequately, as it turned out) to meet the increasing demand for reform. These took shape in the introduction of a bill by Senator John F. Kennedy (D Mass.) designed to assure democratic procedures in the conduct of union affairs through periodic secret-ballot elections of union officials and, by stiffened requirements of disclosure, to stop the mismanagement of union funds.

Senator Kennedy's bill had no trouble being accepted in the Senate, and a broadly similar bill was voted out of the House Committee on Education and Labor, but at that point debate on the issues involved in it hardened significantly. Beginning in 1958 and continuing in 1959, the White House legislative liaison staff, working with like-minded members of the House, both Democrats and Republicans, had been maneuvering to have a bill prepared that would go further toward correcting the conditions disclosed by Senator McClellan's investigation and be more reflective of what were now the stiffened views of the president and of an increasing number of members of Congress. Accordingly, when the Kennedy bill reached the floor of the House, addressing some of Senator McClellan's questions but silent on the amendment of Taft-Hartley, there was an alternative ready to be substituted for it that covered both areas and had broad bipartisan sponsorship.

Introduced by Representatives Phil M. Landrum (D Ga.) and Robert P. Griffen (R Mich.), this alternative bill would amend Taft-Hartley along the lines favored by the White House

(close the no-man's land gap; close loopholes that had weakened Taft-Hartley's restraints on secondary boycotts; outlaw
the so-called "hot cargo" clauses of labor-management contracts that permitted actions akin to secondary boycotts; and
put certain curbs on organizational and recognition picketing).
At the same time, it would give effect in large measure to the
reforms that the McClellan Committee had shown were needed
in the conduct of union affairs, notably in the election of
officers, in the reporting and safekeeping of union finances, and
in the handling of funds held in trust for members. Ultimately
enacted by wide margins in both House and Senate, it was
signed by Eisenhower on September 14, 1959 as the Landrum-
Griffen Act. It remains a landmark in labor legislation.

Thus, from a cautious start in 1954, the broadening and
reform of labor legislation in the Eisenhower period ended in
1959 in a vigorous exercise of presidential leadership and in
important and lasting changes in labor law.

Working for Liberal Policies in Trade and Aid

Like other presidents who have worked for liberal policies in
trade and aid, Eisenhower did not win all the battles he fought
for them. But the losses were not due to any lack of zeal on his
part; indeed, his commitment to internationalism was second
only to his fervent national pride and patriotism.

His position on trade rested on two foundations: one economic and the other political. The economic foundation was
the familiar proposition that the world's work is done best, and
the benefits from it are distributed most equitably, when nations trade freely with one another on the basis of their com-
parative advantages. Eisenhower expressed it adequately
enough on one occasion by saying that a country "should buy
those things it doesn't produce so well and sell (those) in which
it has great efficiency." [88] The political foundation was his
belief that checking the spread of communism in the world
depended heavily on there being "an increased volume of
trade, with decreasing obstacles of all kinds," with the less-
developed countries participating fully in it.[89] Checking com-

munism's spread depended also on bolstering the military defenses of developing countries and helping them develop their economies. Because he regarded assistance to these ends as essential to the protection of U.S. interests in the world, he consistently referred to the measures that gave effect to it as constituting a program of "mutual security," and urged others to do likewise.[90] There was a characteristically strong statement in a May 1957 radio-TV address of the danger he saw in denying adequate funds to the aid program:

> [O]ur Communist antagonists are resourceful and cunning. Their aggression is not limited to the use of force or the threat of its use. They are doing their best to take advantage of poverty and need in developing nations, and so turn them against the free world. Success would enable them to win their long-sought goal of Communist encirclement of our country.[91]

Needless to say, there was no lack of opposition to what these views implied for trade and aid. Then as now, there were blocs in Congress (including not a few from what Eisenhower once referred to as the "ivory fringe" of the Republican Party) that were protectionist on trade, unhelpful on foreign aid, and skeptical of multilateralism in any form.[92] It was the same in the business community. As he wrote in his personal diary, there are

> industries, big and little . . . so concerned for their own particular immediate market and prosperity that they utterly fail to see that the United States cannot continue to live in a world where it must . . . export vast portions of its industrial and agricultural products unless it also imports a sufficiently great amount of foreign products to allow countries to pay for the surpluses they receive from us.[93]

Finally, there was an encrustation of tariffs and other obstacles to trade that had been built up over the years and that, because it could be reduced only at the risk of imposing hardships on industries that had expanded under its protection, made the liberalization of policy a difficult and politically sensitive undertaking. Eisenhower was a realist in facing these obstacles. At a February 25, 1959 news conference, for example, he reminded a questioner:

> We are [not] in an idealistic situation where you start, *de novo,* to solve a thing, you have to take the world as it now is . . . above everything else the United States should keep its cost down and try to liberalize trade.[94]

* * *

The first test of these principles came in 1953 when, unless Congress legislated otherwise, the Reciprocal Trade Agreements Act would expire on June 12. The law had been passed in 1934 as an emergency measure to promote economic recovery by spurring exports, but it had been extended repeatedly and, by 1953, had established itself as essentially the charter under which the United States joined with its Free World trading partners to keep tariffs and other obstacles to trade from rising and, whenever possible, to reduce them. It was not likely that Congress would let the law expire, but there was always the possibility that when it was extended the authority it gave to the president to negotiate tariff reductions would be lessened. From Eisenhower's viewpoint, an extension was needed on terms as favorable as possible. Lower tariffs would help carry forward the economic development that had been boosted in Western Europe and in other industrialized Free World countries by the Marshall Plan. They would do the same for less-developed countries.

Still, there could be hardships for U.S. industries affected by tariff reductions, and the protectionist sentiment that would be aroused by any indifference to this effect could not be ignored. Queried in one of his earliest news conferences on what this implied for trade policy, Eisenhower responded that "some kind of peril point or escape clause" would have to be continued in the Trade Agreements Act.[95] (The "peril point" provision authorized the Tariff Commission to specify a level below which the president could not exercise his authority to grant a tariff concession without giving Congress a written statement of his reasons; the "escape clause" provided that, following study and recommendation by the Tariff Commission, any concession made under the Trade Agreements Act could, at the president's discretion, be withdrawn or modified if it could be shown that serious injury to a domestic industry had been caused or was threatened.) To do so would provide a middle way between ignoring altogether the hardships that tariff liberalization might entail, which a full-fledged free trade position would propose, and raising the tariff barriers, which protectionism would call for.

*   *   *

There were two tests in 1953 of where the new administration would stand on these questions. The first involved an "escape clause" case, in which Eisenhower rejected a Tariff Commission recommendation which, if followed, would have reversed a previously negotiated reduction in the tariff on briar pipes. It was a small matter for the overall economy (a large matter, of course, for the producers of briar pipes), but for the world community it was a sign that the new administration's policies would be in the liberal tradition, directed toward the reduction of barriers to trade.

The second test, involving the Buy American Act, was concluded when Eisenhower accepted a Defense Department decision under which a contract to supply certain items of electrical equipment for a water-resources project (the Chief Joseph Dam) was divided between a British manufacturer and a U.S. company when it might have gone exclusively to the latter.[96] To have settled the question entirely in favor of the U.S. company would have been consistent with the recommendation of the Army Corps of Engineers, which was in charge of the project, and consistent with the way the act had to that time been administered. But it would have been a notorious setback for liberal trade policy.

There were special circumstances surrounding both these tests that, in the end, favored what was done, but the Buy American Act was in any case no favorite of Eisenhower's. He had said at a news conference after only three months into the presidency: "I personally have always felt that there should not be a rigid Buy-American Act, or anything of that nature."[97] In his view, questions dealt with under the act should be decided not by fixed and predetermined rules, as the legislation tended to encourage, but on a case-by-case basis, with the decisive consideration being what was judged to be in the "best interests of the United States." As he put it in the April 23, 1953 news conference:

> If the best interests of the United States require or seem to indicate a broader or better trade with someone else, then we should do that. And when the best interests of the United States demand some other action, we should follow that.

As the record shows, the "best interests of the United States" were more often than not found on the side of freer trade.

*   *   *

Although these 1953 tests were only minor skirmishes, they had a bearing on the main issue, which was whether the Trade Agreements Act would be extended and, if so, on what terms. Should it be extended "as is," which there was reason to believe could be accomplished but which would preserve the "escape clause" and "peril point" provisions that many wished to see removed, or should these provisions be challenged, which might result in the act not being extended at all?

As it happened, circumstances allowed the question to be passed for a time without debate: Eisenhower merely asked that the Act be extended for one year "as is," stating that to do so would "provide . . . the time necessary to study and define a foreign policy which [would] be comprehensive, constructive, and consistent with the needs both of the American economy and of American foreign policy."[98] To carry out the study, he proposed that Congress authorize a bipartisan commission, with members from both the legislative and executive branches of government, to determine how the laws bearing on tariffs and trade could be "modified or improved so as to achieve the highest possible levels of international trade without subjecting parts of our economy to sudden or serious strains."[99]

Congress acceded to these requests and a commission was

appointed, chaired by Clarence Randall, a prominent businessman. Less than a year later (January 23, 1954), it delivered its report; though spotted with dissents on particular points, it was strongly supportive of a liberal trade policy. Two months later (March 30, 1954), Eisenhower had proposals for Congress shaped largely after the Randall Commission's recommendations. These would extend the Trade Agreements Act for three years, not for one; continue the "escape clause" and "peril point" provisions without change; increase the president's authority to make tariff cuts in exchange for reductions by other countries; exempt from the provisions of the Buy American Act bidders from nations that treated U.S. companies equally with their own nationals; increase the duty-free tourist allowances to $1,000, exercisable every six months; and make certain changes in the tax laws to promote U.S. investment abroad. In addition, Congress was notified that the General Agreement on Tariffs and Trade (GATT) would be renegotiated, looking to improvements in its administration, and that proposals would be made later relating to customs simplification, the international aspects of U.S. minerals policy, and Merchant Marine policy.

Anticipating resistance, assurances were given in a news conference directly after the program was submitted to Congress that the authority to cut tariffs would be used with consideration for the impact that reductions might have on U.S. industry. But no secret was made of the intention to move toward freer trade. The president stated:

> The government . . . will take such steps as are necessary to prevent adjustment hardships from becoming widespread or severe. But that there will be some adjustments of that kind is, of course, inevitable.
> I do believe that in this day and time the free world must . . . realize that in an expanding, healthy, two-way trade lies our best insurance that the doctrines of statism [do not] overcome our whole idea of free government.[100]

Predictably, Congress was cool to even the modest liberalizing that the proposals contemplated, and Eisenhower came away with less than he asked for. In deference to the desire of

Congress to hold hearings on the act before extending it for more than a year, he agreed to an extension of one year rather than three. And while it was a disappointment that the authority to make reciprocal tariff reductions was not increased, it was a victory that it was not diminished, as many in Congress would have liked. Finally, Congress made it explicit that its willingness to have the legislation extended implied neither approval nor disapproval of U.S. participation in GATT. Never having accepted President Truman's theory that GATT had been entered into under presidential authority implicit in the Trade Agreements Act, and therefore did not need ratification, Congress went out of its way whenever extending the law to say that the extension it was granting did not signify its recognition of the agreement.

*   *   *

The one-year extension made it necessary, of course, to return to the Trade Agreements Act in 1955. In doing so, the White House repeated its 1954 recommendations (a three-year extension of the law; increases in the president's authority to reduce tariffs when other countries made reciprocal reductions; and certain changes in the tax laws to promote U.S. investment abroad) and added a new proposal that was bound to meet stiff opposition. Congress was asked to authorize U.S. membership in an Organization for Trade Cooperation (OTC) which was being set up (by multilateral action) to provide "a continuous mechanism for the administration of the [GATT] trade rules and the discussion of mutual trade problems."[101]

The outcome was again only a partial success. The three-year extension was granted, with the usual disclaimer that it implied neither approval nor disapproval of GATT. The president's authority to negotiate for tariff reductions was continued, but not entirely as requested (unused portions of the authority to cut tariffs could not be carried over from one year to the next). And it was made somewhat easier for relief to be obtained under the "escape clause" and "peril point" provisions. Membership in OTC was denied. On balance, Congress had taken a step toward trade restriction.

*   *   *

It was evident by 1957, and especially as the economy moved in that year into recession, that when it became necessary again to seek extension of the Trade Agreements Act the resistance would be stiffer than before. With this in mind, consideration was given to a plan designed to cushion any negative impact of trade liberalization on U.S. industry. It would give financial assistance to industries able to show serious injury from increases in imports attributable to tariff reduction.

To have put such a plan before Congress (it had been rejected by the Randall Commission) would undoubtedly have helped achieve the act's extension, and that course was advocated strongly by John Foster Dulles, Secretary of State. But Eisenhower decided not to do so, on the ground that the contemplated relief would be difficult to administer fairly and without considerable waste and that the availability of financial assistance would merely delay adjustments in industry and commerce that in the end would have to be made. As an alternative, it was proposed that corrective action that could be taken under the act's "escape clause" be strengthened.[102]

Obviously, there was a concession in this to protectionist sentiment, but the "escape clause," carefully and conservatively administered, was felt to be a better way of providing relief to injured industries than a program under which they would be entitled to a grant of federal funds. At the same time, it was requested that the Trade Agreements Act be extended for five years (to avoid having it expire before Western European countries had a chance to complete their "common tariff" arrangements), that additional authority be granted to the president to negotiate under GATT for further tariff reductions, and (repeating the earlier request) that the United States be authorized to participate in the OTC, with the understanding that doing so would not diminish the extent of any tariff concessions obtained through GATT.[103]

As described by an ad hoc private group organized to work for liberal trade policies, the response was "the most highly protectionist measure ever passed by Congress in all the reciprocal trade renewals since 1934."[104] The Trade Agreements Act was extended for four years, not five. Restraints were put

on presidential authority to cut tariffs by a provision that allowed Congress to override the president's rejection of a Tariff
Commission "escape clause" finding if it could obtain a two-
thirds vote in both House and Senate. And the time the Tariff
Commission was authorized to take to study "escape clause"
and "peril point" questions was standardized at six months.
OTC membership was again denied.

On this note ended what had been for six years one of
Eisenhower's principal legislative efforts. In several respects,
ground was lost. But, considering the protectionist sentiment in
Congress, which was all the time on the rise, to have held
ground on key positions was no small success.[105] The Trade
Agreements Act was still in place. U.S. participation in GATT
was still intact. Substantial authority to reduce tariffs was still
available to the president. And the difficulty of mustering a two-
thirds vote in both House and Senate to overturn an "escape
clause" finding by the president made it unlikely that such an
effort would succeed.

*   *   *

Obtaining funds from Congress for mutual security programs
was an equally difficult struggle. To many of its critics, foreign
aid was a "give away"; to Eisenhower, it was not only warranted on humanitarian grounds but, as already indicated, was
essential to the nation's military defense and vital to the future
of democratic institutions in the world. When he asked Congress in 1953 for $5.8 billion for this purpose, he said of the
request:

> In my judgment, it represents a careful determination of our
> essential needs [in fiscal 1954] in pursuing the policy of collec-
> tive security in a world not yet freed of the threat of totalitarian
> conquest.
>
> Unequivocally I can state that this amount of money judi-
> ciously spent abroad will add much more to our Nation's ulti-
> mate security in the world than would an even greater amount
> spent merely to increase the size of our military forces in being.
>
> Were the United States to fail to carry out these purposes,
> the free world would become disunited at a moment of great
> peril. . . .

This is the way best to defend successfully ourselves and the cause of freedom.[106]

And of the funds requested for economic and technical assistance the message stated:

> Through these programs, the United States is proving its interest in helping the peoples of these areas [South and Southeast Asia, the Middle East, Latin America, and Africa] to work toward better and more hopeful conditions of life, to strengthen the foundations of opportunity and freedom. To guard against the external military threat is not enough: we must also move against those conditions exploited by subversive forces from within.

It was commonplace in Washington circles in the 1950s to criticize Eisenhower's foreign aid proposals as inadequate, but the reality was that Congress regularly regarded them as excessive, voted less money for them than he asked for, and made it repeatedly necessary for him to go to the program's defense. There was an example of this in his response to a July 22, 1953 news conference question (noting that Congress had cut a billion dollars from his request) in which he was asked whether the program could "operate successfully under these circumstances." He replied:

> I have been around the fringes, at least, of this problem for a long time. I have never looked upon what we now call MSA as giveaway programs . . . I put it right square alongside our own security program, because I think that is exactly where it belongs.
> We are looking at the position of the United States in the free world, its ability to establish collective security, which means its [the U.S.'s] own security; and those two should be viewed together.
> So . . . when we go at that program, I don't think merely of how much are we cutting here and there; how are we affecting the security and the position of the United States of America, that is the way I look at it . . . I think, and I have been doing a lot of studying on it, I think that cut is too heavy.[107]

It was of course also necessary to press these views directly on individual members of Congress. In one such effort, only a day after the news conference cited above, a letter was dispatched to Senator Bridges (R NH.), chairman of the Senate Appropriations Committee and no friend of foreign aid, urging his support for the program and stating: "This, of all times, is not a moment to hesitate."[108]

There was, nevertheless, a good deal of hesitation. There were questions in Congress on what conditions should be placed on the expenditure of funds (Should military aid to Western European countries be made contingent on their ratification of a European Defense Community Treaty?), even on setting dates for terminating the program. In the end, conditions that would seriously limit its effectiveness were avoided, and after the White House had reduced its request to $5.5 billion, a total of $5.157 billion was authorized.

*   *   *

Congress continued in 1955 and 1956 to deal with the aid programs in the same questioning and essentially niggardly manner as before. Then, in 1957, in an attempt to circumvent what to that time had been the principal obstacles to getting a fair hearing for his proposals (the necessity of having every year to prove the program's worth, and the practice of considering requests for military aid separate from what was requested for the Defense Department), Eisenhower proposed a number of fundamental, even radical, reforms in how the annual budget request should be handled.

- Requests for military aid funds would be separated from requests for economic assistance and handled as an integral part of the Defense Department budget.

- Military aid would be handled on a "continuing authorization" basis, as the Defense Department's budget always had been; dealt with in this way it would not be necessary each year to defend the program's existence, just as it was not necessary each year to reconfirm the Defense Department's right to exist; one would have to defend only the amount of money being asked for; the same "continuing authorization" basis was requested for programs providing economic and technical aid.

- A Development Loan Fund (DLF) was requested which would make it possible to substitute loans for grants in carrying out much of what was done to promote economic development in recipient countries; as a banking agency, DLF would of necessity have to operate on a continuing basis, and that status was requested.

- "Special assistance" funds, which were for activities not of a continuing nature, would be handled as a separate category and authorized annually.[109]

It is hard to see why foreign aid programs were ever conducted differently than as proposed in these recommendations, but there were many in Congress who did not believe in foreign aid as a continuing activity of the US government, and when Congress had finished its work on the 1957 request Eisenhower had been rebuffed on most of what he had asked for. A Development Loan Fund was created (made responsible to the president, not to the International Cooperation Administration, as had been requested) but little else of what had been asked for was granted. The request to draw a distinction between military and economic assistance was refused. The proposal to put continuing programs on a continuing authorization basis was turned down. And the amount of money appropriated fell short of what had been requested by about a billion dollars.

Thus, mutual security was left in 1960 substantially as it had been found in 1953—a misunderstood, underfunded, and often maligned activity, with not more than a one-year's hold on life.

*   *   *

Fortunately, there was more success in dealing with the need that emerged during the Eisenhower years to increase the resources of the International Monetary Fund (IMF) and the International Bank for Reconstruction and Development

(IBRD). Congress was asked in 1959 for large additional sub-scriptions to the capital of each of these institutions.[110]

As already noted, making a large contribution to the IMF in 1959 was inconvenient in two important respects. It called for a $344 million transfer of gold when the nation's gold supply was already being depleted from balance of payments causes; and it increased fiscal 1959 budget expenditures by $1.375 billion when the deficit for that period was already destined to be large as a result of the 1957–58 recession. The gold transfer may well have contributed to the Federal Reserve's disposition to keep a tight rein on the use of credit, when any encouragement to do the opposite would have been helpful; and the impact on the budget increased the size of the swing from deficit in fiscal 1959 to surplus in fiscal 1960 for which the administration was later severely (in my view wrongly) criticized. Fortunately, the com-mitment to the IBRD, which was much larger ($3.175 billion) than the subscription to IMF capital, required neither a transfer of gold nor an immediate charge against the budget. Despite the ramifications, both commitments were initiated and supported strongly by the White House. Both were authorized by Con-gress.

*   *   *

There are of course many standpoints from which Eisenhower's record of foreign economic policy can be judged, but judged by what happened during his presidency to the volume of world trade and investment the results were outstan-dingly favorable. It has been estimated that world trade dou-bled in nominal terms between 1950 and 1960, an increase that would average at least 5 percent a year after adjustment for inflation. And the trade deficits that had cropped up in the late 1950s were eliminated. At the same time, several new agencies were added to the roster of those available to help finance economic development in the less-developed areas of the world. The International Finance Corporation (IFC) was set up in 1955 as an IBRD affiliate to make loans that would not qualify under that agency's regular lending program; the De-velopment Loan Fund was formed in 1957 to make loans as part of the Mutual Security Agency program; the Inter-American Agency was established in 1959 to "facilitate the flow of public and private capital to economic development in [the American] hemisphere and . . . [to] supplement existing lending arrangements"; and the Internatonal Development Agency (IDA, an IBRD affiliate) was set up, also in 1959, to make "soft loans" for development purposes on a multilateral basis. In addition, the 1950s witnessed a significant expansion in private foreign investment, with U.S. companies in the lead. As remarked earlier, it was the decade in which the true internationalizing of American business began.[111]

The record is not, however, without setbacks. As every president following Eisenhower has found, it was at times necessary to accept the expedient of voluntary export restraints, regrettable as that was, to avoid the more objectionable protective measures—import quotas, in particular—that Congress would otherwise almost certainly have mandated.

It goes without saying that what was accomplished cannot be attributed exclusively to Eisenhower's personal efforts, nor even to the combined efforts of his administration. But that his attention and support helped bring them about is clearly not in doubt; indeed, there is not the slightest chance that they could have been won without personal involvement of the type the president gave to the effort. The tariff reductions achieved during his presidency were not the largest in the post-World War II years, but they were substantial, averaging about 15 percent on tariffs reduced in the 1955–56 round of GATT negotiations compared to reductions estimated at 26 percent and 20 percent, respectively, in the 1950–51 and 1960–62 rounds. The Buy American Act was not administered in the manner of casting gauntlets before an increasingly protectionist Congress, as some might have preferred, but it was applied in an evenhanded way and less restrictively than before. And the stability of the U.S. dollar on the foreign exchanges, on which Eisenhower placed great stress, was preserved. Considering the circumstances of the time, including the persistent unreadiness of Congress to follow Eisenhower's leadership, it is hard to visualize a context more conducive to the increase of international trade and investment than was achieved in these years.

On the political side, however, with regard specifically to Eisenhower's goal of promoting democratic institutions in the less-developed areas of the world, the results were far below what he had hoped for. It is by no means certain that there would have been greater success had Congress been more willing to follow Eisenhower's lead, but its general reluctance to do so was undoubtedly a factor contributing to the disappointments which abound in this area of the record.

Notes

1. *Public Papers, DDE, 1960–61*, p. 562.

2. Adams, *Firsthand Report,* pp. 204 and 218. A newspaper account of the Kasson speech (*The Wall Street Journal,* September 8, 1952, p. 1) reported that "unexpectedly lavish" promises were made by both candidates. What Eisenhower said was open to the "golden promise" interpretation that was quickly put on it, but when a question at his January 27, 1954 news conference implied that he had done more than merely promise to abide by the farm price-support laws then on the books and in the meantime develop an alternative program he challenged the questioner to find evidence in the campaign speeches that he had done so. Had any been found he would surely have been confronted with it but the subject did not arise again, at least not in press conferences. The Kasson speech is in the *Adams Papers,* Box 6, the George F. Baker Library, Dartmouth College, Hanover, New Hampshire. There are comments by Eisenhower on the problem of developing and winning enactment of an adequate farm program in *The White House Years,* Vol. I, pp. 287–90, in *Public Papers, DDE,* 1954, pp. 206 and 571–72, and in *Public Papers, DDE,* 1955, pp. 465–66. Also, there are comments relevant to the issue in Professor Don Paarlberg's Columbia University Oral History interview, in the Butler Library of Columbia University, New York, New York.

3. Loan balances outstanding and commodities in storage under CCC ownership fluctuated widely, but the trend of both was up and the cost to the budget was immense. With farm prices falling in 1953 from highs reached during the Korean Conflict and with farm operating costs tending to rise, the CCC extended $2.1 billion of loans in fiscal 1953 and the outlays for "agriculture and agricultural resources," of which the CCC accounted for about two-thirds, came to nearly $3

billion, constituting 17 percent of all budget outlays other than those for national security and interest on the public debt (*Historical Statistics,* Part 1, p. 488 and *Budget of the United States for the Fiscal Year Ending June 30, 1955,* p. M33).

4. The July 20, 1953 White House statement announcing establishment of the National Agricultural Advisory Commission is in *Abilene Papers,* Official File, Box 916. The January 1954 proposals were put before Congress in a Special Message (*Public Papers, DDE,* 1954, pp. 23–39).

5. *Public Papers, DDE,* p. 528.

6. *Historical Statistics,* Part 1, Series K330–343, p. 488.

7. The Acerage Reserve is such an ostensibly reasonable idea that it is every now and then reinvented, only to have its weaknesses soon rediscovered. Its attraction is that it holds out the possibility of "using surpluses to reduce surpluses;" that is, commodities already in CCC stocks would be sold to raise the cash needed to redeem certificates given to the farmers who, as participants in the program, agree to cut back cultivation. Its weakness is that the cropland remaining under cultivation is typically used more intensively than anticipated, causing supply to be reduced by less than the expected amount. In the Conservation Reserve, on the other hand, the farmer not only consents to a reduction in the amount of cropland to be cultivated but undertakes to carry out soil and water conservation for a specified period on the set-aside land. Federal funds help meet the cost of transferring land from one use to another for a period long enough to establish the new use. The proposals are described in *Public Papers, DDE,* 1956, pp. 42–62 and in *The White House Years,* Vol. I, pp. 557–63. There are discussions of the Rural Development Program in the Columbia University Oral History Project interviews of True D. Morse, who had principal responsibility for it as Under Secretary of Agriculture, and Professor Don Paarlberg, one of its principal architects. The Annual Report of the program is in *Abilene Papers,* Official File, Box 501.

8. *Eisenhower Diaries,* pp. 217–18.

9. Texts of the veto message and the radio/TV address are in *Public Papers, DDE,* 1956, pp. 385–99.

10. *CQ Almanac,* 1956, p. 391.

11. *Public Papers, DDE,* 1958, pp. 100–107.

12. *Public Papers, DDE,* 1958, p. 251.

13. *CQ Almanac,* 1958, p. 271.

14. The veto messages (one on wheat, the other on tobacco) are in *Public Papers, DDE,* 1959, pp. 476–79.

15. *Public Papers, DDE,* 1960–61, pp. 162–65 and 388–89.

16. *Public Papers, DDE,* 1960–61, pp. 701–02.

17. *Public Papers, DDE,* 1960–61, pp. 922–24.

18. *Public Papers, DDE,* 1960–61, p. 621.

19. Adams, *Firsthand Report,* pp. 202–19.

20. *The White House Years,* Vol. I, p. 563.

21. Eisenhower registered his admiration for FHA's accomplishments at a dinner celebrating the twenty-fifth anniversary of its founding. His remarks are in *Public Papers, DDE,* 1959, pp. 470–72.

22. *HHFA Annual Report,* 1952, pp. 72–83 and the January 1954 *Budget Message,* p. M65.

23. *Abilene Papers,* Official Files, Box 612. There is an indispensable account of how thinking on problems of housing and home finance developed prior to and immediately after Eisenhower's election in Miles L. Colean's contribution to the Columbia University Oral History Project. The full text of the interview was published by the Mortgage Bankers Association of America in 1975 under the title, *A Backward Glance* (see pp. 100–104, especially).

24. January 1954 *Budget Message,* pp. M64–M69, and the Special Message to the Congress on Housing, January 25, 1954 (*Public Papers, DDE,* 1954, pp. 193–201). The initial cabinet presentation on housing proposals (December 9, 1953) is in the *Abilene Papers,* Cabinet Series, Box 2.

25. The plan was to establish a new FHA insurance program under which a family displaced from its home by public action—for example, by an urban renewal project—could obtain a loan on a preferentially-liberal basis to buy a new or rehabilitated private dwelling outside the development area. Also, the terms available on FHA-insured loans to buy existing structures would be made comparable with those available on loans to buy newly-constructed homes (they were less liberal at the time), and FHA would be authorized to make home repair and modernization loans in larger individual amounts and for longer repayment periods than formerly.

26. In the title of his book, *The Federal Bulldozer* (Massachusetts Institute of Technology Press, Cambridge, 1964; reprinted by McGraw-Hill, New York, 1967).

27. *Public Papers, DDE,* 1954, pp. 648–49. The 1954 legislative outcome and the administration's reactions to it are reported at length in *CQ Almanac,* 1954, p. 205.

28. *CQ Almanac,* 1955, pp. 253–58.

29. *Public Papers, DDE,* 1955, p. 779.

30. *Public Papers, DDE,* 1959, pp. 503–6.

31. *Public Papers, DDE,* 1959, pp. 639–41.

32. Edward Berkowitz and Kim McQuaid, "Welfare Reform in the 1950s," *Social Service Review,* March 1980. pp. 450–58.

33. Eisenhower spoke many times supportively of programs to help sustain individual and family income against interruptions (retirement, illness, unemployment) but also stressed the need to provide

216   THE US ECONOMY UNDER EISENHOWER

insurance under plans that were actuarially and financially sound. For examples of this see his August 23, 1954 radio-TV address (*Public Papers, DDE*, 1954, pp. 746–56), the October 8, 1954 speech at Denver, Colorado (*Public Papers, DDE*, 1954, pp. 892–99), and the September 30, 1954 letter to W. Earl Shaefer, a business acquaintance (*Abilene Papers*, DDE Diary Series, Box 8).

34. *Abilene Papers*, DDE Diary Series, Box 8.

35. *The White House Years*, Vol. I, pp. 441–42.

36. Coverage would be extended to "self-employed farmers; many more farm workers and domestic workers than are now covered; doctors, dentists, lawyers, architects, accountants and other professional people; members of many state and local retirement systems on a voluntary group basis; clergymen on a voluntary group basis and several other smaller groups" (Special Message to the Congress Transmitting Proposed Changes in the Social Security Program, *Public Papers, DDE*, 1953, pp. 534–36).

37. *Public Papers, DDE*, 1954, pp. 801–02.

38. Changes in line with White House recommendations included an extension of OASI coverage to 600,000 additional owners or operators of farms and about 225,000 self-employed lawyers, dentists, and others; an increase in federal funds to encourage better medical care for needy aged, blind, or disabled persons and for dependent children; grants to train social workers and to support research on ways to help people overcome dependency; and increased funds for child welfare programs (*Public Papers, DDE*, 1956, pp. 638–39).

39. *Public Papers, DDE*, 1956, p. 636. Governor Adams wrote of this legislation in an August 23, 1956 letter that there was "no question but the disability provisions of the bill were bad" and that the administration had opposed them "from the beginning." But, as Adams pointed out, the bill contained much of what the president had asked for and he was in no position to veto it (*Abilene Papers*, Office File, Box 84).

40. *CQ Almanac*, 1958, p. 157.

41. *Public Papers, DDE*, 1958, pp. 661–62.

42. The original intent in most states was to pay 50 percent of earnings, but most laws were written with a maximum dollar amount in them, and as wages rose with the ceiling unchanged benefits dropped below 50 percent. The administration's proposals were summarized in the *January 1954 Economic Report*, pp. 96–99.

43. See, for example, his June 2, 1949 letter to General Paul Hawley in *Eisenhower Papers*, Vol. X, no. 442.

44. *Public Papers, DDE*, 1954, p. 70.

45. *Public Papers, DDE*, 1960–61, p. 367.

46. *Public Papers, DDE*, 1954, pp. 632–33.

47. *Public Papers, DDE*, 1954, p. 941.

48. *Report of the Health Care Financing Administration* (Bureau of Debt Management and Strategy, U.S. Government Printing Office, Washington, D.C.)

49. *Eisenhower Diaries*, p. 154.

50. *Eisenhower Papers*, Vol. X, no. 208. The response was to a letter from the late R. Gordon Wasson, a former Columbia College instructor and distinguished New Yorker who was a leading investment banker, a trustee of Barnard College, and a great friend of the university.

51. The Gwinn letter is in *Eisenhower Papers*, Vol. X, no. 445.

52. *Public Papers, DDE*, 1957, p. 651.

53. *Public Papers, DDE*, 1958, p. 601.

54. *Historical Statistics*, Part 1, Series A-31, p. 10 and the *January 1960 Economic Report*, Table C-22, p. 141.

55. *Public Papers, DDE*, 1954, pp. 151–52.

56. *Public Papers, DDE*, 1955, pp. 243–50.

57. *Public Papers, DDE*, 1956, pp. 63–71.

58. *Public Papers, DDE*, 1957, pp. 89–93.

59. *Historical Statistics*, Part 1, Series H-499, p. 373 and the *January 1960 Economic Report*, Table C-22, p. 141.

60. *Public Papers, DDE*, 1958, pp. 127–32.

61. *Public Papers, DDE*, 1958, p. 671.

62. Following a July 2, 1954 report to the cabinet by Governor Stassen that dealt with areas of the country experiencing special economic difficulty, Eisenhower directed that studies on federal aid to such areas would be made at the CEA (*Adams Papers*, Cabinet Series, Box 6).

Subsequently (October 14, 1955), a presentation on area-development proposals was made to the cabinet by Dr. Burns (*Abilene Papers*, Cabinet Series, Box 6). There were divergent views about the proposals and Eisenhower requested more work on them. The 1956 State of the Union Message stated that legislation dealing with "pockets of chronic unemployment" would be high on the year's agenda, as it was.

63. There is a good statement of his views on how the problem should be dealt with in the May 3, 1960 Special Message to Congress on the Legislative Program (*Public Papers, DDE*, 1960–61, pp. 391–92).

64. The 1956 proposals and the principles underlying them are set out in some detail in the *January 1956 Economic Report*, pp. 61–63.

65. *CQ Almanac*, 1956, pp. 517–19.

66. It is not unprecedented for Congress to balk at assigning a new function to the Department of Commerce, even when the task, as

in this case, is within the department's basic mandate. Eisenhower's "Memorandum of Disapproval" is in *Public Papers, DDE,* 1958, pp. 690–91.

67. The Cooper letter is in *Public Papers, DDE,* 1960–61, pp. 18–21. Detailed accounts of aid available to communities for development purposes were given in the April 20 and May 1, 1960 reports of the Interdepartmental Committee to Coordinate Federal Urban Area Assistance, referred to in *Public Papers, DDE,* 1960–61, p. 469.

68. Special Message to the Congress on the Legislative Program, May 3, 1960 (*Public Papers, DDE,* 1960–61, especially pp. 391–92).

69. *Public Papers, DDE,* 1960–61, p. 413. The veto message is in the same volume, pp. 417–20.

70. *Public Papers, DDE,* 1960–61, pp. 617–18.

71. Eisenhower's June 1, 1956 letter establishing the Cabinet Committee on Small Business expressed his feeling for the small company as a "dynamic influence" in the economy (*Public Papers, DDE,* 1956, 547–48). So also did his July 15, 1957 letter to the House Ways and Means Committee endorsing Cabinet Committee proposals for changes that would assist small firms (*Public Papers, DDE,* 1957, pp. 538–44) and his remarks to the Conference on Technical and Distribution Research for the Benefit of Small Business, held in Washington under the Cabinet Committee's sponsorshp on September 24–25, 1957 (*Public Papers, DDE,* 1957, pp. 686–88).

72. *Third Progress Report of the Cabinet Committee on Small Business* (U.S. Government Printing Office, Washington, D.C., December 16, 1960), pp. 2–3.

73. *1967 Supplement to Statistical Indicators,* (U.S. Government Printing Office, Washington, D.C., 1967), p. 123.

74. David Gumpert and Jeffrey Timmons, *The Insider's Guide to Small Business Resources* (Garden City, N.Y., Doubleday, 1962), p. 178, and the *Annual Report of the Small Business Administration, 1979* (U.S. Government Printing Office, Washington, D.C. 1979).

75. Not everyone agreed that government should give a preference in the bidding process to any one category of companies, and doing so did indeed conflict with Eisenhower's basic position regarding competition. But the exception was deliberate, believing as he did that to keep opportunities open for small companies had important beneficial side effects for the whole economy. The *Third Progress Report of the Cabinet Committee on Small Business* (December 16, 1960, pp. 4–10) describes what was done.

76. The *Second Progress Report of the Cabinet Commitee on Small Business* (December 31, 1958, pp. 8–10) relates how the conference came to be undertaken, gives the recommendations that came from it, and identifies the persons who (on a volunteer basis) were

principally responsible for planning its agenda and seeing it to completion.

77. The *Third Progress Report of the Cabinet Committee on Small Business*, December 16, 1960, pp. 13–14.

78. On Eisenhower's uncertainty regarding "right to work" laws, see his January 18, 1954 letter to Lewis W. Douglas (*Abilene Papers, DDE, Diary Series, Box 5*) and his responses to news conference questions on May 5 and December 15, 1954 (*Public Papers, DDE, 1954,* pp. 454–55 and 1105–6).

79. Adams, *Firsthand Report,* p. 7.

80. *Abilene Papers,* Cabinet Series, minutes of the December 15, 1953 meeting.

81. At the bottom of this incident there appears to have been a misunderstanding between Secretary Durkin and the president regarding the function of a cabinet officer. See *The White House Years,* Vol. I, pp. 196–99 and Adams, *Firsthand Report,* pp. 300–304. The Adams Papers (Box 8) contain a number of documents on disagreements between the Departments of Labor and Commerce relating to Taft-Hartley.

82. Recommendations to Congress were presented in Eisenhower's Special Message to Congress on Labor-Management Relations, January 11, 1954 (*Public Papers, DDE,* 1954, pp. 40–44). A September 11, 1953 letter from Eisenhower to his brother Arthur stated that Senator Taft, before illness disabled him, indicated his agreement with most of what the administration was proposing in regard to amendment of the Taft-Hartley law. Taft's residual questions had to do with secondary boycotts and "right to work" laws, about which he conceded he was himself uncertain (*Abilene Papers, DDE Diary Series, Ann Whitman File, Box 3*).

83. Minutes of the May 10, 1957 cabinet meeting show that Secretary Mitchell had little enthusiasm for what the McClellan Committee was doing, preferring instead that the administration's legislative program concentrate on the subject (it was less controversial) of protecting funds held in trust by union management for union members. Eisenhower's preference, on the other hand, was evolving toward legislation that would deal directly and severely with the abuses that the McClellan Committee was exposing.

84. *Public Papers, DDE,* 1958, pp. 118–24.

85. *Public Papers, DDE,* 1958, pp. 663–64.

86. *Public Papers, DDE,* 1959, pp. 143–46.

87. *Public Papers, DDE,* 1959, pp. 349, 543 and 551.

88. *Public Papers, DDE,* 1959, p. 215.

89. *Eisenhower Diaries,* p. 249.

90. *The White House Years,* Vol. II, 133–36. One of Eisenhower's

friends, and a frequent correspondent, suggested that "two-way trade, not one-way aid" would be a better phrase than "trade not aid" (*Abilene Papers,* Name Series, Box 31, letter from George Sloan, March 26, 1953), but Eisenhower never viewed aid as a one-way relationship.

91. *Public Papers, DDE,* 1957, p. 350.

92. *Eisenhower Diaries,* p. 249.

93. *Eisenhower Diaries,* p. 244.

94. *Public Papers, DDE,* 1959, p. 215.

95. *Public Papers, DDE,* 1953, p. 65.

96. A first round of bids was turned down on the ground that the specifications needed to be amended. In subsequent bidding, awards were made to both U.S. and U.K. suppliers. Moreover, an Executive Order was issued in December 1954 specifying that the extent to which a U.S. supplier's bid could exceed that of a foreign supplier without being held "unreasonable" would be reduced to 6 and 10 percent (in two types of cases) from the 25 percent that had previously been standard practice. On these incidents see *The White House Years,* Vol. I, pp. 208–211 and Appendix D. Also, there are tracks of Buy American Act discussions in minutes of the cabinet meetings on April 3 and 10 and June 5, 1953 (*Abilene Papers,* Cabinet Series). Eisenhower's March 26, 1953 letter to George Sloan (*Abilene Papers,* Name Series, Box 31) is also relevant.

97. Publc Papers, DDE, 1953, p. 202.

98. Special Message to the Congress Recommending the Renewal of the Reciprocal Trade Agreements Act, April 7, 1953 (*Public Papers, DDE,* 1953, p. 165).

99. Letter to the President of the Senate and the Speaker of the House of Representatives Recommending Establishment of a Commission on Foreign Economic Policy, May 2, 1953 (*Public Papers, DDE,* 1953, pp. 252–54).

100. *Public Papers, DDE,* 1954, p. 365.

101. Special Message to the Congress (*Public Papers, DDE,* 1955, pp. 32–40 and 393–99).

102. The change consisted of shifting backward to July 1, 1934 from July 1, 1954 the base above which the president was authorized to lift tariff rates by as much as 50 percent. Since tariffs were in most cases higher in 1934 than in 1954, the effect was to increase the corrective action that could be taken at the president's discretion.

103. The OTC request was made to Congress on April 3, 1957 (*Public Papers, DDE,* 1957, pp. 283–41) and extension of the Trade Agreements Act was requested in a January 30, 1958 Special Message (*Public Papers, DDE,* 1958, pp. 132–35). Details of the White House requests are in the *January 1958 Economic Report,* pp. 70–72. The legislative history is in *CQ Almanac,* 1958, pp. 165–82.

104. *CQ Almanac,* 1958, p. 175.
105. Eisenhower's efforts in 1958 on behalf of his legislative program on international trade included a speech on March 27 to the National Conference on International Trade Policy (an ad hoc citizens group organized to support the administration's program), remarks on May 6 to the Advertising Council, a letter on June 10 to the Chairman of the House Ways and Means Committee protesting (as a "tragic blunder") proposals that would let Congress override the president in "escape clause" decisions and thus (in effect) give final authority in these matters to the Tariff Commission, and remarks on trade policy in a July 9 address to the Canadian House of Parliament (*Public Papers, DDE,* 1958, pp. 132–35, 243–50, 461–63 and 529–37).
106. *Public Papers, DDE,* 1953, p. 259.
107. *Public Papers, DDE,* 1953, p. 508.
108. *Public Papers, DDE,* 1953, p. 513.
109. Special Message to the Congress on the Mutual Security Programs, May 21, 1957 (*Public Papers, DDE,* 1957, pp. 372–85).
110. Special Message to Congress on Increasing the Resources of the International Bank for Reconstruction and Development and the International Monetary Fund, February 12, 1959 (*Public Papers, DDE,* 1959, pp. 184–88). Also, the *January 1959 Budget Message,* pp. M40–M43.
111. Estimates of world trade are from the National Industrial Conference Board *Economic Almanac, 1967–68,* p. 510. Data on U.S. trade and foreign investment are from the *National Income and Product Accounts of the United States, 1929–74* (U.S. Government Printing Office, Washington, D.C.), Tables 1.1 and 1.2, and *Historical Statistics,* Part 2, Series U-27, p. 869. Estimates of tariff reduction are from John W. Evans, *The Kennedy Round in American Trade Policy* (*Harvard University Press, Cambridge, 1971*), p. 12.

VI. Assessing the Record

Interest is always high in assessing how a president has performed in office, and especially in comparing records among presidents, but making such assessments in a fair and analytically acceptable manner is not easy. There is first of all the difficulty of being objective about a question on which the analyst will almost certainly have some already settled views. And there are technical considerations that will prevent the conclusions from ever being entirely definitive. Thus, how should credit or blame be divided between the president and Congress, or between the president and the Federal Reserve System, when both Congress and the Federal Reserve have the power to set policies independently of the president that can be decisive in determining whether his programs succeed or fail, and on occasion do so? And how does one adjust for features of the economic environment that bear importantly on how the economy performs but over which the president has little or no control, and which can vary enormously from one presidential period to another? For example, did the president's term begin at the peak of a business cycle or at a trough, or at some intermediate point? Was the country going into war, with defense expenditures rising, or was it, as under Eisenhower, making its way from war to peace, with military spending on the way down? Was the president faced at the beginning of his term with the task of bringing the inflation rate down, or was he spared from having to undertake that normally growth-retarding and unpopular exercise? Similarly, what was the condition of the federal budget and of the nation's international economic and financial accounts when he came to the White House, and what was it when he left?

Clearly, no assessment of a president's economic record, whether made on a judgmental basis, as is mine, or on the rigorously-structured statistical basis that is increasingly the style, can claim to have adjusted fully for these and other such complications. All that can be said for the assessment that follows is that it looks at the Eisenhower record from all points of view thought to be relevant and material, stays as close as possible to verifiable facts, and judges it according to what seems fair and analytically correct. As with all presidencies, there were minuses as well as pluses in the record. First, the minuses.

● *There were three recessions.*
Although the president is far more narrowly limited in what can be done about the ups and downs of the business cycle than is commonly recognized, nothing in the usual presidential experience matches recession for blighting the economic record. Accordingly, doing all that can be done to prevent or to moderate recession will have a high priority in every president's program. Certainly it did in Eisenhower's. His administration initiated the systematic use in government of the economic indicators that are now widely employed in economic forecasting, with Eisenhower among the most attentive followers of what the numbers had to say. Both the Treasury Department and the CEA kept regularly in contact with the Federal Reserve authorities and their staff economists and, without intruding on the System's independence, did what they could to influence its decisions along the lines believed to be most appropriate. From the administration's beginning, high priority was given to the development of countercyclical contingency plans, including the preplanning of public construction. Notwithstanding Eisenhower's resistance to tax reductions that could not be clearly justified, he proposed and obtained reductions when they were judged to be warranted. And his administration is outstanding for inventiveness in devising countercyclical mea-

sures, for vigor in applying them when needed, and for support of the Council of Economic Advisers in all of this.

Despite these efforts, the record is flawed by there having been three recessions in eight years, the first two of about average depth and duration, the third of much less severity. And while recession is unwelcome at any time, to have had even a mild downturn in 1960 was extremely awkward from the political viewpoint of the president and the Republican Party. For the party in the White House, there is no substitute in a presidential election year for an economy on the upbeat. The cyclical annals, accordingly, must be judged as major minuses in the Eisenhower record.

● *The growth rate was below the historical norm*
It has been a major point with Eisenhower's critics that the economy's growth during his tenure was below par, and it is true that aggregate output as measured by price-corrected GNP expanded from 1953 through 1960 at a rate that averaged only 2.4 percent a year, well below the 3 to 3.5 percent (depending on the period selected) that was the historical norm up to that time. But because of the inclusiveness that in other respects is one of its principal virtues, GNP is not necessarily a fair measure of economic performance for any specific period. And in my view it is not a fair measure for the Eisenhower years. Changes in the composition of total output in those years held the growth rate down without involving the negative effect on national welfare normally associated with that result.

Chief among these changes was a reduction in defense spending. Doubtless correctly, Eisenhower maintained that the country was getting more national security, rather than less, for the money being spent, but the reduction in defense spending that was carried out during his presidency had nonetheless a lowering effect on the economy's growth rate in those years.[1] There is no official estimate of defense outlays in price-corrected terms for either 1952 or 1960, but a reasonable estimate of them suggests that, but for their decline (and ignoring the secondary and more remote effects of that decline, which were almost certainly negative for the growth rate), growth of real

GNP under Eisenhower would have been around 3 percent rather than the 2.4 percent cited above.[2] In addition, the growth rate was held down by inventory accumulation that was lower at the end of the period than at the beginning and by a shift from a positive to a negative trade balance. Whether the second of these developments should be regarded as necessarily a negative in the economy's performance is an open question; certainly the first should not be.

Finally, it is reasonable to note that the Eisenhower growth record is more favorable when judged by what happened to the output of goods and services touching directly on the consumer's welfare than when the test is what happened to total output. Thus, real output of consumption goods, including the output of housing, rose 3.4 percent a year from 1953 through 1960, well above the 2.2 percent in 1929 through 1952. And goods and services purchased by state and local governments—items that are in the main consumer-oriented—increased at a robust 5.7 percent annually.

In short, they were good times for the consumer. But, reasonable or not, presidential records are typically assessed not by the output of consumer goods and services but by the economy's aggregate output, and judged by that measure the Eisenhower record was on the low side.

● *The structural element in unemployment increased.*

As it does in all presidencies, unemployment during the Eisenhower years moved up and down with the business cycle, but two features of its behavior made it particularly troublesome.

First, as time passed it became apparent that the overall unemployment rate was yielding less and less to economic expansion, and thus was tending to trend upward. After dropping below 3 percent of the workforce in the 1952–53 upturn it fell only to around 4 percent in the 1955–56 boom, and only to 5 percent in the 1958–59 recovery. Conversely, after rising to slightly above 6 percent in the 1953–54 recession, it went to 7.5 percent in the 1957–58 downturn and was headed again to that level as the economy slowed in 1960.

Second, it was apparent by 1958 that in a number of areas high unemployment was becoming more and more a chronic condition, with people out of work for extended periods, perhaps never holding a job, for reasons having little if anything to do with the short-term ups and downs of business. The condition underlying this higher-than-average and more-persistent-than-average unemployment was referred to in the 1950s as the "distressed areas" problem.

Dealing with the tendency of aggregate unemployment to trend upward was of course mainly a matter of working to stabilize the economy and raise its continuing rate of expansion; but dealing with area unemployment that was higher and more persistent than elsewhere called for corrective measures of a selective nature. Some of the latter could be brought into play under powers already available to the president, but (as we have seen in Chapter V) more authority was needed, and it was a keen disappointment to Eisenhower that he was unable to obtain it from Congress in the form he wished.

The second term of his presidency ended without adequate provision having been made for dealing with the "distressed areas" problem. Sad to say, it is still in the main an item of unfinished business.

- *There was less opportunity than hoped for to achieve tax reduction and reform.*

Tax reductions and reform were high on Eisenhower's agenda from the beginning of his administration, and it was a major disappointment that there was less opportunity to accomplish it than had been hoped for and expected. True, for countercyclical purposes, the White House supported and obtained tax rollbacks in 1953 (effective in 1954) that it had initially opposed, sponsored a package of changes in the tax code in 1954 that had important equity-improving and burden-reducing effects, and achieved important tax relief in 1957 for small businesses. But otherwise, in order to bring budget receipts and outlays into a relationship that promised balance over a period long enough to span the normal business cycle, it maintained a "hold the line" policy on taxes when an opportunity to recommend reductions and reforms would have been preferred and would have been politically more agreeable.

In January 1960, conditions came close to matching what, in the president's view, was needed to justify making a major tax-reduction proposal. But conditions were not entirely right, and it was decided to apply the small surplus then in prospect for fiscal 1960 to debt reduction and to conserve the tax-cutting opportunities expected in fiscal 1961 for the next administration, which the White House confidently expected would be Republican.

Had there been no recession in 1960 and had the Republican presidential ticket been successful in the November election it would almost certainly have been possible to propose and obtain tax reduction on agreeable terms in 1961. But economic and political events prevented this from happening, producing again a negative mark for the Eisenhower record, and altering history in many important ways.

- *Eisenhower was outstandingly successful in having vetoes sustained, but less so in winning approval of his legislative proposals.*

Refusing to enact legislation requested by the White House is an obstacle that Congress places in some degree before every president, even when the majorities in House and Senate are of his own party. But in Eisenhower's case, working in all but the first two of his eight years in the presidency with a Congress controlled in both chambers by the opposition, and with deep philosophical differences separating him from many legislators, the handicap was particularly heavy. It is true that nearly all his vetoes were sustained (158 out of 160), but only about half of his administration's legislative proposals were adopted.[3]

The list of proposals turned down included many of critical importance. Among them were bills that would have strengthened the administration's ability to cope with the business cycle. Others would have given greater scope to private effort in meeting the housing needs of low-income families. Still others would have enabled the administration to deal more effectively with excess farm production, allowed the president to move more aggressively against unemployment in "distressed areas," permitted a more rational and stable administration of foreign aid, made it easier to control federal spending, and allowed the federal debt to be managed more in line with market realities.

Rebuffs are understandable, given the philosophical differences that separated Eisenhower from many in Congress, but obtaining legislation to carry out his agenda is properly a test of a president's effectiveness, and by this test there is distinctly a shortfall in the Eisenhower record.

But there were big pluses.

● *The federal budget was brought to structural balance.*
However the federal budget is calculated (whether on the "administrative" basis that was standard at the time, on the "unified" basis that is used now, or as the less commonly cited "cash consolidated accounts") it was balanced in three of the seven full fiscal years over which Eisenhower presided—in fiscal 1956, fiscal 1957 and fiscal 1960. And in the national income and product figures, which are calculated on a calendar year basis and in what is generally regarded as analytically a more meaningful manner, there were surpluses in the federal sector of the accounts in four of the eight calendar years of his presidency—1955, 1956, 1957 and 1960. Moreover, at no time under Eisenhower did the deficit in the unified federal budget exceed 2.3 percent of GNP, and in most years it was well below that; in the 1980s it has been as high as 6 percent.[4]

Achieving these results required resistance to the ever-present pressure to increase spending and, when a persuasive case for doing so could not be made for it, to the intermittent urging to cut taxes for countercyclical purposes. While gained at some cost in popularity, the end result was strongly positive: a relationship between budget receipts and outlays such that, except during recession, there would be a balance or a surplus in the fiscal accounts. In short, the budget was brought to structural balance and kept there.

● *Prices were stabilized.*

Without meaning to underrate the role of the Federal Reserve System in achieving this result, to have presided over a stabilizing of prices must be regarded as one of Eisenhower's major successes. And it was not easily won. There were tests of nerve as well as principle along the way. As we have seen, the first came in 1953, when what to do about the apparatus of direct controls carried over from the Truman period had to be decided. Against much advice to the contrary, including some from members of his own cabinet, controls were dismantled. The results were good: instead of spurting up when ceilings were removed, as some had feared, prices settled onto a flat trend and stayed essentially flat for upwards of three years.

The second test came in 1955–56, when there was a resurgence of increases in the price indexes, but by late 1958 this threat had been overcome, again by relying on monetary and fiscal restraint.

There was still some inflation psychology in the economy when Eisenhower left the White House, but the basis for it had been eliminated more fully than was generally understood at the time; indeed, more fully than was understood by many in the Eisenhower administration. Price indexes were flat or close to flat in 1960, and had been so for two years. In short, the battle against inflation had been won. Undoubtedly and unavoidably, it had been won at some cost to the economy's growth at the time; but price stability was powerfully favorable for the economy's chances of growing at a better rate in the post-Eisenhower years.

● *There were important improvements in personal income and well-being.*

There is more than nostalgia behind the view that the 1950s was a kind of "golden period" in recent American experience. There is a solid basis for it, grounded in large increases in the output of consumer goods and services. The advances in personal income and well-being were not greater in all respects than those achieved in the Truman and Kennedy-Johnson years, but in some important respects they were higher than in either of those periods and high by any standard of longterm achievement. And there was a palpable quality of sustainability about them.

To begin with, there were 5.5 million more civilian jobs in 1960 than in 1952, an average annual increase of 1.1 percent. This was below the exceptionally large increases (1.9 percent a year, on the average) in the sixteen years that followed the Eisenhower period but in line with the 1 percent that was the annual average for the 23 years that preceded it.[5] More jobs in a context of relatively stable prices meant a larger aggregate of personal income payments, in real as well as nominal terms. And income payments adjusted for price changes and for tax and nontax payments (real disposable personal income) rose in the Eisenhower period at 3.1 percent a year, on the average.[6] In addition, it is a plus for the Eisenhower years, as it is a plus for the Truman years, that both were followed by further increases in real personal income.

There were also large improvements in income calculated on a family basis. Thus, with only relatively small increases in the participation of women in the labor force, the median of family incomes, adjusted for inflation, rose 3.3 percent a year from 1952 through 1960, compared with 2.6 from 1948 through 1952.[7] The average annual increase accelerated to 3.4 percent between 1960 and 1968, but dropped to 0.9 between 1968 and 1978. It is estimated to have been roughly zero between 1978 and 1986.[8]

As would be expected, advances in real personal income were reflected in the Eisenhower period in many specific improvements in individual and family well-being: in health and longevity; in personal financial security; in a widening of home ownership; and, as the *January 1960 Economic Report* put it, by "notable gains . . . in education and other cultural areas."[9]

But not everyone in the 1950s was happy with what was happening. There was much decrying of how Americans chose to spend their rising incomes, notably of their preference for automobiles of large size, and of the "tail fins" on them. But if a rising real personal income, however the consumer wishes to spend it, is in any way conclusive as a test of an economy's performance, as it is reasonable to say it should be, the Eisenhower period was one of outstanding achievement.

- *After years of increase, the size of government relative to the rest of the economy was stabilized, and the trend to a greater federalizing of governmental functions was reversed.*

When Eisenhower said in 1952 that he was entering the presidential election campaign as a "Great Crusade" he meant, perhaps more than anything else, that there would be a challenge to the rising size of government relative to the rest of the economy. The ratio to national income of government expenditures (federal, state and local) had been moving up for two decades in a seemingly inexorable manner. It had gone from 12 percent in 1929 to nearly 25 percent in the late 1940s (after having touched nearly 57 percent during World War II), and had gone from there, with only brief reverses, to roughly 33 percent in 1952.[10]

Eisenhower was sensitive enough to the need for much of what government was doing not to seek an abrupt reversal of this trend. In addition, he was enough of a gradualist not to have sought to do so. But he was committed in his basic philosophy to checking the drift to bigger government and turned at once to that task. What that required, of course, was restraint over the increase of public spending, carried out in a context of steady increases in national income. The first Budget Message (January 1954) included a statement of what would be done at the federal level:

> By using necessity—rather than mere desirability—as the test for our expenditures, we will reduce the share of the national income which is spent by the Government. We are convinced that more progress and sounder progress will be made over the years as the largest possible share of our national income is left with individual citizens to make their own . . . decisions as to what they will spend, what they will buy, and what they will save and invest. Government must play a vital role in maintaining economic growth and stability. But I believe

that our development, since the early days of the Republic, has been based on the fact that we left a great share of our national income to be used by a provident people with a will to venture. Their actions have stimulated the American genius for creative initiative and thus multiplied our productivity.[11]

The depth of Eisenhower's commitment to this position is confirmed by his return to it in January 1961 in his final budget message. Repeating what he had said in 1954, he continued:

This philosophy is as appropriate today as it was in 1954. And it should continue to guide us in the future. Over the past 8 years, we have sought to keep the role of the Federal Government within its proper sphere. . . . At the same time, the record of this administration has been one of action to help meet the urgent and real needs of a growing population and a changing economy. . . . The major increases in spending . . . have not been devoted to the tools of war and destruction. A military posture of great effectiveness and strong retaliatory capability has been maintained without increasing defense expenditures above 1953, despite rising costs. . . . We have . . . direct[ed] more of our public resources toward the improvement of living conditions and the enlargement of opportunities for the future growth and development of the Nation. . . . And it is significant that requirements have been met while holding [federal] budget expenditures to a lesser proportion of the national income than in 1953."[12]

When the administration ended the goal had been achieved—the ratio of total government spending (federal, state and local) to national income was the same 33 percent in 1960 as in 1953, the balance between the public and private sectors of the economy had been stabilized. In addition, the trend toward a greater federalizing of government had been reversed. The federal component in total government outlays, which had risen from 26 percent in 1929 to 76 percent in 1952, fell over the next eight years to 68 percent.[13]

Stabilizing the balance between the public and private sectors of the economy was by no means a universally-acclaimed outcome. But in this assessment of the Eisenhower record it is entered as a strongly positive achievement, comparable with bringing the budget to structural balance and with stabilizing prices. And it is all the more positive considering that it was accomplished with no loss of defense capability and with important improvements in individual and family well-being.

- *An historic improvement in the nation's infrastructure was started in 1956 with the launching of the Interstate Highway System.*

After lengthy debates within the administration and in Congress over how it should be financed, an Interstate Highway System was authorized in June 1956. It had been recommended to Congress in February 1955 in a special presidential message, accompanied by the report of the presidential commission, chaired by General [Retired] Lucius Clay, which had studied it in depth. Not enacted in the 1955 session, it was recommended again in the January 1956 State of the Union Message.

The undertaking—40,000 miles in its original format, to be built over 13 years—was the largest single U.S. public works project to that time or since. It was of immense interest to Eisenhower for what it would mean to national security (military experience had underlined the importance of transport) and, equally important, for what it would mean to the nation's economic development. He was acutely sensitive, also, to the possibility that its construction could if necessary be scheduled to help stabilize the economy. It has had good effects in all these respects.

- *Confidence in the enterprise system was strengthened.*

It was a major success for Eisenhower's economic philosophy, and a tribute to the economy's performance during his presidency that, by 1960, confidence in the ability of the market-directed, enterprise economy to yield important improvements in the standard of living was at a high level, well above what it had been for decades. To be sure, the system had its critics, but the demands for greater intervention into the economy by government that had emerged as World War II was coming to a close, and which were of such concern to Eisenhower and his associates in government, had for all practical purposes been silenced. Given the importance for the viability of democratic institutions of a vigorous, market-oriented economy, this must be regarded as the leading plus in the Eisenhower economic record.

● *Finally, the economy was left in good order.*
It is standard in politics that when a new administration involves a change of party the newcomers complain of their "Iegacy," and so it was following Eisenhower. Because the economy was in recession when the transfer took place, there were grounds for some complaint, even though the decline was small. But recession notwithstanding, all the dimensions of the economy that bore on its prospects for growth were in good order. There were no imbalances that would cause the cyclical decline to deepen; actually, activity was on the verge of turning into recovery. There was nothing in money supply growth or in the inflation outlook to deter the Federal Reserve from continuing with the easing of credit that was already well advanced (the consumer price index was de facto stable). There was no yawning federal budget gap to be closed. Federal budget receipts and outlays were so matched that even a mild recovery would produce a surplus. And although there was still an outflow of gold and a volume of liquid liabilities to foreign nationals and international institutions that had the potential of causing the outflow to increase, exports were rising strongly and prospects were good for improvement in the overall balance of international payments. Universally, the U.S. dollar was relied on with confidence as the "key currency" of the world.

Eisenhower got less credit than was his due for having brought the economy to this position, partly because partisan politics does not distribute credit in such matters in an even-handed way, but also because on all sides—among scholars, journalists, politicians and the public generally—there was less recognition in 1960 than there came to be later of how important it is to the economy's prospects to have prices stable and federal finances in good order.

But the importance of having achieved these conditions was

not lost on Eisenhower. In the introductory portion of the *January 1961 Economic Report* (the section that is the president's personal statement), he noted that "a firm base" had been laid for a period of sound economic growth.[14] It was a correct assessment of the economy's condition.

Striking a Balance

It must be plain from the character of the pluses and minuses in the Eisenhower record, as reviewed above, that they cannot be easily netted against one another. Different analysts will weigh the items differently. And they may wish to add others to one side or the other of the books. But it must also be plain that any reasonable assessment of their overall balance will be positive.

That is not to say that the record could not have been better. There might well have been more success in stabilizing the economy, which would have worked wonders for the period's overall growth rate. There was some underrating of the recession risk by the administration on each of the three occasions when a downturn ultimately did occur; the Federal Reserve, as well, could have been more sensitive on this score. Economic growth would almost certainly have been higher and more stable if the rate of increase of money supply had been steadier. Whether the economy's performance would have benefitted from a more liberal increase in the money supply is a debatable question. I believe it would have. For an economy in which nominal GNP increased over the eight years ending January 1961 by nearly 5 percent a year, an increase in the broadly-defined money supply (including time deposits of commercial banks as well as demand deposits and currency) that averaged 3.0 percent a year was surely at the bottom of the range of increases that could be regarded as acceptable, even given some increase in the turnover of money balances. And the 1.7 percent average annual increase in those eight years in the narrowly-defined money supply (covering only demand deposits and currency) was clearly a tight fit. True, there was some inflation psychology still to be extinguished in 1959–60, but it was of diminishing importance. It seems a fair assessment that there would have been no loss in the fight against an uptrend of prices if in those years both the administration and the Federal Reserve, and some of the administration's more vocal supporters outside government, had been quicker to realize that, for the time at least, the battle against inflation had been won. And there would surely have been some gain in the effort to avoid recession, and thus to raise the economy's rate of growth.

It would have been helpful also to have been spared the 1957 bruhaha over the budget, a misadventure for which the administration was largely responsible. The same can be said of the 1959 steel strike, though this was a misfortune over which the administration had no control. And the economy's ability to avoid recession and stage recovery would undoubtedly have been greater, with helpful effect on the average annual growth rate, if the country's large, private banks had been able to set the prime rate with greater sensitivity to the economy's cyclical condition. Finally, it would have been enormously helpful if there had been a more like-minded Congress to work with.

But, despite the obstacles and frustrations, the president's major economic goals had been reached by January 1961. Confidence in the market-directed enterprise system as the vehicle for achieving economic progress was high. The relationship between the public and private sectors of the economy had been stabilized. And a solid foundation had been laid in the federal budget and in the stability of prices for extending economic progress into the future.

In short, the record nets to a strong plus—a constructive presidency that was good for the nation.

Notes

1. In his final State of the Union Message (January 12, 1961), Eisenhower disputed charges made during the 1960 presidential election campaign that his administration's budget policies had resulted in a "defense gap," stating:

> For the first time in the nation's history we have consistently maintained in peacetime, military forces of a magnitude sufficient to deter and if need be to destroy predatory forces in the world. (*Public Papers, DDE*, 1960–61, p. 917)

2. The estimate was made by netting nominal GNP for 1952 and 1960 by the amount of defense spending in those years and deflating the result by the same price index as used to deflate total GNP.

3. *CQ Almanac,* 1959, p. 661, and 1960, p. 93.

4. Data are from the *February 1985 Economic Report,* Table B-72, p. 318 and *National Income and Product Accounts of the United States, 1929–74,* Table 3.2, pp. 96–97.

5. *February 1985 Economic Report,* Table B-2, p. 266; *Long Term Economic Growth, 1860–1970,* Series A-79.

6. *February 1985 Economic Report,* Table B-24, p. 261.

7. *Social Indicators,* 1976, Table 9-1, p. 453.

8. *Economics Reports,* February 1985, Table B-27, p. 264 and February 1988, Table B-30, p. 282.

9. Page 2, Appendix C of the *January 1960 Economic Report* presents a comprehensive set of statistical tables on "The Diffusion of Well-being, 1946–59."

10. Nutter, *Growth of Government in the West,* Tables B-1 and B-4.

11. *Public Papers, DDE,* 1954, p. 89.

12. *Public Papers, DDE,* 1960-1961, p. 1027.

13. Nutter, *Growth of Government in the West,* Table B-6.

14. *January 1961 Economic Report,* pp. iv and 43–44.

Epilogue: Lessons from the Eisenhower Experience

New conditions create new problems, and an economic strategy that had good results at one time does not, of course, assure good results at another. But the basics of what Eisenhower stood for in economic policy have by this time been sufficiently tested to warrant drawing certain lessons from experience during and subsequent to his presidency that can be useful today and in the future. Among these lessons a few stand out with particular prominence.

- *Fundamental to everything else, experience confirms Eisenhower's confidence that if government concentrates on getting the economic environment right it can safely depend for economic progress on individual initiative, self-reliance, and private, competitive enterprise.*

This is the premise on which Eisenhower's whole economic strategy was based, and although the philosophy of government implicit in it commands more respect today than in his time, resistance to it continues. It is anathema to advocates of central economic planning and, at a less sternly ideological level, is resisted by those who desire merely a more interventionist style of government, without basic institutional change. But passing into and out of double-digit inflation in the United States in the 1970s and 1980s made it easier to see that the activism that counts most is that which concentrates on getting the economic environment right—on getting government finances in order; on overcoming inflation or preventing it from

238

getting started; on keeping markets open and competitive; and on strengthening the incentives to work, save and invest.

Also, there is proof of the premise underlying Eisenhower's economic strategy in developments elsewhere in the world, where centrally-controlled economies have of late been re-discovering the power of individual initiative and the impor-tance of open, competitive markets. Recognizing the validity and pragmatic worth of these principles is obviously not the end of what one needs to know about economic policy, but it is surely the beginning.

- *Experience has also confirmed the workability of the mixture of pragmatism and ideology in Eisenhower's political makeup.*

Practical politics is always a mixture of pragmatism and ide-ology, and there was such a mixture in Eisenhower's methods. There was pragmatism in his advocacy of a "Middle Way"; and there was ideology—an unmistakably conservative variety—in his "Bundle of Freedoms" theory, with its endorsement of a free, market-directed economy as the only context in which democratic institutions could be secure. Being such a mixture, his methods were understandably as often a cause of dismay to his more rigorously conservative supporters as they were to his critics on the opposite wing of politics. Still, it is one of the clearest lessons of recent history that his meld of pragmatism and ideology offers a style of government that comes closer than any other to what is appropriate and can be effective in the American context.

- *Equally, experience has confirmed Eisenhower's rule that the art of government consists in good part of finding a workable balance between fiscal conservatism and social liberality.*

Finding such a balance was not easy in the 1950s; if anything, it is more difficult today. The fiscal side of the problem involves finding a match between budget outlays and receipts that keeps the two broadly in balance at a level of taxation that is politi-cally acceptable and not unduly repressive of incentives. On the expenditure side the task is to allocate available funds among competing demands as fairly and constructively as possible without creating, as Eisenhower once put it, a "permanent dependency" in the beneficiaries of social programs.

Little wonder that Eisenhower should have remarked, looking back on his presidency, that finding the right balance between fiscal conservatism and social liberality was the key to achieving constructive results in government. It is the lesson of his experience that, difficult as it is to find a workable balance, it is in the end imperative that one be found.

- *In a different area of policy, experience has demonstrated repeatedly that while it is possible to overreact to a danger of inflation, the more serious mistakes are those made by reacting to it too late, too timidly, or in the wrong way.*

The view has been taken in this book that gold outflows toward the end of Eisenhower's presidency caused both the White House and the Federal Reserve to rate the inflation problem higher than was warranted by what was actually happening to prices at the time, and that the result was to complicate the problem of holding the economy in 1959–60 on a course of uninterrupted growth. But if Eisenhower was wrong in this his error was small compared with the misjudgments that in later years allowed inflation to accelerate sharply. The spiral of rising costs and prices that began in the mid-sixties had finally to be confronted by doses of monetary restraint that entailed heavy economic costs. After reaching nearly 13.5 percent as an annual average in 1980 the increase of consumer prices had by 1985 been reduced to 3.6 percent, but in the interim the economy had passed through two recessions, the buying power of family income had been cut by nearly 10 percent (between 1978 and 1983) and massive imbalances had emerged in the federal budget and in the nation's foreign trade accounts.[1]

Not everything in this unhappy history was the result of tardy, timid and programmatically ill-conceived responses to inflation, but it is a safe surmise that responses more in line with the Eisenhower model—early and firm application of monetary and fiscal restraint—would have made it possible for much of it to be avoided.

- *In addition to what it shows regarding money policy and the stabilization of prices, the Eisenhower experience underlines heavily the importance of money policy in determining how well the economy performs.*

It is difficult in today's complex monetary context to judge what is the most appropriate rate of increase of the nation's money supply, and it was not easy to do so in the Eisenhower years. But it does appear that the increase during Eisenhower's presidency, taking the whole eight years into account, was at best barely rapid enough to give the economy the scope and stimulus for growth that was warranted and was needed. And it is clear that the money supply, however defined, fluctuated too widely.

Drawing on this and subsequent experience, few would deny that it would help greatly toward achieving a better economic performance if discrepancis (plus or minus) between growth in money supply and growth in the economy's capacity to expand output were lessened and if fluctuations in money supply were held within a narrower range.

- *It would be useful also to have a careful and impartial study of the president's role in the shaping of money policy. Should he have a hand in it?*

The record under Eisenhower, no less than under other presidents, does not encourage one to believe that White House contributions to the shaping of money policy would always be well advised. But the importance of money and credit in determining how the economy performs, and the president's accountability under the Employment Act and before the public for what that performance proves to be, demands attention to the question: Should he have a more direct hand in shaping policy in this area?

Eisenhower was tested several times on this question. In the end he satisfied himself that the right answer was to keep the

Federal Reserve System as independent as possible, with his underlying distaste for politics almost certainly taking charge of the argument. But the question is still open. It needs thorough, impartial and authoritative study.

- *Granted it can be counterproductive to try to balance the federal budget during recession, but experience underlines heavily its importance at all other times.*

No defense is needed nowadays of having the federal budget in "structural balance," meaning that income and outgo are so matched as to be broadly equal or showing a surplus when the economy is operating satisfactorily, free of recession. The still unsettled questions are how best to achieve that condition, and how to prevent departures from it.

There was much discussion of these questions at the staff level and among certain of the cabinet officers during the Eisenhower administration, including whether there should be a constitutional amendment requiring a balanced budget, but there was never an official endorsement of any one of the possible legislative approaches and I doubt that Eisenhower could have been persuaded to embrace any one of them, least of all a constitutional amendment. What his record illustrates is that the decisive factor in achieving a balance in budget accounts is not legislation that mandates it but consistent and aggressive presidential leadership at the budget-making and budget-administering levels. There must be resistance to proposals for the increase of spending that cannot be funded out of the prospective matchup of income and outgo. And there must be resistance to proposals for tax-cutting for countercyclical purposes when a strong case cannot be made for it and when the reduction would lessen the tax system's longterm revenue-raising capability below what is needed to support the community's desired level of spending. None of this can be done easily, but Eisenhower's record supports the view that resolute leadership by the president can make it possible.

- *How to moderate the upward pressure on costs and prices of wage increases that exceed productivity improvement,*

*without having recourse to monetary and fiscal restraints
so severe as to risk turning the economy into recession,
continues to be a major problem of economic policy. It is
typically underrated and not well understood.*

In circumstances such as obtained in 1956–57 (the inflation rate
low but threatening to accelerate and unit labor costs tending to
rise), an appeal of the sort made by Eisenhower at that time
that wage demands be held within the limits of productivity
improvement and that prices be set in reasonable relation to
costs may help meet the problem. Indeed, it could be a serious
oversight for the president not to make such an appeal. It can at
least promote a better public understanding of what is at stake
for the country in what is being bargained over by labor and
management, and in that way have a beneficial impact on the
major players in the bargaining process. Any appeal made
must, however, be supported by appropriately antiinflationary
monetary and fiscal policies. And it must be phrased and presented in a way that minimizes the risk that it will lead to direct
governmental intervention in the event it does not succeed.

- *Legislation is urgently needed to put the president in a
  better position to orchestrate a full and balanced economic
  stabilization program.*

The president's authority to deploy the policy tools needed to
help achieve vigorous, inflation-free growth—those that have
an overall (macro) impact, and those that are selective (micro)
in effect—should be as extensive as necessary to enable him to
fulfill his responsibilities under the Employment Act. As things
stand, it is inadequate.

The need to study ways to strengthen the president's hand in
shaping money policy has already been noted. Other powers
are needed. Among them the elusive "item veto" would go
some distance toward enabling him to influence the volume and
composition of budget outlays, but the whole budget-making
process is desperately in need of reform. On an even more
sensitive matter, it is perhaps time to consider giving the president authority, within limits set by Congress, to make temporary changes in tax rates for economic-stabilization or budget-
management purposes. Certainly, the limitations imposed by

Congress on how the Treasury can manage the public debt should be removed. And the president should be given greater leeway to adjust the terms on which loans are made, insured or guaranteed by the federal government. There is a major task here for legislative reform.

- *A major effort should be launched to improve the informational base on which economic forecasts are made and on which programs to smooth the business cycle and promote growth are carried out.*

There are many reasons why activity in an enterprise economy every now and then drifts or plummets into recession or, in an alternative mode, meanders for an extended period along a trend of subpar growth. Whatever the cause, the chances of dealing adequately with these failings of our economic system depend heavily on the availability of reliable, up-to-date information on what is happening. As things stand there are deficiencies in this regard so large and so numerous as to require a major overhaul and strengthening of the statistical programs of government. Drawing on advances in telecommunications and on the gathering and computer-assisted processing of economic data, it should be possible to make enormous improvements in them. It is urgently necessary that such a project be undertaken.

- *Finally, experience teaches that there is immensely more to being right about economic policy than being right about its purely technical aspects.*

More important in this regard than anything else is the policymaker's time horizon—the weight given to a policy's likely longrun effect as against its nearterm impact. Accordingly, there is a heavy premium on the insights and powers of imagination needed to help visualize a policy's effect over time, as there is also a large premium on the patience needed to give policies enough time to do what is expected of them. There is also the fortitude a president needs to resist being drawn into actions which, while they may promise to be beneficial in the near term, have been judged likely to be counterproductive in the long run. And because there are so many essentially subjective factors involved in judging a policy's likely impact, near-term as well as longterm, the premium on experience and intuition is without a doubt heavier than is commonly recognized.

Eisenhower was outstanding for these habits of mind and capabilities. The temper of the day favored a faster-paced, more interventionist management of the economy than he was prepared to accept, and underrated the importance for the economy's continuing health of the conservative handling of fiscal and financial affairs that he favored. Experience has led, however, to his strategies and methods being rated more highly, just as it has increased the respect accorded his underlying philosophy in economic and political affairs. It is in these respects that the record supports the assertion, alluded to in the Prologue to this book, that, in matters basic to the shaping and carrying out of economic policy, "Ike was right."

1. *February 1990 Economic Report,* Tables C-30, p. 328, and C-58, p. 359.

A Note on Sources

In order to avoid a needless proliferation of notes, references have been omitted where factual statements in the text can be verified readily in standard and widely-available statistical sources. My principal reliance for such material was *Business Conditions Digest (BCD)*, a monthly compendium of economic series that covered in detail the period dealt with in this book. *BCD* was published separately by the Department of Commerce beginning in 1961 and through March 1990 but was merged in April 1990 into the department's *Survey of Current Business*. I used mainly the July 1986 issue of *BCD* and the historical series indexed there but published in issues of previous months. I have made some limited use also, with appropriate references, of the unpublished precursor of *BCD* which was produced from mid-1957 through 1960 (a joint effort of the CEA and the Department of Commerce) and ultimately became the basis, in revised format, of *BCD*. The unpublished *BCD* was at the time the most complete and up-to-date collection of "economic indicators," and was relied on heavily at the CEA. Full descriptions of source are given for data such as that drawn from the Commerce Department's *Historical Statistics of the United States, Income and Product Accounts of the United States, 1929–74,* and *Long Term Economic Growth, 1860–1970,* and from the Federal Reserve Board's *Banking and Monetary Statistics, 1941–1970* and *Flow of Funds Accounts, 1976.*

There has also been extensive use, with appropriate acknowledgment, of several collections of personal papers (some published; some not) and of the minutes and other records of various administrative bodies. Materials in this category include the eight volumes of the *Public Papers of the Presidents of the United States, Dwight D. Eisenhower,* 1953 through 1961, which contains messages, White House statements, and news conference records of Eisenhower as president; Volume X of *The Papers of Dwight David Eisenhower,* prepared at Johns Hopkins University by Professor Louis Galambos and published by The Johns Hopkins University Press; papers in the Eisenhower Presidential Library at Abilene, Kansas, including minutes of cabinet meetings and meetings of the president with Republican legislative leaders; the papers of Governor Sherman Adams, held in the George F. Baker Library at Dartmouth College, Hanover, New Hampshire; minutes of the Federal Reserve Board's Open Market Committee, used by me in the library of the Federal Reserve Bank of New York but available now in microfilm from a commercial source; and the Oral History Collection of Columbia University, lodged in the university's Butler Library in New York City. Finally, there was extensive use, with appropriate acknowledgment, of Eisenhower's two-volume memoir, *The White House Years, The Eisenhower Diaries,* edited by Robert H. Ferrell, the published memoirs of Governor Sherman Adams *(Firsthand Report: The Story of the Eisenhower Administration),* the published papers of George M. Humphrey *(The Basic Papers of George M. Humphrey, as Secretary of the Treasury)* and of course of the *Economic Reports of the President,* January 1954 through January 1961.

Index